MARKETABLE VALUES

MARKETABLE VALUES

Inventing the Property Market in Modern Britain

DESMOND FITZ-GIBBON

THE UNIVERSITY OF CHICAGO PRESS
CHICAGO AND LONDON

The University of Chicago Press, Chicago 60637
The University of Chicago Press, Ltd., London

Published 2018
Printed in the United States of America

27 26 25 24 23 22 21 20 19 18 1 2 3 4 5

ISBN-13: 978-0-226-58416-4 (cloth)
ISBN-13: 978-0-226-58433-1 (paper)
ISBN-13: 978-0-226-58447-8 (e-book)
DOI: https://doi.org/10.7208/chicago/9780226584478.001.0001

Library of Congress Cataloging-in-Publication Data

Names: Fitz-Gibbon, Desmond, author.
Title: Marketable values : inventing the property market in modern Britain / Desmond Fitz-Gibbon.
Description: Chicago : The University of Chicago Press, 2018. | Includes index.
Identifiers: LCCN 2018020206 | ISBN 9780226584164 (cloth : alk. paper) | ISBN 9780226584331 (pbk. : alk. paper) | ISBN 9780226584478 (e-book)
Subjects: LCSH: Real property—Great Britain—History—19th century. | Real property—Great Britain—Marketing—History—19th century. | Real property auctions—Great Britain—History.
Classification: LCC HD593 .F58 2018 | DDC 333.30941—dc23
LC record available at https://lccn.loc.gov/2018020206

♾ This paper meets the requirements of ANSI/NISO Z39.48–1992 (Permanence of Paper).

CONTENTS

INTRODUCTION

Locating the Property Market

For Sir Walter Elliot, the spendthrift patriarch in Jane Austen's posthumously published sixth novel, *Persuasion*, the property market was something to be avoided at all costs. Having racked up debt in the name of vanity and status, Sir Walter now faced the need to retrench. Family pride and legal constraint ruled out any thought of selling the family's principal estate, and so Kellynch Hall would have to be let, and the family relocated. The thought of his baronial seat with its pictures, shrubberies, and parks in the possession of strangers filled Sir Walter with dread. To effect the change would be a "trial of fortitude" made manageable only through the deepest of secrecy, "not to be breathed beyond their own circle." Advertising was out of the question; no one should know of the intention to rent, and so the whole business would be transacted at a distance, through the family's solicitor, Mr. Shepherd. The very idea of a commercial transaction was so unpalatable that Sir Walter effectively erased it from his mind and demanded that others do the same. As he instructed Shepherd, "it was only on the supposition of his being spontaneously solicited by some most unexceptionable applicant, on his own terms, and as a great favour, that he would let it at all."[1] Sir Walter thus reimagined the property market as a network of benevolent charity.

There was nothing remarkable in Sir Walter's attitude toward the selling and leasing of property. His desire to keep his estate intact, to protect the family's status and reputation, and to hide any sign of financial trouble from the outside world, reflected common aristocratic assumptions about the importance of landed property as a social and political institution of nineteenth-century British society. There was also nothing unusual about Sir Walter resorting to the market when the need ultimately arose, as it did for many other owners of land seeking to acquire, develop, or consolidate estates; to raise capital; or to pay off debt. Indeed, the commercialization of land—buying it, selling it, leasing it, and borrowing on it—was an entirely recognizable fact of life to the readers of Austen's novels. What troubled Sir Walter most, however (aside from the clearly unpleasant prospect of leaving his estate) was the risk that his social worth might be measured by the visibility of his property being brought to market. The property market might be a necessary recourse at times, but there was still no reason to draw attention to it. Its social and cultural invisibility was one of its essential features, happily reinforced by Austen herself, when she had Mr. Shepherd discover, through private rather than public means, the Croft family and their protagonist nephew, Captain Wentworth.[2]

Less than a century later, the property market looked very different. As one correspondent sarcastically stated in the *Estates Gazette*, a leading property trade journal founded in 1858, the issue was not whether the market should be visible, but rather whether or not it was visible enough. "Where is the so-called 'Property Market,'" wrote "An Old Hand," "and what of its quotations?"[3] The very idea of a property market, the writer continued, was "absolutely a misnomer" in light of the failed institutions that facilitated its operation. The question seemed nonsensical, since, as An Old Hand clearly knew, there was plenty of evidence to be had for the existence of something like a property market. There was, for example, a marketplace: the London Auction Mart, first opened in 1808, where one could go to see public sales of estates, farms, buildings, and houses. There were people whose job it was to advertise and mediate these sales. There were, on a daily basis, hundreds if not thousands of advertisements, notices, handbills, and posters announcing forthcoming sales, both by auction or through private contract. There was the *Estates Gazette* itself, and other periodicals like it, that routinely reported on sales and provided a platform to debate the existence of the market. And there were prices, compiled by professional associations, reported in the press, and commented on by an increasingly vocal body of professional and lay observers. The correspondent knew all of this, had recited many of these examples in his or her letter, and would undoubtedly have agreed—as did many at the time and as have historians since then—that land had been subject to commercial transactions for ages in Britain.[4]

What, then, did it mean to imply that the property market was absent or missing? For this correspondent, the misnomer of the property market hinted at one answer. The property market could not be seen because none of the activity associated with the buying and selling of land conformed to an ideal type of market that could readily be identified for other commodities, such as stocks, corn, or cotton. The word *market* "implie[d] not only a place in which dealings in a special commodity are carried on, but where current quotations affecting such a commodity are the actual prices at which the same may be dealt in"; the stock exchange, corn exchange, and cotton exchange were "all recognized places where buyers and sellers, either themselves or through their brokers, congregate and deal on definite prices, fixed as regards the article itself, but fluctuating according to circumstances and conditions."[5] Property sales were far too varied and idiosyncratic for such certainty. Whereas the property market might have an ostensible home in the auction mart, it could never offer up a definite price for a fixed article. Prices for land, moreover, were "governed by entirely different data to that which affects other 'property.'" Desire and status, no less than reason and investment, guided the decisions of property owners, and the self-evident dissimilarity between properties in different locations made them impossible to compare in anything like the fashion used to guide security or commodity trades. The property market may have looked similar to other markets on the surface, but taken as a whole, as an assemblage of people, practices, and ideas, it did not work as a *real* market should. For all these reasons, An Old Hand struggled to see the property market in any of its more obvious places, but did so from the perspective that seeing it better was a necessary and laudable reform. The letter concluded with a recommendation that advertisements be more targeted so as to increase competition for properties likely to be in higher demand. Both Sir Walter Elliot and An Old Hand questioned the nature of land's marketability, whether or not it could or should be treated fully as a commodity or as something else; but for the latter, what mattered most was how to configure the uniqueness of land in ways comparable to other commodities. These paradoxical desires—to not see the market at all and to see it most clearly—defined the parameters by which Britons invented a new kind of property market.

This is a book about how the practice, organization, and perception of the property market changed over the course of the nineteenth century and in response to evolving debates about the nature of land's commodity status. I argue that, while land had long been subject to trade, it was only during this period that Britons began to think about it in aggregate terms, associating it with the more abstract space of a "property market" that could, despite this abstractness, be made visible in a variety of new ways, from places of sale to the journalistic ventures that amplified the views of practitioners like An Old Hand. Imagining the property market was not simply about importing new ideas about the commoditization of property; nor was it a case of a "market logic" restructuring all property exchange in its own image. Making the property market visible took work—cultural work that was anchored in particular histories of people, time, and place. Rather than treat the property market as a given, as something that was already present in some immutable form, this book demonstrates how the market became culturally visible and normalized in very different ways from what had existed before.

Throughout this period, both the meaning of land's marketability and its institutional organization were debated with varying degrees of intensity and across a range of cultural locations, but always with a sense that the answers were important and freighted with implications beyond the simple act of exchanging rights for money. Indeed, for many, the commodity status of land was part of a much larger "land question" that was argued throughout Britain and its expanding empire and encompassed questions of landownership, social relations, political representation, and imperial power.[6]

Part of the invisibility of the property market, according to many reformers, had to do with legal restrictions placed on it. For example, calls to liberalize the transfer of property were common throughout the mid-Victorian years. Richard Cobden was given the most credit for popularizing "free trade in land" as a slogan in 1864, but the idea was by then well established in radical politics, having emerged alongside the campaign for corn law repeal in the 1840s.[7] Land, insisted James Beal in 1855, was essentially "*extra commercium*" thanks to the shackles of legal entail and primogeniture.[8] Riffing on the same theme in 1870, the *Times* framed the essence of the English land question as whether the law of property would remain forever stuck in the doorway of history, one foot chained to the fetters of feudalism and the other stretching across the threshold to commercial freedom.[9] Still again, in 1885, speaking on the subject of land title reform, the president of the Wonersh District Liberal Association (Surrey) insisted that reform "would give land a real marketable value, and enable an owner to sell a field or an estate with as much ease as he would sell a pig or a bullock in the local market."[10] Up to the mid-1880s, then, calls for free trade in land insisted that the project of reform needed to address the absence of a fully liberalized market.

The passage of the Settled Land Act in 1882, which permitted life tenants of landed estates to sell settled land under certain conditions, did little to appease free traders; but by the mid-1880s their demands appeared far less radical in light of new arguments put forward to address the land question. In 1881, for example, Alfred Russel Wallace founded the Land Nationalisation Society (LNS) to help lobby for an end to landlordism in Britain via the state purchase of all private land.[11] A year earlier, the American economist Henry George had proposed a slightly different plan to tax the full value of land, thereby nationalizing it in all but name.[12] George's supporters established the English Land Restoration League (ELRL) to further the aim of a single land tax. Each of these schemes was revolutionary in different ways—Wallace's by its proposal to vest all ownership in the state and George's by the refusal to compensate owners for their individual losses—but at their core both cast a skeptical eye toward the supposed virtue of privately owned land and its commoditization.

Like all previous land reformers, both the LNS and the ELRL linked the political reform of land with particular ideas about property's commercial status, but now an absent property market had suddenly become an oppressively present one. Whereas free traders insisted that land be considered a commodity like any other, land nationalization advocates firmly believed it was not. The question of land's status, argued F. W. Newman for the LNS, was "not one for Political Economists, it belong[ed] to Morals, Politics, and History."[13] The law, not economics, was the ultimate arbiter of marketability, he wrote, before comparing the injustice of making land marketable with the similar injustice carried out by slavery: "Robbery of men's bodies, and robbery of a nation's land have close analogies."[14] Here was an echo of Ruskin, who had earlier demurred on the question of land's commodity status, writing that the "bodies of men, or women, . . . must not be bought or sold. Neither must land, nor water, nor air, these being the necessary sustenance of men's bodies and souls."[15] The same comparison with slavery emerged again, in 1899, when Wallace himself wrote that history, not justice, explained the buying and selling of both land and slaves; the emancipation of both was an inevitability. "'Free trade in land' has been fairly tried and has conspicuously failed," Wallace concluded, "and men are being driven by its failure in the conviction that land is not a fit subject for trade at all—that it should not be bought and sold as if it were a commodity."[16] Wallace, along with many others, embraced a new historicism by drawing on the work of scholars in comparative history and law, whose research into the history of early Anglo-Saxon communal ownership seemed to support the contingency of individual ownership. Along the same lines, historicism and agrarian radicalism in Ireland and Scotland ultimately pushed the Liberal Party to abandon its earlier principle of free trade in land in favor of legal protection for customary tenures.[17]

Land nationalizers, single taxers, and Celtic radicals fundamentally shifted the politics of land in late-Victorian Britain, pushing from the political center older calls for free trade and law reform and generating conservative responses that more strenuously defended the legitimacy of an open land market. As J. Langdon Parsons pointed out when he reminded his readers of Abraham's first recorded purchase of land for four hundred shekels to bury his wife Sarah, the legitimacy of the property market sprang from the deepest origins of Western history and biblical tradition.[18] Another leader in this defense was the Liberty and Property Defence League (LPDL), founded in 1883, which produced a number of pamphlets attacking socialist land plans.[19] In several of these, the authors actually called into question a premise shared by late-Victorian socialists as well as older conservatives, who argued that land's limited availability made it uniquely unsuited to comparisons with other commodities. To the contrary, as one anonymous author wrote, the availability of land could increase both theoretically and practically through improvements in productivity and the expansion of the market to colonial frontiers. All commodities faced theoretical limits to their production, argued another writer, but the daily notices for free land grants in settler colonies suggested that peak land remained a distant threat. Viewed as an imperial resource, land was no more limited than sugar or cotton, and its market was no less legitimate.[20]

For reformers, as for An Old Hand, locating the property market was inseparable from debating the ambiguous social, moral, and political questions surrounding the buying and selling of land in a society of highly unequal ownership. To focus on the everyday institutions that organized the exchange of property seemed to miss the much larger point of their collective limitations and failures. It was as though the property market was mapped according to two different topographies: one marking out the experience of exchange in everyday practice and the other indicating the landscape as it should have been or would one day be, given sufficient reform, the passage of time, or a more dramatic rupture of the social fabric. Scholars since then have fallen prey to similar thinking, most famously Karl Polanyi, who referred to the creation of a land market as "perhaps the weirdest of all the undertakings of our ancestors," but who also insisted that the logic of what he termed "market society" imposed itself from outside of any existing social institutions—a logic disembedded from a social context of its own.[21] This was the logic of supply and demand, of price quotations as An Old Hand would have wished to see them, a property market, as F. M. L. Thompson once put it, "in the economists' sense" of abstract and generalized exchange relations.[22] The logic of abstraction has thus always stood at a distance from the practice of exchange. To seek out one version of the property market has entailed disregarding all signs of the other.

The history of the property market is best understood as process in which ideas about marketable status and the practice of exchange evolved together. Like all markets, the property market was the achievement of historically specific work that combined ways of seeing with new ways of doing.[23] This market was thus assembled through networks of association that linked people, places, objects, and ideas. Moreover, these associations were variable and dynamic in ways that changed over time, permitting us to trace the reconfiguration of commodity cultures without denying the facts of earlier instances of exchange. The "particulars of sale," a phrase commonly used to advertise nineteenth-century property, mattered for understanding how the property market worked in any given time and place. This sense of markets as networked and contingent processes has recently been emphasized in Michel Callon's discussion of "marketization," a term that I will use broadly throughout this book.[24]

The particulars of the property market were determined by a wide range of actors involved in the buying and selling of real estate. We have already heard from two of them: the fictional Sir Walter Elliot, a wealthy but credit-starved landed aristocrat; and an anonymous writer who nevertheless adopted a moniker of someone with longstanding experience in the business of real estate. We know far more about the likes of Sir Walter, however, than we do about the many intermediaries involved in the marketing of property.[25] Thus, while the perspectives of owners and buyers will be explored in the background of this study, the foreground is occupied by the view from professions like auctioneering, house and estate agency, surveying, the law, and journalism. I am particularly interested in the social and material worlds through which these tradespeople built their identities and mobilized the expertise and institutions required to craft a more visible real estate market.

My emphasis on the contingency and everyday practice of real estate marketization brings this study of land in closer conversation with what has recently been called "histories of capitalism" or the "historical study of economic life." Like others in this field, I am interested in understanding how cultural practice shapes what Kenneth Lipartito describes as "the mosaic of economic forms and fluid institutions that constitute a capitalist system."[26] Land has long been considered an important institution in market societies and accounts of capitalist development, but the central concern has typically been to pinpoint the period in which land first became mobilized as an economic good or a means of capitalist production. Rarely is much weight placed on the fluidity of those institutions that make property marketable in different historical or social contexts. Part of understanding these more local and dynamic aspects of capitalist societies involves paying attention to the "anonymous history" and everyday worlds that give meaning to economic life—worlds like those inhabited by auctioneers, solicitors, and estate agents.[27]

There is also much to be gained from broadening the focus of capitalism studies beyond American capitalism, as this book aims to do by considering real estate in Britain. For all the attention that has been leveled on British economic history—typically under the now questionable rubric of England as the first industrialized nation—scholars have only tangentially scrutinized the formal and informal institutional practices that went into shaping the experience of everyday economic life.[28] From personal debt and labor contracts to joint-stock enterprise and limited liability law, the foundations of Victorian capitalism have been shown to be laid with contested and often ambivalent attitudes toward Adam Smith's legacy of free and open markets.[29] The perennial questioning of property's marketability was thus hardly an idiosyncratic attitude within Victorian commercial culture, even if it was sometimes perceived as such. Therefore, it is important that the marketization of property be understood as part of a larger development of British market culture shaped through different institutional practices.

The practices of the land market are difficult to understand without a brief foray into terminology. *Fee simple*, *leasehold*, *copyhold*, *ground rent*, *ground annual*, *feu*, and *feu duty*—these and other such terms are a bewildering but unavoidable hazard of British land law and its history, but one must be clear about distinctions between land and property. This book is concerned with the social and cultural practice of exchanging for money the rights to land and the buildings attached to land. Land and buildings were used in many ways and for different purposes, and appear in many forms. Changes in land use in nineteenth-century Britain had a profound impact on the organization of commodity exchange. Urban and commercial growth, for example, resulted in the subdivision of larger estates into smaller plots of land and many more buildings, each of which could at some point be brought into the market.[30] The nature of these objects—whether they were houses, estates, farms, commons, or barren plots of building land—is not as relevant to this study as are the means by which they were traded. In fact, the material qualities of land and houses were far less important overall than the rights that were claimed to them. It was the rights to land, not the land itself, that were the true objects of the property market.

The nature of property law in Britain was such that possession of land was never in itself sufficient proof of ownership.[31] The only absolute owner of the soil was the Crown, declared so by right of conquest following the Norman invasion. All other rights were held in estates subordinate to an earlier grant of land by a feudal superior. Tenure referred to the means by which an estate was held—originally as an exchange for service, but in modern times converted into money payments. The most secure and highly valued estate was a fee simple, or freehold estate, held under freehold tenure, which came as close as was possible in the law to absolute ownership. Real property, or realty, referred to those rights associated with freehold tenure. Other forms of tenure existed, as did estates held for a term of years, known as a leasehold estate. The term of a lease could range from a few months to a thousand years, but always included an eventual right of reversion to the original freehold; in London, where leasehold estates were a common feature of urban development, the standard was a ninety-nine-year term. Technically speaking, leasehold estates were classed as chattel or personal property, and therefore not included in definitions of real property or real estate. Finally, there were also important differences between the laws of property in England, in Scotland, and in Ireland, some of which will be discussed elsewhere in this book. Unlike in Ireland, where the land laws were a specific target of English colonialism, the laws of Scotland were explicitly recognized in the Acts of Union that created the Kingdom of Great Britain in 1707; thus its system of feuing—regranting lands between successive superiors and their vassals, without rights of reversion—imparted a unique character to Scottish urban development and real estate culture.[32]

Taking these complexities of built environment, legal distinction, and national custom into consideration, this study nonetheless treats the real estate or property market in more general terms, seeking not to reify particular classes or categories of property, but rather to examine a variety of instances in which rights associated with land and buildings were configured into contexts of alienable or commodity exchange. There were significant differences between renting a cottage and auctioning the fee simple to a large country estate, but these distinctions are as much a part of the history of the property business as they are grounds for considering their histories separately. I therefore use terms like *land*, *property*, *real estate*, and their associated markets as interchangeable and broadly inclusive for the purposes of understanding the longer-term development of commercial culture and practice.

This story begins in the eighteenth century, during a transformation in British consumer culture that resulted in new strategies for marketing, buying, and appreciating an ever-expanding world of goods.[33] Many of these techniques for buying and selling migrated to the world of property transactions. Despite the long history of commercial exchange in land, the widespread use of auction sales and the development of the professional expertise to manage them marked a new and important departure in the history of the property market. As I argue in the first two chapters of this book, auctions of real property borrowed from practices used elsewhere in early modern commercial culture and appear to have become well established sometime in the mid- to late eighteenth century. What made auction sales noteworthy as harbingers of a new commodity culture was the degree to which questions of marketability and the social relations of exchange were raised in an explicitly public forum, made visible to anyone attending a sale. Whereas previously such questions were resolved through private networks of correspondence between owners and their agents, auctions provided a new means of connecting people and information within what James Vernon has aptly called Britain's "society of strangers."[34]

Though it is difficult to establish a direct connection between auction sales and changes in the nature of demand for property, there is at least a correlation between an increase in the use of such collectively negotiated judgments of property value and a parallel growth in what economic historians refer to as the "positional premium" paid for land.[35] This premium refers to the social and political benefits that could accrue from owning land, and it has long been debated when and to what degree such a premium may have factored into the valuation of real property. Some economic historians have concluded that no additional premium was ever reflected in early modern land prices—in other words, that land was treated similar to any other commodity investment; but social historians have insisted that the status value of land (at the very least, of landed estates) was an important and enduring factor of demand.[36]

In two separate studies, however, Avner Offer and Gregory Clark have concluded that while the commodity status of land seems to have prevailed in earlier centuries, some measure of enhanced status value became more apparent beginning in the late eighteenth century, encouraging, for example, tenant farmers to remain in leasehold agreements rather than pay inflated prices for freehold land.[37] These studies have also concluded that a positional premium appeared across the spectrum of property locations and sizes. If it was the case that the demand for property was complicated by more diverse considerations of value, the marketization of property during the nineteenth century undoubtedly played a role. Practices like auctions served well as tools for estimating more uncertain values and for connecting more diverse communities of buyers, leading Arthur Young to speculate in 1813 that "the great influx of wealth has of late years been the means of making property more general."[38] The organization of the property market around the question of marketability thus reflected a distinct shift in the longer history of property exchange.

The suggestion that there was something distinct about the organization of the property market in nineteenth-century Britain might come as a surprise to those familiar with Britain's long imperial history as an occupier of foreign lands. Despite the visibility of late-Victorian land grabs in Africa, the Middle East, and Asia, these events were preceded by centuries of practice with conquering territory elsewhere, such as in Ireland, North America, South Asia, Africa, Australia, and New Zealand.[39] The acquisition of colonies was a complicated and highly contested affair, very often shaped as much by the actions of speculators, settlers, and squatters as by the intentions or policies of metropolitan governments. Equally important, however, was the export of British ideas about property, carried along with the other baggage of British emigrants, and the practices and technologies needed to convert land into a marketable commodity. Cultural notions of improvement and indigenous property; legal regimes of customary and statutory property law; economic theories of land, wealth, and taxation; and technological developments in surveying and cadastral mapping—all played a role in the creation of colonial land markets.

As important as these various exports were, relatively little attention has been paid to the ways in which colonial experience and practice opened up a field of experimentation and intellectual exchange that could influence understanding of the property market at the center of empire.[40] My book identifies several points of contact. The most immediate was the above-mentioned influx of wealth from colonies and the new buyers for land who aspired to invest this wealth in the status and power of English landed estates. The marketing of estates to these new groups is discussed in chapter 1. A more detailed engagement with the intercourse between colonial and domestic property markets comes in chapter 4, where I discuss the ways in which land title registration traversed the British imperial world and brought both types of market into a comparative analysis of property market culture. The development of cadastral cartography in England using Ordnance Survey maps (an issue closely related to the registration debate) also demonstrated the degree to which technologies refined in the service of colonial rule circulated to reshape the meaning of marketable property at home. Much like the history of political liberalism—which, as Andrew Sartori has demonstrated, found independent and vernacular purchase in places far removed from the center of empire—the construction of the property market in Britain emerged from networks of association that were not so easily traced to linear paths of teleological metropolitan development.[41]

Despite the emphasis in this study on the particular practices and contingencies that went into the construction of a nineteenth-century property market in Britain, there can be no denying the important parallels that also existed in real estate marketization elsewhere. In France, for instance,

Alexia Yates has examined the commercialization of property in fin de siècle Paris and found similar concerns and debates over the question of real estate's alienability and its relationship with other markets of modern capitalism—in particular, the stock market.[42] The legal classification of real estate within French civil law appeared to contradict the evidently speculative nature of its existence as a commercial object shaped by new forms of advertising, marketing, and corporate investment. No such distinction existed in English law, but the desire to define land in more marketable terms was evident in debates about title registration. Similarly, the conceptual emergence of the property market as an object of discrete analysis took place within the same decades in both countries. Thus, in the same years that the *Estates Gazette* reimagined its coverage of the real estate market in England, daily and weekly reports began to appear sporadically in *Le Figaro* (1881) and *Le Temps* (1885), followed by more consistent and wider coverage in the 1890s.[43] The marketization of property followed distinct historical paths, but in response to a clearly transnational logic of uneven capitalist development.

The anecdote of An Old Hand interrogating the effectiveness of property market institutions was notable in part because of how rarely contemporaries commented on them. This study therefore takes the approach of examining several different sites of market practice, tracking within each of them changes over time in the organization and meaning of marketability. Chapters 1 and 2 explore the history of property auction sales from the perspective of those who mediated these sales and in terms of the coordination of spatial practices that emphasized the universal alienability of property. Chapter 2 examines another mediator of market exchange in the form of the estate agent, arguing that both agents and auctioneers faced the difficult task of asserting their expertise in the liminal space between market exchange and a supposedly disinterested professionalism. Chapters 3 and 4 consider the property market in the more abstract space of market calculation and legal reform. Chapter 3 follows the history of property market journalism, from its origins at midcentury to the proliferation of different forms of reportage that emerged in the 1880s and 1890s, all focused on ways of representing in general terms the ebb and flow of local real estate transactions. Part of the difficulty in tracking these transactions stemmed from the lack of a central registry of land titles, the creation of which is the subject of chapter 4. Title registration has long been maligned as a century-long effort at failed Benthamite reform, but what is less acknowledged is the degree to which the debate over title reform introduced a persistent desire to mobilize land with the same fluidity and freedom thought to characterize other commodities, like stocks, ships, and watches. Having thus focused on four sites where the desire to see property in marketable terms was most explicit, I explore in chapter 5 the opposite question: how the *inalienability* of land came to be enshrined in one of the founding institutions of the land preservation movement and how this movement shaped and responded to the dynamic negotiation of the property market's limits.

CHAPTER ONE

The Marketplace

In English usage, the word *market* has long embodied two very different meanings: one having to do with an older, socially embedded *place* and the other referencing an abstract *space* of generalized exchange relations. This conceptual dichotomy—and, in particular, the emphasis on the relative autonomy and immateriality of the market space—is entirely modern, entangled within the same histories of commercial transformation that gave birth to new, more visible forms of property market organization. In medieval and early modern Europe, markets were fixed places, often marked by a cross in the center of towns and governed through dense social and cultural networks of ritual and custom. From the fifteenth century onward, however, the abstract market emerged, less as a place than a principle—a generalized encounter determined not by physical markers or local custom but, as Adam Smith would elaborate, by the opposition of competing self-interests. The very concept of modernity is often narrated through this historical parting of the ways between marketplaces and the growing dominance of market space across all fields of society.[1]

In the nineteenth century, the distinction between the marketplace and market society lodged itself further in the differing epistemologies of modern social science. Economists like Antoine-Augustin Cournot developed mathematical expressions for supply and demand curves. Scholars of jurisprudence and comparative anthropology like Henry S. Maine examined the histories of marketplace institutions in village communities, and, as it happened, re-situated them to the periphery of the modern world. Distinction also bred disdain: for Enlightenment thinkers like Smith, Jacques Turgot, and Nicolas de Condorcet, the marketplace was inherently vexatious, characterized by the corrupting interference of local corporations and government, a sclerotic burden on what might otherwise be a more rational form of economic calculation.[2]

Even the most sympathetic treatments of the marketplace, such as those written on the "moral economy" of local market practices, have only reinforced a persistent binary logic between a socially embedded marketplace and an abstract market space defined purely in terms of a disinterested cash nexus.[3] However, the effort to rid the market of its localism has never been completely successful, and critics of the market idea continue to point to the importance of social and spatial practices in situating the reification of market ideologies. The cultural meanings of market exchange may be more mobile and diffuse today than they were in the more strictly delimited practices of the medieval village marketplace, but they are no less dependent on or constitutive of these situated geographies of exchange. Thus, in considering the relationship between place and space in the configuration of the property market, this chapter begins with a set of seemingly straightforward questions about the geographical organization of property exchange in eighteenth- and nineteenth-century Britain, and particularly London: Where was property traded, how did the geographical organization of property exchange evolve over the course of the period, and what did such changes mean for understanding the property market?

My initial answer to these questions is that, while a significant portion of property transactions continued to be carried out in private—behind the hedgerows and office doors of estate owners and their solicitors—the public sale of property was transformed in ways that gave the property market greater coherence, meaning, and visibility. From the prevailing practice of private treaty sales and public auctions held in inns, taverns, and coffeehouses, metropolitan auctioneers and estate agents designed and constructed purpose-built spaces for property exchange, the most important being the London Auction Mart, first erected in 1808 and subsequently relocated to a new building in 1867. The auction mart provided a place in which to imagine a coherent and abstract market space; but this process was invariably a negotiated one, filled with the tensions and ambiguities associated with making marketable something as socially, politically, and culturally important as real estate. The auction mart created a spectacle of exchange comprising many different actors and observers, and its principles of bringing the market into the view of the public were eclipsed only at the turn of the nineteenth century, when the geography of property exchange proliferated into a kaleidoscope of suburban and provincial offices and salesrooms.

THE DEVELOPMENT OF PROPERTY AUCTIONS

Though it was built in the nineteenth century, the London Auction Mart had eighteenth-century origins. Its significance must be understood in the context of a broader transformation in British social and economic life that set the conditions for new commercial cultures and practices like public auctions, for new categories of marketable urban and suburban property and property buyers, and for new kinds of commercial and institutional spaces in London and elsewhere. This period was marked less by the overall growth in the quantity of goods consumed than by changes in taste, quality, and consumer demand; a nation of consumers became accustomed both to new goods and to new methods for marketing them.[4] Commerce likewise depended on the greater movement of goods and people and the extension of social networks between individuals living and working across greater distances—be it within cities, or between city and country, London and provincial towns, or the metropole and its expanding imperial network. These changes also generated forms of economic abstraction that reconfigured how people thought about the economy and their own economic lives.[5] In terms of real estate, urban development and the demand by new classes of investors further encouraged the use of commercial practices that could communicate information to a broader public. Commerce, finance, and empire all found institutional expression in the development of London, and, in particular, the City. London thrived as a central place of commercial and imperial power, and its institutional fabric reflected this in the design of new spaces like the Bank of England (opened in 1734, but greatly expanded under the design of Sir John Soane after 1788), the corn exchange (1749), the coal exchange (1770), the stock exchange (1801), and the auction mart.[6]

From the late seventeenth century, auction sales developed as a popular institution of British commercial culture, though not one that was initially used for many real estate transactions. As Brian Cowan has noted, auctions were integral to the forms of genteel sociability that shaped British metropolitan consumer culture, but he also demonstrates that the overwhelming majority of public auction sales at this time—88 percent, according to a survey of printed advertisements from the 1660s through the 1690s—concerned works of art and rare books.[7] These were the sales "by candle" that took place in London's proliferating coffeehouse culture and that so fascinated contemporaries like Samuel Pepys, John Evelyn, and Robert Hooke. Auctions similarly linked and facilitated the movement between the expanding networks of British imperial trade and commerce; many of the great trading routes that fueled British expansion relied on auctions as the primary method of sale. This was true for slaves in the West Indies and the American colonies, for bulk imported goods carried back to London docks, and for the diverse and exotic luxuries made available in the metropolis through colonial trade.[8]

Following the growing popularity of auctions for personal property, public sales of real property became more common from the mid-eighteenth century. Based on a survey of printed advertisements, Peter Ash established that the first auction of land or house property likely took place in the 1730s and was probably the work of the most prominent auctioneer of the day, Christopher Cock.[9] Cock hosted auctions in his Covent Garden office, and, though he was initially known as a bookseller, one advertisement in the spring of 1739 included the sale of two houses among the other property being sold from a bankrupt tradesman.[10] By the 1740s the same office routinely posted advertisements for the public sale of land and houses, along with continued sales of personal property. In 1766, when James Christie opened his great room in Pall Mall, he likewise featured auctions of landed estates and other real property. By the late eighteenth century, auctions—for real and personal property—had spread throughout the country and were so associated with the consumption of luxury goods as to become subject to state regulation. Under the Auction Duty Act of 1777 (17 Geo. 3, c. 50), taxes and license fees specifically distinguished between sales of real and personal property.[11] Regulation played an important role in defining auctioneering as a distinct occupation, but so too did a process of specialization that resulted in auctioneers developing expertise in particular branches of trade. Thus, an article written for the *Penny Magazine* in 1844 observed that the "connoisseur in pictures and prints, goes his rounds regularly through one series of rooms. . . . The book-collector has his special haunts. . . . Furniture occupies the principal attention of a third class of auctioneers, carriages and horses of a fourth."[12] Finally, there were "the mighty ones of the calling"—those who traded in estates.[13]

Modern social theory argues that auction mechanisms flourish in social contexts where more heterogeneous populations no longer view traditional networks of privately exchanged information to be effective or reliable.[14] As a general principle, this would suggest that the development of real estate auctions in late eighteenth-century Britain reflected a reconfiguration of exchange mechanisms, perhaps in response to uncertainty in the value of new forms of property or as a means of connecting more socially or geographically distant sellers and buyers. Neither of these was universally true, however, since private treaty remained the more common means of exchanging property. Indeed, there are many examples of large-estate owners trusting in private mechanisms to find buyers and negotiate market values, turning to public sales only as a last resort.[15] When the London solicitor James Coulthard organized the sale of the third Duke of Chandos's Radnorshire estates in the early 1770s, for example, he combined the use of private networks of professional contacts with public printed advertisements, employing a competitive bidding mechanism and the threat of a public auction sale if the property (or portions of it) failed to attract interest.[16] Sales of estates were also often driven by debt, and many families on both sides of an exchange preferred the less exposed and more trustworthy route of private negotiation.[17] Suspicion over the public exposure of an auction sale persisted into the nineteenth century. When the solicitor in charge of selling the Rushall estate in Wiltshire wrote to the Duke of Wellington in 1837, he confided that the owner, Sir Edward Poole, feared an unsuccessful auction might depreciate the value of the estate. Asking about the advisability of an auction sale, the agent wrote, "I have no right to ask *your* opinion, but I should like to have it."[18] Wellington declined to purchase the property, but it was ultimately advertised for sale at the auction mart the following year, suggesting that Poole and his lawyer overcame their initial hestitation.[19]

In the case of the Rushall estate and for many others, public sales offered a valuable mechanism for attracting a diverse community of spectators and bidders. This was certainly true for the kind of large sales that drew national attention, such as one in 1824 that put Richard Arkwright into possession of Sutton Hall for £482,432 or one that enabled the Duke of Devonshire to sell his estate at Wetherby for £168,561.[20] There is no historiographical consensus on the degree to which new wealth aspired to settle in estates, but it is clear that there were enough new purchasers from the ranks of urban business and professions to justify new marketing techniques. John Habakkuk has suggested a list of possible purchasers that includes returning nabobs, politicians, clergy, merchants, bankers, lawyers, West Indian planters, seamen, and industrialists.[21] Moreover, the market for smaller properties was not necessarily less diverse, as B. A. Holderness has shown was the case in Lincolnshire, where a steady volume of smaller sales fed the demand of local farmers, regional merchants, and professionals, and even distant metropolitan investors.[22] Auction sales contributed an important marketing mechanism to this process.

Auctions were also used for many different types of property, from very large estates to much smaller parcels generated through the breakup of estates and urban development. At the aforementioned auction of the market town of Wetherby, the Duke of Devonshire disposed of his nearly 1,500-acre estate in 170 lots of farm, residence, and commercial property; this kind of subdivision appears to have happened with greater frequency throughout the nineteenth century. "Experience goes to prove," stated one guide to estate management from 1868, "that, in disposing of any extensive estate to secure the largest price . . . sell it in lots."[23] The author gave the example of a small estate outside London, initially purchased for £1,600 but then broken up and sold in lots for a total of £21,980. Such subdivision often preceded more intensive urban expansion and development, though this process started well before the nineteenth century. For the counties surrounding London, land began to be subdivided into mini-estates for retiring professionals early in the eighteenth century. At this time, Daniel Defoe remarked on the many "handsome large houses" on the border of Essex.[24] The growth of London thereafter generated new residential properties on planned estates in west London by the likes of Grosvenor, Portland, and Bedford, as well as speculative house building there and elsewhere across the city.[25] Later in the nineteenth century, building societies and freehold land societies would also use auctions as a means of disposing of improved building lots.[26]

The forces of estate improvement and urban development produced exactly the kind of property that was typically advertised for sale by auction in London around the time of the auction mart's construction.[27] In a single issue of the *Times* from 1805, for example, the firm of Winstanley & Son advertised a wide range of upcoming real estate auctions, including the following: the 1,073-acre estate and manor of Warkworth in Northamptonshire, a mini-estate "in the Vicinity of Clapham" with a "New erected Villa" and fourteen acres of land, and a sale in multiple lots for a mix of freehold commercial property (shops and public houses) and dwelling houses situated on Bull Inn Court and Maiden Lane, the Strand. A week later, the father-and-son firm previewed another auction for a leasehold residence on 58 Gower Street, held by the Duke of Bedford on an eighty-two-year term. Elsewhere in the paper, a great many advertisements gestured to London's outward expansion, such as in the ad published for Allport & Son for a three-acre leasehold farm in Hackney, "eligible for carrying on the gardening business or [that] at any easy expence [*sic*] might be converted into a desirable residence for a genteel family," or another ad by Smith for a leasehold timber house and yard in nearby Hoxton, "well calculated for building a manufactory and dwelling-houses in a populous improving neighbourhood."[28] Across the city—from residential villas to public houses and riverbank manufactories—auctions sales mobilized the commoditization of property by alerting prospective buyers to sales and convening them to negotiate values and prices.

Finally, though auction sales were used throughout Britain during this period and were regulated by similar laws, differences in practice were seen by some commentators to stifle the more widespread use of public sales outside England. In Scotland, for example, where auctions were commonly referred to as roups (and auctioneers known as roupers), the English practice of reserving a final bid for the seller was instead addressed through the use of upset prices, which often meant that properties started bidding at higher prices, thereby suppressing further competition. Bids for real property were also taken to be contractual in Scotland, even before the fall of the auctioneer's hammer, whereas in England they could be withdrawn in the course of the sale.[29] The "English mode" further required an immediate deposit of 10 percent, which gave vendors insurance against phony bids as well as a means of paying any auction duties. Finally, the close of a public roup in Scotland offered little protection to anyone who may have offered an earlier bid, since, in the case of the highest bidder failing to complete the sale, the seller reserved the right to force a sale on the next highest offer. This last custom, complained one Scots commentator, was "a barbarous condition . . . which would not be tolerated in England for one moment."[30] As the same writer noted, none of these conditions were likely to have a noticeable impact on sales of larger estates; houses and other smaller properties were another matter.

Despite regional variations in practice, however, property auctions had clearly become well established by the nineteenth century. By 1853, Alfred Cox, an estate agent practicing in London, supposed that

> those who would at one time have recoiled from the rude exposure to public gaze which they consider inseparable from a public auction now frequently resort to it without reluctance; and this change of feeling arises partly from the altered tone of public opinion on these matters, and partly from the increased advantages and facilities of that mode of transferring property.[31]

Cox rightly pointed out that selling property by auction involved a whole change in "public opinion" regarding how property should be treated in the marketplace. Unlike transfers by private treaty, auctions entailed a significant degree of commercial spectacle, a "rude exposure to public gaze," that could be deeply unsettling to more traditional notions of propriety and ownership. This gaze depended both on the existence of new publics interested in the purchase of land and houses and on the ability to reconfigure the marketability of real property in the public space. Marketability in this sense refers not only to the strictly legal conditions often used at the time to define "marketable" titles, but also to a broader spectrum of new material and spatial practices, cultural configurations, and social dispositions. These collectively enabled and made meaningful the buying and selling of real estate. The cultural construction of public marketability was particularly noticeable where the spectacle of an auction sale was most visible—which is to say, at the auction itself. It should therefore be of no surprise to see those with the most to gain from auction sales paying close attention to the design of auction space, which is exactly what happened in the opening decade of the nineteenth century.

AN IMPROVED PROPERTY MARKETPLACE: BARTHOLOMEW LANE

One anonymous author announced a call to reform the marketplace in a pamphlet published in 1807.[32] The overlap in style and content between this document and the prospectus for the new auction mart that was circulated only months later strongly suggests a single author, which a later source would identify as George Edmund Shuttleworth.[33] Shuttleworth became a founding director of the London Auction Mart, and though he was not listed as an original shareholder, it is nevertheless reasonable to suppose that it was he who led the effort to build it. In *An Address to the Auctioneers of the Metropolis*, Shuttleworth celebrated the development of auctions in a phrase that was subsequently copied into the company prospectus. "Public Auctions," he wrote, "have . . . been adopted as an impartial and just medium for the exercise of individual competition—to accelerate the Transfer of Property—to open the Channels of Commerce—and to promote the Spirit of Enterprize and Speculation."[34] Unfortunately, despite the progress of auctions, Shuttleworth complained that the "present accommodations for Public Sales in London [were] totally inadequate."[35] He then offered a detailed critique of Garraway's Coffee House on Exchange (or Change) Alley—a place well known for stock trading in the history of eighteenth-century finance, but which had also become the leading place for auction sales by the turn of the century (see fig. 1).

Though it is difficult to say how or precisely when Garraway's assumed its reputation as an informal institution for auctioneers, the shift may have represented a greater specialization in metropolitan auction sales. Up to that time and continuing into the nineteenth century, many auctions were typically held either "on the premises" or in local inns and taverns. Based on a sample of auction advertisements in the *Times*, Brian Learmount has estimated that, as late as 1788, most sales still took place in this way; by 1805, however, a similar sample suggests that Garraway's and a few other

FIGURE 1. Frederick Napoleon Shepherd, *Change Alley*, 1873. Watercolor on paper. View of Garraway's Coffee House. Reproduced by permission of the London Metropolitan Archives, City of London. http://collage.cityoflondon.gov.uk. Image 1623.

private salesrooms, like Christie's offices on Pall Mall, had come to host well over 90 percent of all auctions for real estate.[36] All the same, the rising status of Garraway's did not stop Shuttleworth from charging its owner, "Mr. H." (a.k.a. William Howell), with being "extremely negligent of his duty" to the seventy or so auctioneers estimated to be using the institution.[37] He accused Howell of refusing to give auctioneers sufficient advertising space for handbills and particulars of sale, of discriminating against certain individuals, and of charging unjust fees for the use of rooms. Shuttleworth also complained more generally that the arrangement of rooms at Garraway's made it difficult to attract the public to sales because the rooms most commonly given for auctions were located on the uppermost floors and there was little signage to guide visitors upstairs. The lack of maps for the city and country as a whole also made it challenging for auctioneers to point out "the local advantages of Property."[38] Finally, Shuttleworth pointed out the difficulties of negotiating the sea of information available in newspapers (briefly suggesting that auctioneers should set up their own press dedicated to announcements) and railed against unqualified practitioners and mock auctioneers operating in various parts of London. While the idea of a purpose-built marketplace was not explicitly raised in this pamphlet, it did conclude with a call for the city's auctioneers to convene as a society that could help reform Garraway's and defend the best interests of the profession.[39]

No records survive of the meetings that took place during the winter of 1808, and though Shuttleworth had initially expressed a willingness to work with Howell, it is clear in hindsight that attention quickly settled on a more ambitious plan to construct a new building exclusively for the benefit of auction sales. Perhaps the gathering decided to follow Parisian notaries, who had made a similar decision to open an auction room for realty in 1804. The choice may also have reflected general sympathy with Shuttleworth's enthusiastic call for professional independence and autonomy.[40] In any event, considerably more than fifty auctioneers invested in the initial shares that were distributed on February 4, 1808. The laying of the foundation stone for the auction mart was celebrated that September, with a procession of workmen, directors, and city officials (including the lord mayor) who convened at the London Tavern on Bishopsgate Street before parading down to the site on Bartholomew Lane.[41] Fifteen months later, in January 1810, the auction mart opened for business, with public sales of property located in London, Middlesex, Surrey, Hertfordshire, and Suffolk. These sales consisted of a variety of property, such as leasehold and freehold commercial property, building land, dwelling houses, and landed estates, as well as canal shares, insurance policies, and other annuities.[42]

When the directors of the London Auction Mart published their prospectus in 1809, they imagined a marketplace that would both elevate the status and prestige of a profession and respond to the practical concerns outlined in Shuttleworth's pamphlet. The combined aspirational and practical purpose of the building perhaps said something about the individuals who built it. Those behind the mart's initial construction—the directors listed in the company's prospectus—came from a cross section of London's most elite auctioneers, nearly all of them having established their businesses in the last quarter of the eighteenth century. Richard Winstanley, for example, opened his office on Paternoster Row in 1783. John Prickett expanded his father's carpentry business in 1789 to include auctioneering and surveying, and Henry Robins (whose son George would become the nineteenth century's most famous auctioneer) entered business with his brother, John, in 1790. Harry Phillips left his job as a clerk at Christie's auction house to set up his own firm in 1796. Phillips could obviously boast of establishment connections, but others, like Prickett and Robins, arrived at auctioneering via neighboring trades in agriculture, building, and furniture.[43] Three of the twelve directors listed in the prospectus—Robins, John Page, and Richard Jaques—had also been among the founding members of the oldest known professional association for auctioneers, the Select Society of Auctioneers, established in 1799.[44] As an expression of particular interests, therefore, the auction mart captured the view from the top of this particular branch of commercial society.

Many of the auction mart's founders held specific ties to the trade in real estate. Winstanley, Prickett, Robins, and Phillips regularly advertised sales of land and houses in the *Times*—as did other directors, such as Jaques, Daniel Rolfe Munn, and John Anthony Hermon. In fact, beyond the circle of directors, the majority of the investors in the auction mart held some connection to the sale of realty. The surviving register of proprietors lists fifty-six original shareholders.[45] Sixteen of these sold their shares within a year or two of the initial distribution in 1808, leaving approximately forty owners who were either invested for a longer term (often until their death) or were already prominent real estate auctioneers. Of these, approximately twenty-seven, or two-thirds of the more committed investors, can be identified as having advertised real estate sales on a regular basis around the time of the auction mart's founding. Of course, it is unlikely that many of these auctioneers had specialized to the point of working exclusively with real estate; the auction mart itself was, at least initially, intended to include sales of personal property. All the same, some specialization had undoubtedly begun and would continue, and the bulk of those most active in the auction mart's construction spent much of their time selling estates and other residential and commercial property located in and around the metropolis.

For these founders, the work of imagining a new kind of real estate market required a new kind of institution, set at the heart of Britain's commercial and imperial metropolis. Such an institution would provide "an accumulated source of intelligence, so methodically disposed, as to render the most accurate information, readily attainable."[46] "Existing practice[s]," noted the prospectus, left the public "exposed to so many inconveniences, irregularities, and unpleasant alternatives, that long experience, has impressed the absolute necessity of more extensive, and superior arrangements." The directors also sought to link the auction mart to a broader geography of commercial landmarks found nearby in the City. The prospectus, for example, praised the "almost mechanical precision" by which the new Lloyd's Coffee House, which had been relocated to the Royal Exchange in 1774, had managed to organize the "intricate, diversified, and multifarious" transactions of the maritime insurance market.[47] The authors of the company's prospectus self-consciously positioned the auction mart within "immediate contiguity to those active scenes of business, the Bank of England, Royal Exchange, Lloyd's Coffee House, the Stock Exchange, and other Public Offices," whose proximity to their establishment "[could not] be too highly appreciated."[48] The corner of Bartholomew Lane and Throgmorton Street placed the auction mart only short steps from the City's major credit and securities markets. This undoubtedly lent prestige and convenience to the new institution, though it also acknowledged the social fluidity and ambiguity that still existed between different kinds of commercial and financial activity. The London Stock Exchange had only just begun to effectively limit its membership to jobbers and brokers, and as late as 1845, David Morier Evans complained of "little go" or "alley men" loitering in the court joining the stock exchange to the auction mart and speculating in second-rate shares.[49]

To convey the novelty and vision of the new company, its owners took particular care to advertise the precise details of the auction mart's exterior and interior design. Based on an architectural plan by John Walters, the auction mart rose two stories above the ground floor, with a mezzanine and a basement containing offices and cellar space for a coffeehouse. The mezzanine offered ten office rooms overlooking the central hall. Salesrooms were located on the upper two floors and were allocated for sales of estates on the first and sales of personal property on the second, with special turret lights in the latter rooms for the display of artwork.[50] Each of these floors also included side rooms for private consultations during public sales. The coffee room (see fig. 2) was located on the side of the building opposite the Bartholomew Lane entrance, accessible from the main stairwell of the auction mart as well as from Throgmorton Street. The rear entrance to the coffee room also linked the auction mart directly to the stock exchange via Shorter's Court. The room was thus positioned as a liminal space between the formal hall and salesrooms of the auction mart and the nearby market for securities. Its inclusion undoubtedly represented a concession to the prevailing culture of commercial sociability, but it is interesting to observe that its location placed it in a subordinate position with respect to the main entrance and the more formal spaces of the building. At least in theory, the auction mart demarcated spaces of private and public exchange in a pattern that echoed the City of London's changing commercial geography, from a mixed-use central district with a resident population to a space of purpose-built commercial and financial infrastructure.[51]

The most extravagant feature of all was the auction mart's central atrium, or saloon (see fig. 3). This hall was accessible from the main ground-floor

Figure 2. Augustus Charles Pugin, *Bartholomew Lane*, 1811. Engraving. Interior view of the coffee room at the Auction Mart, Bartholomew Lane. Reproduced by permission of the London Metropolitan Archives, City of London. http://collage.cityoflondon.gov.uk. Image 1043.

Figure 3. Augustus Charles Pugin, *Bartholomew Lane*, 1811. Aquatint on paper. Interior view of the hall in the Auction Mart, Bartholomew Lane. Reproduced by permission of the London Metropolitan Archives, City of London. http://collage.cityoflondon.gov.uk. Image 1041.

entrance and was connected to all other functions of the building: salesrooms on the upper stories, offices on the belowground floors, and the coffeehouse in the rear. The prospectus for the auction mart gave the greatest attention to the details of the saloon, going so far as to offer a pullout plan for the space that enabled viewers to reconstruct its dimensions by raising its four walls off of the page. Within this space, the directors promised to "obviate" the "evil" of limited market perspectives "as speedily as the effect of time, and industry [would] permit." The auction mart would be made "the grand, and central point, for the most prompt information, immediately connected with, or bearing the remotest affinity, to the various denominations of property." At first glance, what most defined the vision of the saloon was this function as a vast repository of information, more efficient than newspapers, greater in scope than any individual firm, and more accessible than the research of any single individual.[52]

Even more important than the amount of information gathered in the auction mart, however, was its organization in space and time. Arranged on each of the four sides of the saloon, notice boards offered prospective buyers concise listings of the particulars of sale for each form of property. Real property dominated both the north and south sides, with a portion of the latter arranged to display fine art and merchandise and a smaller compartment on the west side for other personal and commercial movables. The remaining compartments on the west and east sides contained general information, notices of postponed sales, and of sales made by private contract. The hall likewise offered a collection of maps and atlases: of the world, of England, Wales, Scotland, and Ireland, of the City of London, of individual counties, and of water and road transportation networks. Daily, weekly, and periodical newspapers from London and from leading provincial towns were offered, indexed, and archived for future reference, and it was similarly proposed to keep at the auction mart county and city district registers in which property for sale by both auction or private treaty would be gathered together for ready viewing. In addition, the auction mart would appoint provincial agents responsible for gathering and transmitting information between city and country agents and owners, and it would offer distribution services for those wanting regular updates on forthcoming sales and particulars.[53]

Alongside this coordination and representation of the property market, the saloon offered devices for managing and regulating the market in time. For example, a large stove set in a hexagonal frame at the center of the hall contained a weekly register of approaching sales and a large clock and bell mounted on its top, with which to monitor the pace of sales going on throughout the building. "The sales commence immediately on ringing the bell," noted a sign along the staircase to the upper salesrooms. The various registers and notice boards also corrected another time-related problem that the prospectus identified with the existing system of advertisements, which were often placed in papers subject to the needs of other political, social, and journalistic schedules. A heated debate in parliament or a particularly exciting scandal might cause havoc with the proper timing of advertisements for upcoming auctions.[54] The clock and calendars in the saloon insulated the world of property exchange from outside events, focused the attention of buyers and sellers on the flow of upcoming sales, and thereby reinforced the distinction between commercial life inside the auction mart and the world beyond.

Via this grand assemblage of spatial and information technology, the associated salesrooms and offices of the mart would "be rendered efficient" and "by this arrangement every person, comprised in the extensive population of this great commercial Empire, may at one concise view . . . ascertain if any situation adapted to his avocations, or suitable to his convenience, be attainable, or if any other object of his pursuit, can be accomplished."[55] The auction mart held out the promise of a public institution through which sales of property in the country and beyond would be effortlessly made available to potential buyers. The time and space of the property market were compressed, ordered, arranged, and made visible and predictable to a disinterested audience of vendors, agents, brokers, speculators, and the general public.

It was not enough for the auction mart to just gather and organize information, however; to operate most effectively, it also needed to organize people. Charles Knight gave a sense of this function in his three-installment series on London auctions, published for the *Penny Magazine* in 1844. Knight encouraged his readers to imagine themselves as visitors to the saloon, situating them as direct observers of a supposedly comprehensive and universal field of market information. "Even as we pause in the hall to look around us," he wrote, "the systematic arrangements for the management of the business of the mart, that meet the eye, convey a forcible impression of the extent of that business." Seeing the market was the essential step to participating in it, but this act required discipline and adherence to a prescribed order of operations. After first consulting announcements of postponed or canceled sales, "the eye falls upon the tables that show us the sales of today," followed by a careful study of the calendar for future sales and their associated salesrooms.[56] Once again, the mart both configured the market and empowered new forms of disinterested agency.[57]

The same article explicitly contrasted these arrangements with the more modest amenities found at Garraway's. While the coffeehouse "still flourishe[d] in a kind of immortal youth" amid the "dingy-looking shops or dungeon offices" that lined Change Alley, the magazine quickly passed over its salesrooms, noting that they "present[ed] nothing remarkable."[58] A city guidebook published around the same time admitted that, regarding Garraway's, "an introduction to it, under other circumstances than that of a sale of landed property, would scarcely induce the visitor to believe that it had ever been appropriate to such a purpose, or was calculated to attract the attention it does."[59] Such contrasts based on the themes of disorderliness, informality, and historical association became common tropes for underrating the continued use of Garraway's as a competing market for property auctions.

With few exceptions, published representations of the auction mart rarely investigated the salesrooms themselves. When they did, it was often with a tongue-in-cheek swipe at the pretensions of auctioneers and their performances behind the rostrum. In *Portraits of Public Characters* (1841), for example, James Grant wrote a humorous profile of the legendary "prince of auctioneers," George Robins, in which Grant offered another tour of the mart, but with a focus on the "celebrated locality" of Robins's first-floor salesroom. Commanded at the front by Robins's raised rostrum, the room was otherwise small, "notwithstanding the amount of business done in it, and the importance of the transactions of which it has for so many years been the theatre," and with space for "[no] more than 150 persons, even in a standing position." Grant poked fun at Robins's reputation for elaborate and exaggerated descriptions of property, writing that, despite his "athletic figure," Robins had conveniently placed a single armchair at the back of the rostrum "into which he [was] accustomed to throw himself . . . when fatigued by his exertions." "Such is the place," wrote Grant, "in which property of the value of £50,000 or £60,000 is often, in the course of two or three hours, transferred from one person to another; and in which, from first to last, estates and houses worth millions, have, through Mr. Robin's potent agency, been made to change hands."[60] Through his satire, Grant revealed the spectacle of auction sales and hinted at the energy and anxiety associated with such dramatic transfers of ownership. In this sense, the salesrooms stood in contrast to the more orderly view of the property market that was represented by the saloon.

Contrary to the ambitions espoused in the prospectus or in these other published accounts, the auction mart was not, and never would be, a universal marketplace for the sale of property in London, nor could it offer a "concise view" of property for sale across all of England, the United Kingdom, or the British Empire. However, it does appear to have quickly secured its position atop the hierarchy of metropolitan property marketplaces.

Whereas Garraway's had hosted the majority of real estate auction sales in 1805 (166 of 183 sampled ads), by the summer of 1810—six months after the auction mart had opened—that proportion had fallen to only 26 percent, significantly eclipsed by the mart's share of 61 percent (131 of 215 ads for that year).

The mart also attracted the attention of readers outside London and the home counties through advertisements for provincial estates. On July 2, 1810, for instance, the *Gloucester Journal* posted a notice for the auction of the Pontrylas estate, in Herefordshire, which was to be sold by the firm of Hoggart and Phillips at the auction mart on July 27. Provincial papers also advertised estate sales beyond their own localities, such as when, on September 16, 1830, the *Leeds Intelligencer* posted ads for sales to be held at the mart by George Robins for properties in Shropshire, South Wales, and Bristol. The predominance of estate sales in these ads spoke to the broader national audience for this type of property, though it was not uncommon to see sales for smaller farm property as well. By midcentury, sales at the London Auction Mart were routinely advertised in provincial papers across Britain.

Nearly all the above-mentioned representations of the auction mart, though produced in different times and addressed to different audiences, echoed and reinforced a vision of the property market that the institution's founders had carefully implanted into its social and material designs. This was as much an ideological project as a practical one, reconfiguring in spatial terms an ideal field of commercial relations that simultaneously problematized the existing order of property exchange. Its arrangement anticipated a world in which property information would circulate unhindered between vendors and buyers; a world in which local notices of property sales would be readily amalgamated into a comprehensive perspective; a world inhabited by a public whose encounters in the auction room would be mediated by nothing more than their own commercial disinterest. This was a very different world from the existing one, which was characterized by informal institutions facilitating personal and local exchanges. Understanding this ideological function of the auction mart is at least as important as measuring the extent of its practical achievement, since doing so reveals the social and cultural terms through which nineteenth-century real estate was made marketable.

That being the case, the auction mart could just as easily function as a space to debate the uncertainties and opportunities of marketability as to project and affirm them. Thus, while Grant celebrated the commercial spectacle of Robins swinging a hammer to market landed estates, he also cautioned his readers to consider the auction mart "as a place possessing peculiar claims to the attention of the moralist"; the auction room was "rife with the records of the ruin and wretchedness which noblemen and gentlemen [had] brought on themselves by their extravagance, their dissipation, and their folly."[61] The specter of aristocratic debt haunted the sale of many estates, and its murmurings could never entirely be drowned out by the shouts of bidders, no matter how well the latter were accommodated in the halls and rooms off Bartholomew Lane. In theory, at least, the auction mart isolated the marketability of property by "disentangling" it from its own historical, geographical, and moral associations; in practice, the entanglements of social relations were never so easily kept out.[62] The cultural conditions of sale, so to speak, were always and everywhere negotiable.

This was particularly true when it came to questions of disinterest and anonymity among participants at auction sales, and among visitors to the auction mart in particular. Unlike the stock exchange or Lloyd's subscription rooms, the auction mart was built with the intention of providing information about real estate for sale to any member of the public, not just subscribers. The marketability of property was premised on the supposed virtue of strangers availing themselves of timely and trustworthy information. "The public indiscriminately may avail itself of the advantages connected with [the facilities at the auction mart]," wrote Ackermann—but even his optimism quickly followed with a note of suspicion: "It is but justice to add, that a system of order, regularity, and propriety prevails throughout this whole establishment; that the utmost attention and civility is paid to every individual; [and] that the most minute information on all subjects connected with trade or sale, is frankly communicated."[63] Here Ackermann implicitly contrasted the auction mart with less reputable establishments, but he also sounded a note of caution that could easily reverberate back into the salesrooms.

Of course, fears of collusion and fraud at "mock auctions" were perennial worries in the nineteenth century and reveal the inherent ambiguities of value and social trust that characterize this type of exchange context; these fears could seem particularly acute—not to say humorous—when it came to sales of real estate. For example, in her short story "Purchasing a Property" (1841), Julia Pardoe explored the ambiguities of trust and agency at the auction mart by implicating its practices in a satirical morality tale of commercial fraud.[64] The story relates the misfortune of Launcelot Barham, an ex-stockbroker retired to a "comfortable little independence" and dignified in his distant connections to a baronet and London sheriff. Desiring to leave his flat in the City for the "babble of green fields" he explores various suburban villages advertised for private sale in newspapers, but his quest for the perfect home is frustrated until, several months into his search, he is caught walking in the street during a sudden rainstorm. He finds shelter "as if by a singularly happy chance, in the Auction Mart, where a sale was at the moment going forward, of estates and houses in and about the metropolis."[65]

Barham's indifference to the goings-on at the auction mart is soon tempered by the "strain of elevated eloquence" coming from the auctioneer, who at that moment offers "an elegant and substantially-built stone residence, on the banks of the Thames, with right of fishing in the river, right of common on Runnymeade [*sic*], and sundry other immunities." Seduced by the auctioneer's assurances and by the energetic bids of several curious characters in the salesroom, Barham purchases the property for £700. He sets out to celebrate in the offices of his childhood friend, the solicitor Henry Hotham, whose practice Barham tellingly ridicules: "Here you are, up to your neck, as usual, in papers and parchments, making out titles for pigsties, and spoiling parchment, while I have contrived, without a single stroke of the pen, to become proprietor of a freehold estate, and the master of a stone-built residence on the banks of the Thames."[66] Unimpressed, Hotham questions his friend and is shocked to learn that Barham did not inspect his purchase beforehand. The two depart to visit the property, where they ultimately discover, to Barham's chagrin, that the stone-built residence is nothing other than an abandoned tollhouse at Staines Bridge.

Through the character of Barham, Pardoe depicted an experience in the auction mart different from the one envisioned in the institution's prospectus and celebrated in other descriptions of its operation. It is telling, for example, that Barham happens upon the auction mart by chance, his decision to enter forced on him by a downpour of rain. His entry by a back door bypasses the saloon entirely and instead throws him directly into a salesroom, where the auctioneer and the duplicity of the gathered audience gradually disarm his suspicions and lead him into a series of uninformed bids. Barham surely fits the definition of a stranger to property, but nothing in his experience conveys the ordered and rational calculation that the auction mart is ostensibly intended to offer such strangers: there is no "concise view" of the property market, nor any sign of "systematic arrangements" other than those suggesting collusion and deceit. Indeed, Barham's experience at the mart is implicitly contrasted with his solicitor's more secure and trustworthy world of parchments and private exchange networks. As a stranger to property in a community that in reality was anything but disinterested or anonymous, Barham experiences the moral dangers of questionable marketability in a place built to eliminate them. Pardoe's message of caveat emptor was as clear as it was unsettling to anyone seeking a shortcut to property via the auction mart.

If Launcelot Barham suffers for being a stranger at the auction mart, Thomas Frewen might best be described as having thrived as a stranger by design. Frewen was a landowner who occasionally employed proxy bidders to hide his identity and maximize his economic advantage as a purchaser of property. For Frewen, being a stranger in the auction mart (or at least *acting* like one) really did offer advantages—perhaps not in the way intended by the mart's creators, but certainly in contrast to the less anonymous world of private or local exchange networks. Frewen moved to his family's Sussex estate at Brickwell in 1836, managing his family's other properties in Sussex, Leicestershire, London, and Ireland from then until his death in 1870. Throughout this time, he assiduously worked to expand his holdings through a number of private and public purchases, and his estate correspondence—in particular, the letters exchanged with his personal solicitor, William Nanson—discuss a number of auction room tactics that add further insight and nuance to an already complicated picture of the auction mart and the marketability of property within it.

In one letter, penned April 9, 1841, Frewen informed Nanson of an estate in the parish of Brede, adjacent to Brickwell, advertised to be auctioned in May by Shuttleworth & Sons at the auction mart. "One of these lots [Shearfold Farm] I wish to buy," he wrote, "as I fancy if I can purchase by some *secret agent* it will be bought cheap" (my emphasis). Frewen then asked Nanson to obtain particulars of the sale but cautioned him to act "informally, through a London agent who should be told not to mention for whom he wants it for if *you* write in person Shuttleworth will make enquiry from Smith [the tenant] down here & it may possibly be surmised that you are asking on my behalf" (original emphasis). Though Frewen wanted only a single lot, he also thought it better for Nanson to "enquire about the whole as it will look more like an indifferent purchaser." Assuming that all was well with the estate, Frewen then requested Nanson "to appoint some stranger to bid for me."[67]

Such attempts at anonymity were not uncommon in trying to gather information about properties for sale, but they do seem to have been particularly viable when it came to sales at the London Auction Mart, where distance from the locality made it easier to hide Frewen's intentions from his neighbors. In another example, from letters exchanged in the summer of 1858, Frewen strategized over an upcoming auction of Mill Corner, a nearby property owned by a resident of London, referred to in the correspondence by the last name Cox. Frewen had made earlier attempts to purchase portions of the estate from Cox but had been rebuffed with offers that Frewen found exorbitant; Cox's decision to sell the land now provided a new opportunity for Frewen to obtain it by auction rather than through direct contact. Since both knew each other well, the ability to feign disinterest by proxy was essential to Frewen's plan, and so he asked Nanson "to get some one who would not be supposed to be connected with me or you [to] attend the sale" because "if either Cox or Barnes [the auctioneer] think I want it they will make me pay."[68]

In these examples, Frewen skillfully disentangled himself from the geographical and social associations that he feared would bias others against him as a bidder and would increase the costs of purchasing the properties in question. Pretending to be a stranger to property leveled the economic field and reconfigured the conditions of marketability in ways that avoided the entanglements of social intimacy and local proximity. And though such strategies could be and certainly were used for a variety of public and private property sales, the auction mart undoubtedly made it easier to employ them. The mart was no place for neighbors. Frewen ended up the purchaser of both the above lots, at prices below what he initially feared he would be forced to pay.[69]

Thus the auction mart could provide, in some instances, an effective stage for performing disinterest. This was not always the case in local settings, where Frewen faced a much greater degree of exposure, albeit in ways that sometimes played to his advantage. When Frewen's solicitor in Leicestershire, Benjamin Adam, received a visit from a Mr. Duncan in February 1869, it was because Duncan had already suspected that Frewen might bid against him for a freehold estate that would soon be put up for sale at the Crown Inn in Oakham.[70] Anticipating competition, both Adam and Duncan agreed that "of course there could be no personal feelings in the case."[71] All the same, it was arranged that Frewen would refrain from bidding, on the condition that Duncan take only the portion of the estate that he desired and sell the rest to Frewen at a discount. Summing up the arrangements after the auction, Adam reassured Frewen: "You save a good deal of money, by getting rid of Mr. Duncan's competition and as you suggest it is the more neighbourly course."[72] A month later, Adam wrote to Frewen again with news of another purchase made on the latter's behalf, this time for a house. It might well have sold for less than the closing bid of £200, presumed Adam, had the local mason who was bidding against Frewen recognized the agent Adam had employed for the sale. It was only after Adam himself bid that the mason understood he was bidding against Frewen and so declined to compete any further, afterward telling Adam that "he would not have bid so high" had he realized sooner.[73] For better or for worse, these local sales involved forms of scrutiny, deference, cooperation, and "neighborly" obligation that contrasted sharply with Frewen's earlier success as a stranger to property at the auction mart.

In Frewen's case, anonymity worked in different ways than it did with the character of Lancelot Barham. In several of Frewen's purchasing strategies, he expressed deep concern about being known in the auction room, particularly by the vendors of property or their agents, who might be able to ascertain his identity and use this information to demand a higher price. By employing "secret agents" to bid on his behalf, Frewen was able to get the cheapest possible price from his neighbors. Without question, the marketability of property was still embedded in the local relations between Frewen and his neighbors; but the auction mart provided a means for hiding those relations behind a mask of disinterest. If Pardoe's story of fraud at the mart offered a warning to would-be bidders who were strangers to the marketplace, Frewen's experience demonstrated an opportunity for those who could combine inside knowledge with perceived anonymity. The appearance of anonymity, however, was far more useful than its actual experience, and in this way the auction mart provided a new social and symbolic field for exploring the complexities, ambiguities, and threats that shaped any supposedly disinterested exchange of property.

In contrasting its representational prescriptions with its potential as a place of social practice, the auction mart promised more than it could deliver, on the one hand, and delivered on more than its promise, on the other hand. By midcentury it had moved from coffeehouse startup to the preeminent destination in London for real estate sales. If pressed to measure the mart's cultural visibility at this time—to say nothing of the ongoing anxiety that some property sales could generate—one needed simply to point to the sale, held at the mart on September 16, 1847, of William Shakespeare's home in Stratford-upon-Avon. "Certainly never was such an Auction ever conducted before at the auction mart nor probably ever will again," wrote the surveyor Edward Ryde to himself after returning home from the sale that evening.[74] And while some viewed the property pragmatically, as little more than a freehold plot with a cottage and attached public house, others considered it a "national relic or monument" that should never have been despoiled by being placed in the market.[75] "Considering the worship which Shakespeare has in England," wrote Thomas Kibble Hervey in the *Athenaeum*, "there is something remarkable in the very language which announces the fact—that a dwelling which has been glorified by his familiar presence should have found its way to the auction mart, as if it were any other hereditament—and its 'haunting memories' have become an argument for the cant of the auctioneer."[76] There was even talk of a new breed of stranger to the mart—Americans, who, it was rumored, were preparing to purchase the house and export it wholesale. As the auctioneer mounted the rostrum before an excited and star-studded crowd, it was clear, for better or for worse, that the London Auction Mart had become the premier stage on which to witness the spectacle of marketability.

"HEADQUARTERS OF THE REAL ESTATE MARKET": TOKENHOUSE YARD

As revealing as the design of the original London Auction Mart might have been of the social and cultural conditions under which real estate was commoditized in the first half of the nineteenth century, what mattered most to the auctioneers, surveyors, and other persons of property who owned and used it was the institution itself, and its function as a marketplace. Another possible measure of the institution's success, therefore, might be the relative ease by which its reputation shifted from one location to another during a period of urban redevelopment in the 1860s. Those who spoke of the London Auction Mart in the nineteenth century invariably referred to a single place and a single institution, but the former changed in 1867 with the opening of a new auction mart in nearby Tokenhouse Yard. The institution retained its centrality to the real estate market, however, and even improved on it up until the end of the century, when changing market patterns once again reconfigured institutional organization. Other aspects of the institutional arrangement of the market, such as trade journalism, helped bring further attention to the goings-on at Tokenhouse Yard and further amplified its functions as both a place of business and a place to contest and negotiate the meaning and limits of marketable property.

The sale of the first London Auction Mart took place against the backdrop of one of the most substantial and extensive transformations to London's urban fabric since the rebuilding of the City after the fires of 1666. Demand for space skyrocketed in large part due to the reconfiguration of the City's corporate financial structure, which resulted in the construction of new headquarters for such entities as joint-stock banks and insurance companies.[77] This creative destruction the London landscape put sustained pressure on urban land values and a new demand for lots, both of which made it increasingly difficult for the auction mart to continue operating in its turn of the century establishment. The minutes of the auction mart board of directors reflect keen awareness of these pressures. In 1858 and 1863, for example, the board had received unsolicited bids for the property, the first from the Liverpool and London fire and Life Insurance Company and the second from the Alliance Bank of London and Liverpool. In the first instance, the shareholders equivocated for too long; but in the second, they agreed to open the sale to a public competition. The mart was then sold for £115,255 10s. 6d. and subsequently leased to the Alliance Bank. Limited revenue streams may also have strained the mart's operation and added pressure to the decision to sell. On at least two occasions, the board of directors had tried to reconfigure the mart's internal layout so as to improve its monthly rental income by offering larger office spaces (including a retrofit of the saloon). That said, a report presented to the general meeting of shareholders in January 1863—just months before the decision to sell the premises—referenced the "satisfactory condition" of the company's finances.[78]

Shortly after the sale, several leading London auctioneers circulated a prospectus for a new limited liability auction mart company. The prospectus outlined a plan to build a new mart on Tokenhouse Yard, abutting Lothbury Avenue and only a short distance around the corner of the old mart (see fig. 4). Less grandiose than its predecessor, the new building promised a more pragmatic array of office space and salesrooms, as well as a restaurant to replace the now outdated coffeehouse.[79] Delayed by litigation opposing the design of the building (having to do with neighboring claims to ancient lights), the new salesrooms did not open completely until 1867. Unfortunately, very little evidence remains of the second mart's internal features, making it harder to judge its prescriptive designs. The *Builder*'s report on the new premises did note the increased amount of office space, made possible through the addition of another floor (the source of the lighting litigation) and the larger-size salesrooms.[80] The emphasis on flexible and rentable office space conformed with prevailing trends in commercial building design, and were clearly aimed at addressing the revenue limitations of the previous mart.

In keeping with the design legacy of its predecessor, the new auction mart repositioned itself at the summit of a national real estate market. One way it did this was by integrating into its offices the estates exchange, which was in its time the most ambitious and successful central registry of real estate price information in England (and discussed further in chapter 3). Though never attaining the degree of national coverage intended, this registry came the closest to realizing the aspirations first identified in the original 1808 London Auction Mart prospectus. Housed within the same premises as the new auction mart, the exchange added to the central functioning of Tokenhouse Yard in the real estate market. The auction mart continued to dominate public sales of property, with one scholar estimating its share of all property sales in the second half of the century at around half.[81] Indeed,

FIGURE 4. C. Smith, *Auction Market, Lothbury*, 1867. Wood engraving. This illustration of the new auction mart at Tokenhouse Yard was published in the *Builder*, December 6, 1867, 891. Reproduced by permission of the London Metropolitan Archives, City of London. http://collage.cityoflondon.gov.uk. Image 316471.

the reconstruction in a new location hardly disrupted the auction mart's reputation at all, to the point where the familiar reference to "the mart" seamlessly traveled the short distance to the new offices. "To-day," wrote one anonymous report, "the returns of the sales here transacted [in Tokenhouse Yard] represent a sum never perhaps dreamed of as attainable by the first promoters of the old Auction Mart; and so entirely has the place and its business become a part and parcel of the commercial life of the great City, that 'Tokenhouse-yard' is known the whole world over as a notable centre."[82] It was, said another popular city guide in 1891, "the chief mart in the city for the sales of estates and houses by auction,"[83] or, as another headline put it toward the end of the century, "the Headquarters of the Real Estate Market."[84]

Regulating the tone of the auction room was a necessary part of framing the auction mart as a place of business. Thanks to its increased public visibility and the attention it received from an expanding world of news and trade press, this work was both easier and more difficult. Easier thanks to a trade press that could offer editorial commentaries and prescriptions for appropriate behavior; more difficult due to the growing number of occasions when the auction mart, as revealed through the press, became a platform to challenge dominant value regimes through the juxtaposition of alternative social worlds.

An important tool for regulating the salesroom came in the form of weekly commentaries published in the professional trade press. In 1894, for example, the *Estates Gazette*'s "Mems from the Mart" column, a weekly commentary written under the pseudonym "Onlooker," attempted to distinguish between visitors to the auction mart who attended with a legitimate intention to purchase property and those who attended for purposes of leisure only. The latter, complained Onlooker, came with false intentions and did nothing but create disruptive noise in the salesrooms. "As far as I can judge," noted the columnist, "it is not those who attend *bona fide* and for the purposes of business of whatever nature who are the offenders, but either individuals who seem to regard an auction as a form of entertainment which ought never to be missed at the price, or even more simple-minded persons who drop in in a vague sort of way, and act at the Mart like the old agricultural labourer of the story did at church—namely, sit down, stretch out their legs, and think about nothing." Conversations about "aspects of politics" or "the last sensational case in the law courts" or "anecdotes of how the narrator's great grand-uncle once bought a farm in Sussex for less than half its value" distracted the so-called bona fide visitors from focusing on the central purpose of the salesrooms, which was the deliberation of market prices. "Order and silence," Onlooker admonished, "are courtesies which I think even the careless will, on reflection, admit to be due to the gentleman conducting the sale, and to the majority of those attending it."[85]

Policing legitimate from illegitimate visitors to the mart was easier said than done, however, as was demonstrated a month after the debate about noise. In this instance, another correspondent wrote to complain of "mashers" visiting the salesrooms, but here Onlooker chose to err on the side of restraint. Whereas the correspondent thought that mashers were "as much out of place as a bull in a china shop," Onlooker disagreed, noting that a masher might still have legitimate intentions to buy and that this, above all, was the primary purpose of attendance. Onlooker's earlier complaint, he clarified, was "meant to apply to obstructionists and talkers, who actually interfere with the comfort and business objects of others."[86]

These examples of indirect interference with the business of the auction mart paled in comparison with more direct and hostile conflicts, which regularly tried to interrupt the protocols of the salesroom and to broaden the meaning of a property beyond the question of its market value. The *Estates*

Gazette and *Property Market Review* invariably reported these events in condescending and dismissive tones, but on many occasions it was impossible to hide the raw emotions that threatened to unsettle the mart's image as venue of rational and disinterested calculation.

One report from "Expertus," whose "Week at the Mart" was published in the *Property Market Review* and closely paralleled the style and format of Onlooker's column, demonstrated clearly the contrast between the two worlds of the mart and real estate's broader social context. The sale concerned a leasehold house in South Kensington, No. 35, Drayton Gardens, presented for sale at the mart by the firm of Moss and Jameson in November 1895. The young woman who came to protest the sale arrived, said the article, "in great trepidation, and her teeth chattering with nervous excitement." As the sale began, the woman rose and announced in a "calm and deliberate" tone that the house belonged to her and had been "stolen from me by perjury!" "Then," reported Expertus, "failing to maintain the self-imposed restraint, she broke away into invectives, and in bitter and vituperative phrases charged all those concerned in the matter with dark designs and unnameable misdemeanours."[87]

The most revealing moment of the confrontation occurred shortly after, when, amid the shouts and turmoil of the exchange, a "representative of the press" suggested to the auctioneer that "perhaps it would be more satisfactory to you, Sir, to give some explanation of the cause of the grievance." On recording this remark, Expertus pounced on the journalist, arguing that he "had, in the keen pursuit of his journalistic duties, somewhat lost sight of the unsuitability of the auction room . . . for any such discussion." The auctioneer similarly dismissed the request outright, but in the ensuing call for bids, the damage had clearly been effected to the "malignant satisfaction" of the woman. When the auctioneer, having failed to meet the reserve price, withdrew the property from auction, the female visitor celebrated the fact by exclaiming to the gathered crowd, "I have done my work!"[88]

For Expertus, the episode underscored the same issue raised by Onlooker in the question of noise in the auction room. The marketability of land depended on a strict regulation of both the participants to an auction and the content of what would be allowed to influence the assessment of value; any behavior that distracted from the auction mart's formal and informal protocols or that threatened to call into question the underlying legitimacy of the mart's practices faced certain censure. As Onlooker commented regarding a similar outburst by another female protester in 1894, "There is a time and a place for everything. Family matters are best kept to the family circle. . . . Men go to Tokenhouse-yard to buy and sell property, and though occurences [*sic*] like that to which I have perhaps given too much space may be amusing, they cause inconvenience and a plentiful loss of time."[89]

Onlooker's gendering of legitimate auction room participants was likely not meant to imply that women were foreign elements in auction sales, but rather that their participation should be guided by behavioral modes that Onlooker considered distinctly male. In fact, women featured quite regularly in press reports of sales at the auction mart, despite their lack of representation among auctioneers; and Expertus appeared more willing than Onlooker to grant them a degree of independent aptitude for public competitions. For example, in one weekly report, Expertus profiled a Mrs. Moses whose success in purchasing weekly rental property in the East End had made her "a well-known personage in the property-dealing world."[90] In another column, he asserted that women, more so than men, "displayed the greater *sangfroid* under the exciting influences of a competition," and he cited as an example a woman who had recently challenged an auctioneer to put to lots together so that she might bid on them both.[91] Expertus attributed the subsequent laughter of the other auctiongoers to them having "been immensely tickled, both by the demand itself—so familiar in their own mouths—and the curt peremptory manner in which it [had] been formulated."[92] The point, in other words, was that even when practiced by a woman, expertise in the auction room only underscored a still largely male domain.

Despite the best efforts of journalists and professionals to manage more disinterested forms of etiquette, the auction room remained an enticing stage on which to contest the emotional, social, and political contexts of property for sale. Two final examples of disputes in the auction mart demonstrate the contrast between efforts to frame property sales in the limited terms of the auction room and those aiming to situate them in a larger social context. They also demonstrate how the prevailing logic and protocols of auction practice could be used to invert the meaning of marketability. In the spring of 1888, the *Times* published several advertisements on behalf of the executors of the late Earl of Cavan, whose property in Somerset and County Mayo, Ireland, was to be offered for public competition at the auction mart. The estate consisted of more than two thousand acres of freehold and leasehold lands on the island of Achill and "adjoining the Protestant colony at Dunwort." In addition to the fine shooting, fishing, and yachting, the advertisement noted the unusually low reserve bid of £1000 and alerted readers to the "above unprecedented BARGAIN."[93]

On the day of the sale, before what one newspaper described as "an unusually large attendance," the auctioneer from the firm Dowsett and Co., offered further evidence of an unusual sale, noting in his introduction that "this property possessed remarkable features of sport, and men of enterprise and pluck, who did not mind roughing it a little, and to whom a sentiment of danger, fancied or actual, was an attraction, would find in the purchase of this estate a desirable venture." The auctioneer and various members of the assembled crowd then proceeded to debate, over a series of verbal jousts, the real marketable value of the estate:

> (A gentleman in the body of the room asked if there were no danger from an armed Connaught peasant, ready with his bludgeon or gun, behind a fence, to pop down the Saxon purchaser of this West of Ireland property.) (Laughter) [Auctioneer:] Men like Barnaby, who rode to Khiva; and men like Livingstone, who pierced the centre of Africa; and of Franklin, who penetrated the icy wastes of the North Pole, were those who would find this romantically-situated island in the western province of Ireland healthy and profitable recreation. (A laugh) Besides all these attractions a purchaser would find himself surrounded by a devoted and attached peasantry. (A Voice: 'To shoot him at the earliest opportunity,'—loud laughter)—if on purchasing the estate he presented the 243 acres leased to the forty-seven tenants absolutely to them with a free conveyance—this he could do at little legal expense by having the conveyance printed. A question was asked how much the present tenants were in arrears, and amidst considerable laughter, the auctioneer answered close upon three years. (Renewed laughter.) The bidder: Then there is no chance of recovering the arrears. (Roars of Laughter.) Another: Why not make a present of the land to the tenants, and save the trouble of collecting the rent? (Renewed merriment.)[94]

Clearly exasperated, the auctioneer reminded the auctiongoers that the executors, aware of the problems with the estate, had further reduced the upset price to £600. With this reminder, biddings commenced and the estate was eventually knocked down for £630. The sale concluded with a final exchange between the skeptical audience and a now grim auctioneer, the latter suggesting that the settled price was "really tantamount to giving it away, considering the many attractions it possessed of fishing, shooting—(A voice: 'Shooting landlords'; laughter)—and yachting."[95]

The effort to assess the value of a colonial estate hinged on a number of unpleasant assumptions held by the bidding audience and was expressed in the form of sarcastic heckling. The auctioneer's attempt to restrict the proceedings to establish protocols—through innuendo ("roughing it a little"), colonial motifs, or establish marketing features (hunting, fishing, etc.)—did not prevent the auctiongoers themselves from exposing the underlying social conflict inherent in the property and its proposed sale. The critical function of the auction room as a place for validating the market value of a property was redirected, with the auctioneer's proposed value coming into direct conflict with that of the crowd of bidders. The repeated laughter and derision during the proceedings undermined the effort to create consensus on the value of the estate property, and in so doing made a mockery of the subsequent price. The auctioneer's suggestion that the property had not *really* been sold at all—that it had been given away—perfectly captured the inversion that had taken place in the norms of auction room practice.

The final example of social contestation in the auction mart concerns a campaign waged by members of the clergy in the 1880s against the sale of advowsons—incorporeal hereditaments originally granted to the patrons of local churches for the right to name candidates to ecclesiastical office, but routinely tied to the real property associated with the office. Not all advowsons were sold by auction, but many were; and a House of Lords select committee report and a royal commission report on the sale of benefices, both published in the 1870s, brought the issue to public light and provoked a number of protests at Tokenhouse Yard.[96] Unlike the sale of Irish estates, in which the relative value of the property was called into question through the skepticism of the auctiongoers, the sale of advowsons involved opponents challenging outright the very marketability of certain types of real property. These category distinctions were nonetheless made using the language and practice of the market itself.

The campaign was most heated during the summer of 1882, when several activist members of the Curates' Alliance, a group organized around objections to the sale and purchase of church livings, attended sales at the auction mart in the hopes of disrupting them and bringing public attention to the "traffic in souls," as one paper put it.[97] On several occasions, clergymen used modes of legitimate auction practice—such as requesting copies of particulars of sale, posing questions to the auctioneer related to the particulars, and offering bids for the property—to expose the immorality they viewed as inherent in the sale of church livings. At the sale of an Essex estate and advowson at the auction mart, reported on July 8, Rev. G. Hennessey and the secretary of the Curates' Alliance, Rev. E. G. O'Donoughue, engaged in all three of these tactics, recorded in the *Bristol Mercury and Daily Post* as a verbatim exchange between attendees and the auctioneer:

> Lot 1 being offered, the Rev. E. G. O'Donoughue . . . asked whether this lot included the advowson. Auctioneer—Are you a bidder? The Rev. E. G. O'Donoughe [*sic*]—How can I bid unless you supply me with a copy of the particulars of sale? Auctioneer—You will not have one. I really must appeal to this company to support me ("Hear, hear," and cries of turn them out). The Rev. G. Hennessey—Withdraw the advowson. Auctioneer—No, I will not withdraw it, but somebody may be withdrawn presently (laughter). The Rev. E. G. O'Donoughue—May I ask whether the advowson is included in lot 1? Auctioneer—Yes. Rev. E. G. O'Donoughue—What is the age of the present rector? . . . Mr. Cheffins expressed regret that the clergymen should think it becoming in them to hinder a legal sale, and, addressing the last speaker, he added—If you are not quiet, as sure as you are a living man you will have to go out. The Rev. G. Hennessey—Surely this is a public auction? Here a clergyman made an ironical offer of a shilling for the "lot." . . . A gentleman present, speaking as a lay member of the Church of England, said he regarded the interruptions of the clergymen as "indecent." The Rev. G. Hennessey replied that that was the only effectual way in which they could protest against the sale of souls.[98]

By refusing to give copies of the particulars of sale, the auctioneer implicitly rejected the right of O'Donoughue to stand as a legitimate bidder in the auction. The clergymen, in turn, staked their right to participate based on a claim of public space and offered their own bids for the property in accordance with auction practice. By participating in the auction in this way, the members of the Curates' Alliance subverted the routine codes of the auction room in order to draw new boundaries around what could be considered a legitimate commodity. Their participation, they argued, was "the only effectual way in which they could protest against the sale of souls."[99] The auction room, with its conventions for making property marketable, suddenly became a contingent site for negotiating the social and spiritual limits of marketability.

Most of the abovementioned practices for governing auction sales applied to auctions wherever they were held. The importance of the London Auction Mart, however, was not that its rules were necessarily unique, but rather that its public visibility as a central place for auction sales provided different communities of participants with opportunities to frame and contest the social and cultural relations of property sales. Despite efforts to present the mart's purpose in strictly disinterested terms—arguing, for example, that "men go to Tokenhouse-yard to buy and sell property" and nothing more, or that questions of a property's family, colonial, or religious context were not relevant conversations for the auction room—many visitors to the mart were able to use its own social conventions to invert its assumptions about marketability, and thereby broaden the politics and meaning of the property marketplace.

By the end of the nineteenth century, the London Auction Mart had realized, albeit in a limited way, the vision of a national market for property first set out in its prospectus, now nearing its centenary anniversary. At least symbolically, Tokenhouse Yard had become the reference point both for indexing general trends in the market and for debating the limits of the market. The experience of the Edwardian period, however, disrupted this vision and gradually eroded the coherence of the London Auction Mart project. The forces of change were numerous, and included the rapid rate of urbanization that defined the post-1870 decades in Britain and the Edwardian property market crisis. The latter saw dramatic falls in the value of real property—in particular, urban property—thereby significantly increasing the competition between those professions that survived on charges from property services. F. M. L. Thompson has further argued that in the aftermath of the 1860s property market boom, with demand slack and the advantages of a London sale questionable, many sales reverted to local markets. Over the course of the last quarter of the century and first decade of the next, London's share of the country's total real estate sales likely fell to a third, sustained even at this level largely thanks to the city's dominance in the house market.[100] The end result of these structural changes was a much more differentiated market, with multiple sites of sales both within the metropolis and in the provinces. By the end of the first World War, Tokenhouse Yard had again been sold. It would not be replaced for several years, and by that time there were few who would speak of it in the same terms as its predecessors.

Signs of tension between London and provincial markets were evident as early as the 1890s. In 1893, for example, the *Estates Gazette* reported on the construction of new salesrooms in Shrewsbury, paid for by the firm Hall, Wateridge and Own. As was typical in the less specialized provincial markets, the company handled all forms of property at auction, and the premises were outfitted accordingly, with both storage facilities and salesrooms. A partner in the firm, F. Wateridge, explained to the *Estates Gazette*, however, "that the primary object in building these rooms was, in the first place, to provide accommodation suitable for the holding of monthly property sales; for they saw no reason why the sale of large properties should be taken to London or elsewhere, especially if proper salesrooms were provided in the country town."[101] Such contrasts between London and provincial marketplaces could also be made in less direct fashion, such as by simply promoting the legitimacy of provincial salesrooms through evidence of their success. The card advertisement for one Coventry firm, printed in the *Gazette* in 1895, that promoted its own mart added in brackets at the end of its particulars: "N.B.—Special attention given to the sale of estates, residences town properties and local shares, and the frequent periodical sales in the above Mart are always well attended, and an acknowledged medium for the disposal thereof."[102] Another card in the same issue, for a Sheffield company running an "Estate and General Auction Mart," provided direct evidence of its success the previous year, in which it had offered 482 lots of property and sold 368 of them for total sales of £297,625.[103] In promoting strong attendance, public recognition, and good sales, provincial auction marts staked claims for themselves as legitimate alternatives to the metropolitan property marketplace.

In addition to competition from provincial marts, the London Auction Mart faced the growing independence of other metropolitan firms, particularly those in the suburbs and the West End. The author of one guidebook cautioned new agents to avoid the City and to focus their initial efforts in suburban estate agency, with offices located on high streets, near rail and commuter lines, and in greater proximity to residential areas. "An office should be in as bold, convenient, and conspicuous a position as possible," advised the author, "for it will be seen that the extra cost for a fairly good position may be compensated for in the reduction of expenses in other directions, the principal of which would probably be advertising."[104] The new estate salesroom and auction house opened by J. C. Platt in 1899, on the ground floor of No. 2 Broadway in Hammersmith, provided a good example of suburban expansion. Platt's offices were located directly across from both rail and underground stations, and a photograph in the printed notice for the opening depicted a bustling street view of the premises situated amid the activity of other merchants and traders.[105]

The firm of Knight, Frank and Rutley, founded in 1896, demonstrated the increasing visibility of West End auctioneering firms. In 1910, the *Estates Gazette* printed a detailed report on the company's new office on Hanover Square, and on the company's head of land and estate sales, Howard Frank. At thirty-nine years of age, Frank was reputed to have sold more than one hundred thousand acres of land in England alone, and under his management the company had begun an aggressive overseas expansion, opening offices in New York and Winnipeg. The *Estates Gazette* boldly proclaimed the Hanover Square headquarters as "probably the most comprehensive premises in the profession."[106] The implicit message of this new marketing geography conveyed the declining potential for a centralized real estate marketplace. The Platt offices in Hammersmith and Knight, Frank and Rutley's offices in Hanover Square were two of five private salesrooms which the *Times* in 1921 attributed to a new pattern of real estate sales, in which the former prominence of the auction mart no longer figured.[107]

All these trends culminated with the sale of the Tokenhouse Yard Auction Mart in 1918. The end was swift and brutal for many of the auctioneers who still rented rooms. In early November, the board of directors issued a circular to shareholders alerting them to the receipt and conditional acceptance of an offer from the Bank of England in the amount of £120,000.[108] At the next shareholder meeting, a small minority of auctioneers spoke out against the sale. The board chair noted that the minutes of the previous annual meeting had already recorded the trends undercutting the mart's performance: declining income from room rents, paltry dividends, and outside competition. Bentley J. Bridgewater, speaking in favor of the sale, also "spoke of the decentralization in progress, and of the tendency to hold sales in the country and the West End, whilst suburban sales were also increasing."[109] In futile opposition, the auctioneer Alfred Moore could only characterize both the sale and the board's handling of the matter "as a bombshell."[110]

Both the *Estates Gazette* and the *Times* offered sanguine, if pragmatic, hopes that a central auction mart could be reconstituted in some form, with a more mixed view emerging in the correspondence solicited and printed by the *Estates Gazette* the week after the shareholder vote. Most authors acknowledged the decentralizing trends and expressed regret at the closing of a historic institution, but opinion was divided on the consequences and future prospects of another centrally located marketplace for real property. Some dismissed outright any hope of a new beginning. On the question of where a new mart should be located, one correspondent emphasized the importance and public recognition attached to Tokenhouse Yard: "The market for ordinary small property has been established at the Mart so long that more and more has it assumed the gathering place for London's public and the resort for all people dealing with property owners. . . . People will continue to go to the City in preference to any venue elsewhere, because it has long been the recognized and accepted centre for all classes of property."[111] Despite the significant restructuring of the real estate market's institutional geography and the decline of central London as a landmark within that geography, Tokenhouse Yard remained, for at least a few, the symbolic headquarters of the real estate market.

The institutional configuration of the real estate market in nineteenth-century London evolved in response to the process of urbanization that so dramatically transformed the city from a population of around one million inhabitants in 1801 to more than six million by the end of the century. The practice of real estate auction sales popularized in the eighteenth century and set in the city's inns and coffeehouses brought greater visibility and a more dynamic sociability to the transfer of land and buildings, as did the transformations of the urban fabric associated with such things as railway development, infrastructure improvements, and suburb growth. Though the commercial sale of property had long existed in Britain, the tempo of exchange in and around London generated the kind of pressures that would lead the city's auctioneers and property agents to conceive and build a more formal marketplace. The three iterations of that marketplace discussed in this chapter—from an initial marketplace on Bartholomew Lane to a consolidated institution in Tokenhouse Yard and, finally, to a more decentralized geography of multiple salesrooms—offered different social, spatial, and material arrangements for creating marketable land. These arrangements expressed in spatial terms the novel idea of the property market as a visible, calculable space. The stories of those who visited the mart as vendors, agents, speculators, onlookers, or provocateurs underscored the continual and contingent effort required to build and sustain this idea. As we have seen, it was not an effort that all were willing to see in the same beneficial light. Rather, the London Auction Mart was an artifact of its creators—the property professionals whose job it was to facilitate the public negotiation of exchangeable value. The next chapter thus turns to the growth, development, and function of these professionals in the creation of the property market.

CHAPTER TWO

Market People

Edward Ryde (1822–1892) was a property man through and through, one whose life was shaped by the development and sale of real estate in nineteenth-century Britain. Born in Woking, Surrey, he began his career as a land surveyor for a partnership in Sunbury, but was soon swept up in the early-Victorian railway boom that brought new fame and quick fortune to many able (and even lesser-abled but well-advertised) practitioners.[1] In 1855, after several years of freelance work, in which he promoted himself as a land surveyor and agent, he accepted a position with the South Eastern Railway Company and later contracted with the Charing Cross Railway, the London Central Railway Company, and the London & South Western Railway Company. In his formal capacity as a company surveyor, Ryde regularly attended sales at the London Auction Mart, often to sell surplus railway land; but he also attended there on his own accord, such as in 1847, when he witnessed the sale of Shakespeare's birthplace.[2] He published a number of technical manuals on surveying and valuation, as well as a general textbook on property,[3] and became widely known as an expert witness and arbiter for the valuation and compensation of public works projects, such as the 1875 Artisans' and Laborers' Dwellings Improvement Act (38 & 39 Vict., c. 36). In his private dealings, Ryde valued, purchased, sold, let, brokered, managed, and developed real estate on his own and on behalf of others throughout the southeast of England. He was also an early promoter and defender of the professionalism and integrity of surveyors, writing to the *Times* in 1864, for example, to refute accusations of collusion in compensation cases for railway development.[4] In 1868 he attended the inaugural meeting of the Institution of Surveyors (forerunner to today's Royal Institution of Chartered Surveyors) and eventually served as its president from 1880 to 1883.

In the very broadest sense of his intellectual, professional, economic, and political engagements, Edward Ryde was a person steeped in the knowledge of property, accrued through a lifetime of everyday practice. He wrote about this activity in his personal diaries, one for each year between 1844 and 1892; these records reveal a man deeply and regularly engaged in the commercial exchange and development of land:

> March 6, 1849: "Received instructions from Mr. Impey by letter to dispose of Sunbury Windmill by Private Treaty for £1200."
>
> January 4, 1855: "At 20 minutes past 12 I mount the [auction] Rostrum for the first time, and a most excellent Sale ensues."
>
> February 26, 1855: "To Lewisham by 11 o'clock train. Look at some surplus land there; walk on to Blackheath; take next train to Gravesend; look at some surplus land there."
>
> March 4, 1864: "To Hanworth with Wm Mills to look at 70 Acres of land belonging to him there. Advise him to sell if £15,000 is offered him."
>
> April 12, 1872: "Go to Surbiton and view four houses for Sale by Auction, on account of Paine and Brettsel [solicitors] at Chertsey."[5]

From Sunbury to Surbiton, by foot, fly carriage, and, above all, by the very same railways that he helped to construct, Ryde labored to connect property and people to the calculation of market values.

Throughout his life, on census returns, and in his professional associations, Ryde identified himself as a land surveyor, but his diaries gesture to the expansiveness of the term and its fluidity between other would-be professions—in particular, those of estate agency and auctioneering. Ryde undoubtedly took well-earned pride in his efforts to raise the public status of surveying, and historians have often emphasized the professionalization of property work in the nineteenth century and the struggle to secure status, marked by the rise of organizations like the Institution of Surveyors (1868, granted a royal charter in 1881), the Estate and House Agents Institute (1872), the Auctioneers' Institute (1886), or the merged Auctioneers' and Estate Agents' Institute (1912).[6] Identity and public recognition came slowly, however—very slowly in the case of auctioneers and estate agents, who were not given statutory registration until 1979. For most of the nineteenth century, the census offered little help: occupational descriptions of surveyors, land surveyors, building surveyors, rent collectors, auctioneers, appraisers, land agents, house agents, and estate agents comingled with the promiscuity of a charivari. The only relative certainty was that, until 1881, none of these occupations qualified for professional status. After this time, all but surveyors remained within the class of commercial trades.[7] The boundaries and status between one form of practice and another were perennial sites of struggle. Thus, rather than reify ambiguous distinctions, one could just as easily imagine Ryde belonging to what Sir Alexander Carr-Saunders, writing in the early twentieth century, termed the "unnamed profession, whose diverse functions have little in common save that they all, directly or indirectly, have property in land for their subject matter."[8] Along with many thousands of others in the unnamed profession, Ryde worked to mediate the exchange of real estate in Victorian Britain. This chapter, therefore, is not about the particular life and career of Edward Ryde, but is, rather, about the development of new kinds of careers that connected people and property, as well as the sorts of everyday practice that shaped the meaning of property in the market. As an expression of collective practice, the property market would not have existed in the form that it did without these individuals and their actions.

The word *mediate* is used here in a general sense to refer to the kind of practices that configured the "commodity potential" of real estate, its exchangeability in particular social and historical contexts.[9] Like all potential commodities—perhaps even more so, given the spatial fixity of land and houses—real estate was entangled in dense and elaborate networks of social, political, economic, and ethical association. Property law, land use, rents, mortgages, titles, dynastic ambitions, family ties, neighbors, history, landscape, memory: each lent specific character and authority to the social world encompassing a plot of ground. The moment of sale thus marked a reconfiguration of social worlds through the perceived alienation of one set of associations and the re-entanglement into another. This process was never absolute—social worlds always overlapped—and, as we will shortly see, the inevitable ambiguities or controversies of exchange demanded careful management on the part of those who helped bring property to market. What mattered most at the moment of sale was the *potential* for alienation over and above any other form of association; this in turn required that land be measured, valued, described, and marketed in ways conducive to such estimation.[10] The collective or distributed calculation of market value thus depended on the work of those like Ryde, who constructed such exchange encounters and thereby made meaningful both the objects and subjects of the real estate market.

This chapter begins with a broad typology of the people most directly involved in the mediation of property exchange and pays particular attention to the historical development of two fields within the unnamed profession, auctioneering and estate agency, both of which came into view in the early decades of the nineteenth century. It then explores from a more qualitative perspective some of the practices—such as auction advertisements, property registers, and orders to view—that defined these commercial fields and that placed professionals in the unique and often socially contentious position of having to mediate the public and private exchange of real estate.

THE DEVELOPMENT OF REAL ESTATE SERVICES

The broad definition of market agency that I have suggested could easily encompass a much wider range of actors than surveyors, auctioneers, and estate agents. As both sellers and purchasers of land, individual and corporate landowners regularly made decisions that determined when, how, and under what circumstances real estate would be made available for sale.[11] Most often these decisions were shaped by questions of debt and financing, which further included the input of bankers and other lenders and investors.[12] Architects, urban developers, builders, and contractors also played roles in defining the timing and nature of property brought into the market.[13] Journalists, printers, and publishers made visible the work of marketing property to potential investors and the public in general. Finally, working in conjunction or even competition with all these actors were lawyers, and in particular, solicitors.

Throughout the eighteenth and nineteenth centuries (though originating well before then), solicitors had two separate but related functions in mediating the sale of property. The first was as conveyancers of legal title, which included the work of investigating titles and preparing the abstracts, deeds of conveyance, and other legal instruments that transferred ownership between exchanging parties. This was the staple work for many offices. Conveyancing had been associated with lawyers from their earliest late-medieval origins, but the increasing frequency of transfers in the sixteenth and seventeenth centuries, as well as the proliferation of new forms and precedents involved, brought greater importance and profit, particularly for provincial practitioners.[14] Professional guides cited conveyancing as being of greatest importance to attorney practice, and a study of two firms in eighteenth-century Yorkshire has shown that conveyancing fees and commissions amounted to between 40 and 50 percent of revenues.[15] These were income streams worth fighting for, and so, to protect their interests, solicitors successfully defended themselves in court against competition from the likes of London's Company of Scriveners. Protection was further extended in 1804 when, in exchange for increased stamp and license fees, the government granted solicitors a legal monopoly over conveyancing practice. This monopoly entrenched the profession in the process of property exchange and secured for it what one historian of the late-nineteenth century termed "a permanent rent-charge on the value of land and buildings."[16]

The second function joined a solicitor's legal work to the general world of business and estate management. Of course, there were some critics content to see solicitors restricted to a legal role. "I have known so many instances of disadvantages arising from suffering mere men of the law to intermeddle in the purchases of lands, before the preliminaries of agreement have been adjusted," cautioned William Marshall in his 1804 guide to property.[17] Except for occasions when deceit was suspected, Marshall, acting as an advocate for the professionalization of estate management, thought that a solicitor need only be engaged for the actual conveyance. But, in fact, a solicitor's legal work was routinely associated with property brokering and capital financing. As early as 1747, Campbell's *London Tradesman* conceded that attorneys often combined conveyancing work with "the Trade of a Money-Scrivener; that is, they are employed to find out Estates to purchase, or have Money to lay out for some, and borrow for others."[18] During this period, with their numbers increasing in London and in provincial towns and cities, solicitors also often worked as land agents or estate managers, which could include planning and advising on strategies for the sale and purchase of lands. Mr. Shepherd, the solicitor to the Elliot family in Jane Austen's novel *Persuasion*, demonstrated a wide range of services in advising the family on its financial affairs, using his own personal and professional connections to locate a suitable tenant for Kellynch Hall, and drafting the legal contracts.[19] By the mid-nineteenth century, the specialization of land agency and surveying came to dominate estate management; but in both town and country, lawyers remained indispensable hubs in the information networks that facilitated public and private treaty sales.[20]

Like lawyers, surveyors had long been associated with the management of land, and in particular its measurement and valuation, both of which functioned to situate property in a commodity context. From the mid-sixteenth to mid-seventeenth century, for example, published guidebooks, such as John FitzHerbert's *The Boke of Surveying and Improvements* (1523) and William Leybourn's *Compleat Surveyor* (1653) promoted a discourse of improvement and economic rationalization in estate management.[21] Similarly, in 1667, William Leybourn published *A Platform for Purchasers*, "intended chiefly for the information of such persons as were concerned either in Letting, Buying, Selling or Building of (or upon) Ground then in the Ruins of the City of London."[22] "Such a work," observed F. M. L. Thompson, "heralded a land market which was to some extent operating impersonally, with information supplied by sellers indifferently to any who cared to offer, a market which was breaking away from the closed charmed circle of those in the know, the hangers-on with well-placed acquaintances and well-developed sensitivity to the financial implications of the gossip they gathered."[23] As direct facilitators of exchange, however, surveyors likely played a greater role as land agents in the colonies than they did in Britain before the nineteenth century. The exception was the acquisition of land for public purposes, such as turnpike trusts, canals, and railways—the last being the kind of work that would later prove so formative to Edward Ryde's career.[24]

Compared with lawyers and surveyors, auctioneers and estate agents represented a more novel nineteenth-century specialization of real estate services. Neither auctioneers nor estate agents were mentioned in Campbell's 1747 guide that discussed conveyancers and money scriveners. Toward the end of the century, in 1789, a London directory included the name of James Christie, the well-known auctioneer of both art and estates, along with nineteen other auctioneers, but still no estate agents.[25] Then, in 1802, the number of auctioneers in the *Post Office Annual Directory* nearly tripled and was accompanied by reference to two West End land and house agents, W. Blogg (Pall Mall) and George Crosby (Berkeley Square). More dramatic growth followed, and by 1841 London was home to 274 auctioneers, 71 estate and house agents, and 27 land and estate agents.[26] Within a few decades, auctioneers and estate agents had thus become far more recognizable as distinct trades.

One factor that helped to define both of these trades was state regulation—first of auctioneers, later of house agents. In addition to imposing a tax on auction sales, the Auction Duty Act of 1777 required auctioneers throughout Britain to take out a license to practice. The initial license duty was set at twenty shillings for London practitioners and five shillings for auctioneers in the country.[27] This was a base rate; further licenses supplied the rights to sell other articles of commerce, such as spirits or plate. Though the duties levied on auctions were charged at different rates for personal and real property, there does not appear to have been a distinction made in the license duty, despite the fact that several auctioneers who testified before the Royal Commission of Inquiry into the Excise Establishment in 1834 did identify themselves as primarily auctioneers of real estate. In 1846, the auction duties were reformed by eliminating charges on the auction sales and the required annual license fee of £10.[28]

House agents were more loosely regulated and licensing was not imposed until later in the century. In 1861, the chancellor of the exchequer (and future prime minister), William Gladstone, revised the stamp duty that had applied to some short-term contracts and moved to an annual license fee of £2. This license applied to any agent wishing to sell or rent furnished houses at a value higher than £25 per year; solicitors and licensed auctioneers were exempt. Despite fears expressed in the Commons debates on the matter, Gladstone insisted that the purpose was not to regulate the house agency trade, but to improve the collection of tax revenue.[29] As if to underscore this point, the licensing scheme allowed a major loophole for unfurnished property, which could be let or sold at any price and for any length of time, without need of a license. As licensed house agents would regularly point out, this left many speculative builders—particularly those operating in London's growing suburbs—free to "have tacked on the words 'House Agent' to their other qualifications and designations."[30] The scale of estate and house agency could thus be perceived only in general terms from license figures alone.

What license data show is a pattern of overall growth, at times correlating with broader shifts in the economy of real property. Figure 5 shows the number of licenses issued for auctioneers and for appraisers and house agents from the late eighteenth to early twentieth centuries.[31] The lack of data for agents in the early part of the century makes it difficult to relate these numbers on a per capita basis, but, for auctioneers at least, the number of licenses per ten thousand people declined in the early decades of the century, to around 1.4 in 1840, before rising again to approximately 1.9 in 1900. What is more pronounced, however, is the correlation with the building cycles of the Victorian period. The years of growth in the 1860s, 1870s, and 1890s were associated with increases in the number of practicing auctioneers and estate agents. In contrast, license figures fell during the downturns of the 1880s and 1900s. Both trades offered a precarious livelihood, with relatively high rates of bankruptcy even at the best of times. As was the case with solicitors, auctioneers, and estate agents "grew when property thrived and stagnated when property sales went down."[32] Still, on the eve of the First World War (1910), there were more than thirteen thousand licensed auctioneers, appraisers, and house agents in Britain, eleven thousand of them in England and Wales alone. These figures compare with approximately seventeen thousand solicitors and eleven thousand surveyors licensed or enumerated in the same period.[33] Despite vagaries of a precarious trade, auctioneers and estate agents had established themselves over the course of the century as important intermediaries and providers of real estate services.

Census data and figures from professionally produced directories give a clearer picture of the distribution of auctioneering and estate agency. The inconsistent use of occupational categories makes it difficult to interpret census returns prior to 1871, but in the 1901 census—which returned nearly fourteen thousand self-identified auctioneers, house agents, valuers, and appraisers—London is clearly a predominant center. There were 16 agents for every square mile in the county of London that year, compared with 2.5 agents per square mile in Middlesex. York held more agents per capita than London, but at a density of only 1 agent per 4.5 square miles. Commenting on the returns from 1891, the *Estates Gazette* also noted the prevalence of auctioneers and agents in large provincial towns. In addition to London, seventeen cities with populations more than fifty thousand people contained at least fifty auctioneers; six of these—Manchester, Liverpool, Leeds, Birmingham, Nottingham, and Brighton—supported more than one hundred.[34] Similar patterns were found in Scotland: Glasgow counted 145 auctioneers and house agents; Edinburgh had 118. In fact, the larger urban region surrounding these two principal towns (comprising the counties of Lanark and Edinburgh) was home to the majority of property trades, more than four out of five of the 790 agents included in the census.[35]

These trades concentrated in cities for a number of reasons. As important as sales were to the professional identity of auctioneers and estate agents, most businesses drew income from a variety of services, including insurance sales, mortgage lending, rent collecting, and property maintenance. The growth of urban rental markets for middle- and working-class housing were often at least as important as sales of property, and thus provided ample opportunity for new intermediaries. One of these was Mr. Lickcheese, the fictional house agent portrayed in George Bernard Shaw's play *Widowers' Houses* (1892), whose work extracting rents from London's East End slums served to fuel Shaw's critique of Victorian landlordism. The reality was more complicated, with auctioneers and estate agents sometimes acting as both owners and managers of urban property. In Birmingham, for example, several firms counted among the largest owners of ratable working-class housing and held significant control of all managed house property in the city.[36]

In Scotland, house factors, as they were more commonly called, were even more important to the management of urban property, which might explain why the ratio of auctioneer and estate agent licenses was so different there. In 1900, there were approximately three licensed auctioneers for every two house agents in England and Wales. In Scotland, by contrast, the ratio was essentially even.[37] The difference was due largely to the tenement housing that became so characteristic of Scottish industrial cities. As in England, Scottish

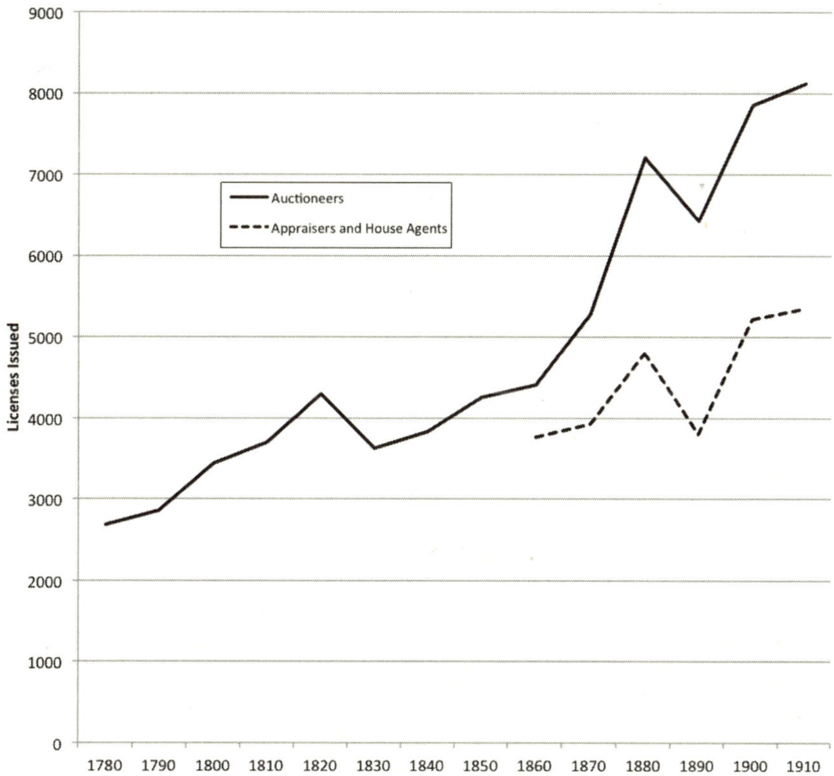

FIGURE 5. Auctioneer and house agency licenses in Britain, 1780–1910.

factors sometimes combined ownership with management, but control over working-class housing was far greater north of the border. Both the concentration of housing and the desire to maintain social distance between owners and tenants sustained a high reliance on factors for advertising, vetting, and managing tenement blocks. As a result, in Glasgow one contemporary estimate suggested that 80 percent of working-class housing was managed by factors.[38] And also unlike in England, factors were much more closely associated with the interests of landowners, even going so far as to form a joint association in 1865. In both England and Scotland, however, the development of real estate trades was virtually synonymous with urbanization, and this may help explain why (among other factors), on a per capita basis, so few licenses were issued in Ireland during in this period.

For what were the more generalist of real estate trades, success as an auctioneer or estate agent required a variety of learned skills, plus a willingness to adapt and the tenacity to seek commissions in every flat, farm, estate, and street corner of the land. As one writer observed, "Auctioneering must, of necessity, have its more varied characteristics, and consequently its broader and more varied types of business men."[39] The tabulation of census or license figures thus presupposes a set of practices and identities that were in fact still being defined throughout the century. If solicitors anchored their expertise in the law and surveyors theirs in metrologies of space, the agents of the property trade ultimately resorted to an expertise of the market itself. How did such expertise operate? By what means did auctioneers and estate agents come to define themselves and their marketable objects, and how did these practices come to shape the larger meaning of property and its market? The rest of this chapter will explore these questions more directly by examining some of the norms, techniques, and competencies defining auctioneers and estate agents.

AUCTIONEERING AND THE LANGUAGE OF PROPERTY SALES

When he died at his home in Brighton in 1847, George Robins left a lasting legacy as the most famous auctioneer of the nineteenth century. Byron dined with him, Carlyle criticized him, and Jerrold, Thackeray, and Dickens (among others) lampooned him. According to Henry Mayhew, Robins's prodigious and ebullient salesmanship was even celebrated in penny songbooks sold on the streets of London.[40] To some of his contemporaries, he was known as the "Cicero of the Saleroom" and "Prince of Auctioneers," though his satirists often chose less laudable pennames, such as Mr. Hammersmith, Mr. Triptolemus Scattergoods, and Mr. Redbreast.[41] Known for an all-embracing enthusiasm for sales of every kind, Robins's role in the sale of Horace Walpole's Strawberry Hill estate in 1842 nonetheless revealed his professional strengths in real estate (he ultimately passed the job of auctioning the books and prints to the more expert hands of Leigh and Sotheby).[42]

Like most other practitioners of the time, Robins traded in both personal and real property, but his reputation was arguably built as a premiere marketer of estates. During the most productive decades of his fifty-year career, Robins was estimated to have sold a total of 687,395 acres of property valued at £9,324,878; these statistics provided an unofficial benchmark for professional success for the remainder of the century.[43] Through his florid descriptive style on the pages of handbills and newspapers and his wit behind the rostrum of his salesroom at the London Auction Mart, Robins fixed the marketing of property squarely in the consciousness of nineteenth-century popular culture. His career and legacy, however, revealed more than just the antics of a particularly colorful salesman. In balancing the line between fact and fiction in his descriptions of property, Robins exposed both a defining competency of auctioneer and estate agency and the crucial dependency on identity and social relations in mediating the exchange of real property.

Born in London in 1777, Robins spent his teenage years surrounded by the sound of auction hammers, and the history of his family's business offers an anecdotal account of the quantitative growth of real estate auctioneering discussed above. His father, Henry Robins, and his uncle, John Robins, began their auctioneering business in 1790 in Covent Garden, when the two men took over the offices of another auctioneer whose father had taken up book auctioneering earlier in the century. The business assumed by the brothers Robins had already begun to specialize in real estate sales, and both Henry and John moved into the trade from their occupations as upholsterers and furniture dealers.[44] City directories of the time regularly noted overlaps between auctioneering, furniture, and undertaking trades, but Henry and John's decision to specialize in real estate epitomized the more general trend, especially in London.

George Robins was often reputed to have officiated his first auction at the age of only 19, but he officially joined his father and uncle in business in 1806 (at age 29). When both Henry and John died in 1821 George took over the business and worked to establish his reputation as one of London's elite practitioners. He publicly stamped his first sales catalog in 1822, and in 1824 he was invited to auction off the English estates of the late Marquis de Ormonde. Those estate sales reached nearly half a million pounds, and were considered at the time to have been among the largest property auctions in memory.[45] Over the following decade, Robins developed and perfected a marketing style that attracted wider public attention for its poetic and embellished description of estates and houses.

The "Robins school," as it was later dubbed in the press, produced descriptions of property that would appear sarcastic to modern consumers but which, at the time, were clearly enjoyed for their romantic wit, tongue-in-cheek modesty, and sense of playfulness with the formalities of aristocratic culture. In one such advertisement, for the sale of the "Greenway mansion" in Devon in 1832, Robins began with typical reserve, noting that "to do [the property] justice, and yet avoid the charge of making the picture too vivid, is by no means an easy task; and conscious of the feeble hand that has to portray many of the beauties of THIS FAIRY LAND, it may in truth be stated he approaches the task with almost fear and trembling." The ad continued:

> THE WOODLAND SCENERY within this Demesne extends itself in all directions, and is diversified by so much of hill and dale, aided by distant and mountain scenery, where the verdure is conspicuous to the mountain top, that it will not fail to remind the beholder of The BEAUTY and WILDNESS of SWITZERLAND; while the River Dart, flowing in placid beauty, pursues its irregular and circuitous course, winds in so many varied forms about this EARTHLY PARADISE. Indeed, so perfect is the illusion, that it really puts on the appearance of enchantment rather than reality.[46]

However much Robins was at pains to remind his readers that his accounts took little from "fancy's sketch," he nonetheless endeavored to entice potential buyers to imagine themselves in possession of properties for sale, with their attendant advantages. In the case of the Devon mansion, Robins calculated that "the healthy appearance of the woods is a pretty strong symptom indicative of health and consequent longevity; and it may be added, that East Indians, and invalids disposed to pulmonary attacks, will find this abode a very great solace."[47] "The climate," he observed, "yields not in its influential powers to the South of France."[48] In another ad, for a mansion in Dorset, Robins spelled out the political influence that could accrue to a future purchaser: "It has long since been the subject of regret that an abode in every respect so well calculated to afford the desired accommodation has not been selected for the M.P. of Bridport. . . . This may, however, be remedied by the new possessor at the approaching election."[49]

Whereas consumptive nabobs and aspiring politicians might fit the bill for certain of his properties, Robins was equally attuned to other speculative possibilities, such as urban development. In a description for a small farm on the outskirts of Hastings, to be sold by auction at the London Auction Mart in July 1830, Robins mused that while the existing farm constituted a "snug Little Residence, most agreeably placed in a fertile Valley. . . . A nobler and more exalted character appertains to this Estate, no less an object than creating upon this fine Domain THE NEW TOWN OF HASTINGS." "In days of yore," he hypothesized, "it would have been accounted romantic to have hazarded such an opinion," but the recent growth of the town as a watering hole for "FASHIONABLE AND OPULENT GUESTS" promised future returns from further development. "In this refreshing valley," concluded Robins, "methinks I hear exclaimed, 'Who could resist a Villa in such a situation?' By a parity of reasoning, 'Who can for a moment doubt the success of a building operation?'" He was equally circumspect several years later, in an ad for another "FAIRY LAND" wherein "surrounded by such a splendid picture, profit appears a by-gone word, a secondary thought; and yet so fertile is the land—so rich in its varied scenery—that an immense annual revenue may be secured by indulging the wealthy merchants of its neighbouring . . . city with sites of ground."[50]

Given the more economical and typographically restrained descriptions offered by Robins's competitors, it is not surprising that he quickly came to the notice of critics and commentators. The *Morning Post*, the chief daily newspaper for his advertisements, regularly expressed its enthusiasm, often directing its readers to the end pages filled with descriptions penned by the supposed "Archon of Auctioneers." In 1833, claiming (erroneously) to have been the first "to call its [the public] attention to a treasure too long hidden," *Tait's Edinburgh Magazine* compared Robins to Wordsworth, adding that in terms of remuneration for his art, Robins held a clear advantage over the famed poet, "the Knight of the Pulpit realising hundreds sterling, whilst he of the Lakes turns tens." "The auctioneering line," stated the journal, "erewhile a despised calling and a low, has, by his means, been elevated to the dignity of an art; and he proudly stands, at this day, an artist, first and alone, in a department which his own genius has made excellent."[51]

His genius was not universally admired, however. For political satirists, Robins's reputation lent itself more toward a parody of unrestrained commercialism, as when, in 1843, *Punch* offered to sell, in the name of George Robins, by "public competition" at the auction mart, "all that valuable Lot and Royal Lifehold Property, the **YOUNG QUEEN OF SPAIN**."[52] Thomas Carlyle similarly agreed that Robins made a good stand in for all that was immoral about the cash nexus. In 1850, he evoked the auctioneer in a political essay about British colonial policy. The value of colonies, he wrote, rested on more than simply the financial cost of their acquisition and possession. He mocked the notion of Robins auctioning the empire on behalf of the principles of political economy: "All men know . . . that to men and Nations there are invaluable values which cannot be sold for money at all. George Robins is great; but he is not omnipotent. George Robins cannot quite sell Heaven and Earth by auction, excellent though he be at the business."[53]

In linking Robins with colonial policy, Carlyle may have had in mind Robins's ambitious attempt in 1842 to sell an estate—or, in the words of the prospectus for the sale, a "principality"—in the Cape Colony. In an ironic twist to his usual blandishments for retirement to the pleasing climes of southeast England, Robins advertised that the Cape's climate was "so congenial to health and consequent longevity, that few, if any, [would] be inclined to return to England." Asserting that the land on the estate could support upward of thirty thousand sheep, Robins gave only the slightest hint of caution, promising that "at the outset, and until he [the emigrant] has made his bed of roses, he should calculate upon trifling personal discomfort; but, it may be asked, where is independence to be procured without it?" This sale appears to have failed only after a correspondent to the *Times*, writing with firsthand knowledge of the actual state of the land, insisted that Robins recall his prospectus on the grounds that the estate held nothing of the promise attributed to it.[54]

Robins died in February 1847, leaving his business to his cousin Edmund Robins (who shortly thereafter auctioned Shakespeare's birthplace). In death even more so than in life, however, Robins came to be associated with the excesses of modern marketing. His descriptions of property were cited in handbooks and histories of advertising, in popular books of logic (under the category of descriptive reasoning), and in many other novels and periodicals. The idea of a particular "Robins school" even found credence in the subsequent career of one of his advertising clerks, who went on to write a book of landscape poetry (and who credited his former employer for giving him "opportunities of indulging in the descriptive and the beautiful").[55]

In an article on the "age of veneer," published in *Fraser's Magazine* in 1852, Robins's influence was contextualized within a larger and more general transformation toward a modern industrial age. It was argued that the George Robins "school of advertising" represented a transitional moment in the general diffusion of marketed falsehoods, brought about by the expansion and integration of markets and the rise of various new media—notably, newspapers—for communicating between buyers and sellers. Robins represented the blurring of a line between charlatanism and professionalism that was quickly dissolving in "these days of manufactured opinion." The author acknowledged the skill with which Robins had adapted new forms of publishing to pursue familiar tricks of deception:

> If a redeeming feature appeared in his catalogue of sale, it was cast in type the largest—all qualifying particulars found publicity in miniature. Facts were marshaled in the poster by notes of admiration, and pleasant fictions, based on "ifs," and leaning on hypotheses, got patented in print by doubtful punctuation. Truth, hyphened to exaggeration, set paradox at nought, and an anti-climax was often saved by an accommodating comma.[56]

What set Robins apart from both the quackery of the pre-industrial age and the more systemized dissemblance of modern marketing, however, was his reflexivity and manipulation of self-conscious exaggerations. His descriptions "bore the genuine marks of fabrication or exaggeration. Everybody knew that he dealt in fiction, and that his surcharged promises were intended to tickle the public curiousity, and were not deliberately framed to deceive."[57] It is not clear why the authors chose to shield Robins from the immorality that they attributed in part to his legacy, but their analysis identified several themes that bring us back to the role of auctioneers in the marketing of real property. These are, first, the importance of description in the process of valuing and exchanging property, and second, the often troublesome division within this process between market facts and market fictions.

As much as his contemporaries and successors tried to distance themselves from the excesses of Robins's style, few would have denied that describing property was one of the primary tasks carried out by auctioneers. This task was evident both in the verbal play of the auction room and in the written documents that ultimately formed the legal contract enforcing the sale. Indeed, newspaper advertisements of the kind discussed earlier by George Robins were commonly abstracts or even verbatim copies of one of the documents—the "particulars of sale"—included in the contract for a sale of real property. In professional terminology, such a contract included the "particulars of sale," the "conditions of sale," and a memorandum of purchase. Whereas the particulars of sale described the nature of the property, its legal identity, its primary features, and its liabilities, the conditions of sale established the rules by which the sale would be carried out (conditions *preliminary* to the sale); the extent, limitations, and liabilities for the rights to be transferred (conditions *concurrent* to the sale); and the provisions governing breach of contract (conditions *posterior*).[58] Although the contract itself could be made with little more than the signature of each party and a reference to the particulars and conditions of sale, the more common practice was to complete, at the close of an auction, a memorandum of purchase printed on the reverse side of the conditions. Together, these three documents constituted the contract for sale and provided the legal basis on which all auction sales took place.[59]

A common point of professional contestation between auctioneers and solicitors involved the question of who was properly qualified to prepare the documents in a real estate contract. Many guides to the law and practice of property sales implicitly recognized the role of auctioneers in drafting particulars of sale, even when it was conceded that questions of legal title should naturally be referred to a vendor's solicitor for review.[60] It was less clear whether or not auctioneers were qualified to prepare conditions of sale, since these conditions often dealt more directly with matters of law; but toward the end of the century, at least one handbook noted that many elite country and London auctioneers routinely prepared both the particulars and conditions of a sale. In principle if not always in practice, auctioneers believed that the description of marketable property distinguished their own expertise from that of the legal profession, and this division could be read in the component texts that formed the contract for public sales of land. Wrote one auctioneer: "The preparation of the particulars of sale ought—either as a matter of etiquette between the one and the other [auctioneers and solicitors], or from the fact that the auctioneer's calling naturally fits him for the task—to be not only the duty, but the legitimate office of the auctioneer."[61]

The importance of the particulars of sale as devices for framing the commoditization of real property was reflected in the large body of legal decisions and opinions that circumscribed their content and presentation.[62] Neglect on the part of the vendor to describe a property "accurately, and in unambiguous language" constituted "misdescription," and could occur in one of three ways: misrepresentation, omission, or ambiguity.[63] Evidence of misdescription could provide the grounds for a buyer to rescind the contract or, as was more often the case, to seek compensation from the vendor. The language contained in a description was deeply coded, with many words and phrases having legally fixed definitions. An acre, for example, should refer to a statute acre, not any of the many local variations of the measure. A "valuable tavern lot" could not describe a property in which the vendor was restricted by covenant from using the land for any purpose other than a private residence.[64] In most cases the onus was on the vendor and his agents to describe a property in such ways "as to convey clear information to the ordinary class of persons who frequent sales by auction."[65]

Given these protections from and legal strictures against acts of misdescription, the career of George Robins should rightfully have fizzled with his first rhetorical flourish. Robins was saved, however, by the widespread acceptance within the law of nonfactual statements, or what one legal textbook referred to as "laudatory epithets"; these statements "as to the value of the property, or as to probable profits, chances, risks, or other matters of opinion" avoided censure so long as they were not deemed to misrepresent specific statements of fact. The classic example was the case of a property described as having "uncommonly rich water meadow land," when in fact the land was poorly irrigated. When the case was brought to trial, the courts concluded that "uncommonly rich" referred to the land, not to the state of its irrigation. In another case, one settled in 1860, the courts accepted the descriptions "substantial and well-built" and "having five bedrooms" despite the fact that the property in question had one wall only half a brick thick and two questionably sized rooms. In each of these cases, the law distinguished between what vendors and their auctioneers offered as opinions of value from what they specifically stated as matters of fact.[66]

Particulars of sale and other verbal descriptions of property made during an auction sale revolved around subtle distinctions between matters of fact and matters of opinion, and it was the job of auctioneers to negotiate the space between legal truth and market imagination. Despite the cultural anxieties posed by the marketing tactics of George Robins, all auctioneers could recognize in him the skills involved in deftly sailing, as one authority put it, "on the windy side of the law."[67] Moreover, at the heart of that tension were two differing notions of agency at work in the marketplace. The first, articulated in more strict legal terms, accepted the use of laudatory epithets by insisting that they should have little effect on the autonomy of liberal and rational market actors. "The theory," stated one guide to real estate contracts, "is that praise conferred by the vendor and the vendor's estimate of the value of his own property do not influence, or at all events ought not to influence, the purchaser's judgment, and that, even if they are unfounded, the purchaser has suffered no wrong because he relied on his own opinion, or accepted the vendor's opinion at his own risk."[68]

A second theory of agency, however, articulated by Robert Squibbs in his 1891 guide to auctioneering, gestured to the greater power of sentiment and desire. "Where auctioneers are concise and to the point," he warned, "they run the risk of attracting attention from those people only who are independent of susceptibilities." "There are many," he continued, "who, whatever regard they may have for plain matter-of-fact descriptions, are equally susceptible with the auctioneer of all that may be charming and attractive—people who, though they may *look* at, will not be tempted to *think* of, a plain description." Central to this theory was a more fluid and dynamic sense of the cognitive processes involved in making market calculations, and here the auction room presented a particularly powerful example of the contingency of these calculations. Later in the same guide, Squibbs noted that the power of the auctioneer depended on the ability to shape ideas during the "spirit of competition" that arose over the course of bidding:

> Men may go to an auction with their calculations well established as to value and what they are to bid; and though they may say that they are not to be netted by any auctioneer's eloquence or earnestness, there is still the liability to temptation left, to be charmed, to be led, to be influenced, to go beyond all their original ideas.[69]

Auctioneers were less like mirrors to reality than they were shapers of it, disrupting "original ideas" and "calculations well established as to value" so as to introduce new associations and possibilities.

Much earlier, in 1840, Douglas Jerrold alluded to a similar set of impulses when he caricatured George Robins as "Mr. Georgious Redbreast." Using as an example the auctioned sale of a share in the Drury Lane Theatre (with which the real Robins had a long and very public association), Jerrold deftly teased apart the dynamic operating between fact and the desire for what today might be thought of as cultural capital. "There is a strange, mysterious connexion," he wrote, "between the advertised commodity and the glorious objects touched upon by the Auctioneer; the 'share' is hallowed by its compelling association with so many brilliant images, that incapable, or even unwilling to separate the real from the fanciful, the reader purchases, and the eloquence of Mr. Redbreast has its wished reward." An auctioneer, concluded Jerrold a few paragraphs on, is "a dealer in words" who, with the "mere artillery of syllables," could capture alike the reason of the "illiterate countryman" and the "man of many thousands."[70]

It is possible to read into Jerrold's and Squibbs's statements the belief that the development and subsequent visibility of auction sales had shifted the dialectic somewhat between these two very different views of auction discourse—the one dismissing the value of words altogether, the other insisting that they were essential. Nevertheless, implicit in many satirical accounts of George Robins's marketing was the idea that reason and desire operate exclusive of each other, and that a barrage of words silences more sober deliberation. Auctioneers' descriptions were little more than puffs of air, lacking in substance. Nonetheless, the distinction noted above between *looking* and *thinking about* descriptions of property is closer to the mark, for it recognizes a deeper social logic at work in the making of marketable property. Matter-of-fact descriptions satisfied the legal conventions against misrepresentation, but, in the end, they offered insufficient information to entice outside buyers to consider a purchase. In order to think about a property for sale, buyers needed to be able to imagine themselves somehow connected to the property; they required a path linking their own social world to that of a future world of ownership, and the means by which this was done was through the use of auction narratives.

Storytelling, in other words, lay at the core of Robins's style. Narrative filled in the space between "East Indian valetudinarians" returning from their colonial postings and finding recuperation in the "FAIRYLANDS" of the Channel coast. Narrative was the bridge across which aspiring estate owners could travel to see themselves as respected holders of the county seat.

Narrative recast small farms on the outskirts of coastal towns as future opportunities for urban speculation and development. Narrative, moreover, was a particularly powerful tool for marketing real property, whose immobility lent itself to the collection of strong historical associations. Indeed, market value was demarcated through specific associations of time and place that were just as important as facts about acreage or drainage. An emphasis on the local and the particular in these stories sustained a more abstract encounter in the auction room by linking individual experience to future states of possession. The career and legacy of George Robins, and the ornate images that shaped his advertisements and auction room banter, brought into relief a process endemic to all property auctions, one in which auctioneers negotiated the values and identities necessary to bring properties into a commodity state and coordinated the market encounters that would transfer them to new ownership. Even if few auctioneers seemed to have been inclined to copy from the Robins school, all would have recognized in him a practice that was central to the trade.

There was also something about auction narratives that gestured to the broader tensions of a more commercial age. As Cynthia Wall has pointed out, the literary imagination of auction sales bore striking resemblance to innovations in modern literature itself. Auction catalogs and particulars of sale, for example, regularly presented the names of auctioneers in formats that mimicked the title pages of books, framing auctioneers as authors of dramas that began with the death or departure of one estate owner and concluded with a new owner restoring the social identity of estate ownership. Both the written description of property and the spectacle of its public sale served to reaffirm the stability of social relations in the context of uncertain commercial exchanges. The narrative function of auctions offers a compelling cultural explanation for the rise in popularity of auction sales during the late eighteenth century. As "narratives of dismantling," writes Wall, auction particulars acted "as important cultural, physical, and textual intermediaries between shifting social, economic, and aesthetic boundaries."[71]

The discussion of George Robins and the various responses to his marketing tactics demonstrate the significance of auction discourse to Britain's broader nineteenth-century consumer culture. More specifically, they show how auction narratives functioned as part of the networks of association needed to make markets and the marketability of property possible. Particulars of sale mediated between the practice of the auction room, the social and cultural expectations of ownership, the legal parameters governing property transactions, and the wider world of changing consumer cultures in the eighteenth and nineteenth centuries. If the kind of agency that makes market encounters possible depends on the coordination of "possible states of the world," then it was the descriptions of property offered in particulars of sale that linked these worlds and further established the ideas of value through which one could be related to another.[72] Auctioneers and particulars of sale were just some of many agents and objects that made these encounters possible, but their proximity to market contexts and the cultural anxieties generated by those contexts shed a particularly insightful light on the means by which a property market came into broader public view.

The public debate over George Robins's legacy continued long after his death, but nowhere was it more pronounced than among auctioneers themselves, who wrestled with his role in shaping their professional identity. Correspondents writing in the trade periodicals that appeared during the second half of the century tried to distance themselves from the excesses of Robins's descriptive style while at the same time holding to a belief in the need for, as one correspondent put it, "local colouring." Along these lines, one conspiracy theory quickly arose accusing Robins of having employed a professional writer to draft his advertisements, with the hope that it might have been possible to celebrate his success without acknowledging his methods. Edmund Robins vigorously defended his uncle's name, claiming that a search of the business's records revealed no evidence of a client ever complaining of misdescription.[73] Once again, the strictures of the law protected the ambiguities of the market.

In truth, late-century auctioneers depended on George Robins as a foil with which to contrast their own independence and respectability. If there was a consistent theme in the treatment of Robins's legacy, it was in situating him in an immediate past of a more prosaic and professional age. Auctioneers repeatedly asserted that the age of puffery was over, replaced by a more sober assessment of market value; but the many pages in professional handbooks dedicated to discussing the potential pitfalls found in drafting particulars of sale belied such confidence. As one guide noted in 1910, "Although this duty [to describe property] may appear to be a very simple one to discharge, nevertheless it would be no exaggeration to say that breaches of it have been the cause of more disputes between vendor and purchaser than any other matter."[74] In the end, it proved easier to celebrate the "humours of auctioneering" through the life and myth of George Robins, whose indispensable talent was "able to lure the Muses from their woodland retreats and render them at home in one of the busiest centres of the busiest city in the world" (fig. 6).[75] In fact, caricatures of Robins marked less of a decline in the art of connecting the social worlds of purchasers and vendors

FIGURE 6. Sketch of Mr. Redbreast (a.k.a. George Robins). Reprinted from Kenny Meadows, *Heads of the People* (London, 1840), opposite page 105.

than they did a displacement of one form of expertise for another. Professionalizing auctioneers could point to the restraint of their own market discourse as evidence of an improved, more objective competency, but this did nothing to change their fundamental role as dealers in the words and worlds of property exchange.

HOUSE AGENCY AND THE "HORRORS OF HOUSE-HUNTING"

From the practice of auctions and the property sales market, we turn to the rental market and the practice of house hunting. Writing about house hunting at the end of the century, H. G. Wells contended that it represented an age-old pilgrimage of the young, tinged with the themes of expulsion and earthly toil: "Since Adam and Eve went hand in hand out of the gates of Paradise, the world has travailed under an infinite succession of house-hunts. Today in every eligible suburb you may see New Adams and New Eves by the score, with rusty keys and pink order-forms in hand, wandering still, in search of the ideal home."[76] Victorian writers generally shared the sense of drudgery associated with the subject of house hunting, but unlike Wells, a great many of them saw in its specific features and cultural anxieties a novel experience of the modern age. A number of factors, including the rise of a middle-class with deep cultural attachment to homes and the rapid expansion of an urban landscape that made it harder to find suitable houses, lifted Victorian house hunting to the biblical importance noted in Wells's description.

Auctioneers and house agents became central figures in these new cultural relations of property, offering to mediate the private exchange of property through their inside knowledge of markets and market practices. Once again, since auctioneers regularly practiced in both public and private property markets, the distinction between auctioneering and house agency should be made with caution, especially since doing so also excludes several other professions who carried out estate and house agency, such as solicitors, surveyors, builders, and home furnishers. Lacking any monopoly power over the sale or letting of property, estate and house agents worked under conditions of constant competition, often visible on the street in the form of competing notice boards attached to homes on the market (see fig. 7).[77] House and estate agents were most often associated with house hunting, however, and their efforts to rationalize and normalize this practice reinforced their own position as mediators of property exchange while simultaneously determining the material and cultural relations of the market itself.

The kind of house hunting described by Wells and others was a decidedly middle-class affair, made possible both by the increase in wealth and number of that class during the nineteenth century and by the development of new sensibilities placing the home as a space of security, identity, and status. The gradual process of distinguishing between the workplace and

A CHOICE OF AGENTS.

FIGURE 7. A cacophony of house agent advertisements posted at street level. Reprinted from George Robert Sims, *Living London: Its Work and Its Play, Its Humour and Its Pathos, Its Sights and Its Scenes* (London, 1902), 220.

the home coincided in the late eighteenth and early nineteenth centuries with the construction of the first suburban estates, whose location on the edge of towns permitted both literal and symbolic distance from the social and moral evils of early industrialization and urbanization. By the 1820s, the house and the idea of home were already on their way to an intimate union. In a world of commercial risk and speculation, the home held an immutable symbolic position in middle class culture, a bastion from the public sphere and the marketplace where the bourgeois might protect and rejuvenate its moral universe. House and home became, in the words of one historian, "the central institutions of civilized life."[78]

The apparent stability of the home as a cultural institution, however, belied the transitory nature of most middle-class accommodation. With few exceptions, homeownership was rare in most parts of the country, particularly in London; and since most houses were therefore rented and required as little as a few months' notice to quit, families could, with relative ease, change homes according to shifts in family structure and income. It was hardly surprising, then, to see Isabella Beeton—the doyen of Victorian middle-class house management—complain of the "horrors of house-hunting" and to offer her readers advice on the essential criteria to be used in judging the quality of a new house.[79] As objects of status, however, houses also fell victim to fashion, and by midcentury the capriciousness and mobility of middle-class housing taste had become a subject of satire. "We change our dresses, our servants, our friends and foes," wrote George Augustus Sala, "how can our houses expect to be exempt from the mutabilities of life?"[80] He elaborated sardonically on an experience increasingly familiar to many middle-class families:

> We tire of the old friend, and incline to the new; the old baby is deposed in favour of the new baby . . . we change, and swop, and barter, and give up, and take back, and long for, and get tired of, all and everything in life—why not of houses too? So the Supplement of the Times can always offer Houses to let; and we are continually running mad to let or hire them, as vice versa, six months hence, perhaps, we shall be as maniacally eager to hire or to let.[81]

Sala equated houses with other seemingly permanent social institutions—friendship and family—and yet viewed them as equally adrift in an ocean of neurotic consumerism.

As unsettling as was the idea of houses used and discarded like cheap stockings, residential mobility was a widespread feature of nineteenth-century British urban life. Over the course of the century, the urban population of England alone grew at more than double the rate of the overall population, and by 1911 the nation was not only overwhelmingly urban (79 percent by then), it was also concentrated in many large cities, with nearly half of the population living in towns with more than one hundred thousand inhabitants.[82] London was the largest city by far, reaching its peak dominance in 1901, when its residents numbered more than a fifth of the total population of England. Much of this urban growth came from migration into cities, either from the countryside or from other towns, such that in 1851 two-thirds of those over twenty years of age in urban Britain had been born elsewhere.[83] And since most housing was rented on short-term leases and provided limited tenure, families continued to move once they had arrived in cities. This was true for working-class families as well as for middle-class families, though homeownership and higher incomes did correlate with greater persistence. Half or more of the working-class families surveyed in two London districts in the 1840s had moved within the past year, and similar rates were found for the general urban population in the Edwardian period. Families across different social classifications thus moved

FIGURE 8. Surveyor and estate agent's office on Euston Road, London, 1907. Reproduced by permission of the London Metropolitan Archives, City of London. http://collage.cityoflondon.gov.uk. Image 107372.

house often, albeit with varying means and aspirations.[84] In the search for greater respectability and higher status, house hunters thus faced a proliferating vocabulary of "mansions," "residences," "villas," and "cottages," each of these claiming to offer better returns of social and cultural capital.

Cultural and spatial complexity spelled opportunity for those willing to coordinate the meeting of buyers, renters, sellers, and lessors. Estate and house agency therefore became a common side business for auctioneers and a primary one for those taking out the cheaper (but more limiting) house agents license. If auctioneers provided coordinating functions by bringing interested parties together in the space of an auction and by connecting their different social worlds through different descriptions of value and identity, so too did estate agents. In the latter's case, however, the field of practice was a more open one, with a potentially greater number of properties available for consideration and with far more varied contexts of social interaction, from the offices of individual agents to the streets and doorsteps of properties placed in the market (see fig. 8).

House agents had a natural interest, of course, in cultivating public ignorance and naivety of the housing market. Doing so only reinforced the need for professional guidance. In his undoubtedly self-promoting property guide and quasi manifesto published in 1853, Alfred Cox, a London estate agent, conceded that "house-hunting is but poor sport. . . . It is rather tedious, troublesome, and expensive toil, attended by disheartened failures, irritating rebuffs, annoying contests with cupidity, exaggeration and deception, and consequently followed by disparagement of the world in general, and landlords in particular." His proposed solution engaged a "*prearranged system*," carried out in part through "the established, and therefore the most complete and expeditious, channels of communication." Inquiries through friends, in newspapers, or on foot—each involving investments of energy, social capital, and time—ignored the advantages to be had through the modern division of labor. "A very little reflection will show that, in an employment requiring so much knowledge of 'ins and outs' as the hiring of house and land, the inexperienced can have no chance of competing successfully against the practiced hand." Unless one was unemployed and "fond of mere drudgery," it was better to hire the help of an agent.[85]

Despite the strong warnings from house agents, many young families continued to follow more traditional methods for locating houses, such as newspapers, local and family networks, and perambulations of desirable neighborhoods. Walking was, in fact, the primary method employed in one early account of house hunting from 1827, involving a family in receipt of a small inheritance who set aside "a certain portion of every day of the ensuing week to various peregrinations of discovery."[86] Similarly, Edward Ryde and his sister Ellen "look[ed] all over the town for empty houses" on a house hunting trip to Romsey, Hampshire, in 1860.[87] Nonetheless, anecdotal evidence suggests that the use of "prearranged systems" likely became more common as the century progressed, aided by the growing number of house agents operating in London and elsewhere. Later accounts of house hunting on foot, for example, regularly included reference to lists of properties provided by one or more firm of estate agents.

To be sure, most depictions of real estate agents were far from flattering, with plotlines that emphasized the ubiquity of misrepresentation and even outright collusion against buyers and renters. In one particularly exhaustive search, a young couple sought out advice from their local firm, modestly titled the "East of England House and Estate Agency Office" (see fig. 9). The lists offered from this local agent failed to produce a suitable house, and so the couple searched the county directory for names of town agents. After a few inquiries, however, they climbed the hierarchy once more: "We will no

FIGURE 9. W. Brunton, "House Hunting," *London Society*, July 1867, 21. Reproduced by permission of the British Library Board. P.P. 6004.gp Vol XII.

longer trust to country agents, we will write to London men."[88] Ultimately, the husband and wife set out alone to search for eligible properties, only to find themselves resigned to remain in their home and determined to never set out on a house hunt again. In each case, the inability of estate agents to offer a desirable property was matched only by their dissembling of that fact through puffed promises of ideal homes.

The difficulty in establishing professional credibility was endemic to the profession, and had been discussed publicly since at least the 1830s, when Alexander Rainy first called for stricter licensing of auctioneers in order to effect a closer approximation to professional conveyancing practice.[89]

Two of the more common targets for complaints included the practice of employing more than one agent and of agents competing unfairly among one another, such as by not sharing commissions for sales benefiting from the work of more than one agent. Whereas solicitors would occasionally argue that auctioneers and estate agents should not receive standard compensation for work undertaken—that they should, instead, "find their own level in public estimation according to their qualifications"—auctioneers and agents, in letters and in editorial opinion, insisted that just as a doctor would be paid for his services no matter the outcome, so too should similar professions be paid for work undertaken, regardless of the ultimate result.[90]

Such concerns gave Cox's "prearranged systems" all the greater importance, since they offered both a means of coordinating market information and of securing for estate and house agency a form of credible expertise. This point was made even more emphatically in another guide to estate agency published by R. Ernest in 1905, which distinguished between what Ernest termed "in-the-rut" agency and more modern and progressive business practice built upon a systematic coordination of the market. Expertise, Ernest insisted, was essential to a progressive practice: "Remember, this is an age of specialists."[91] Only by securing such expertise could estate agents legitimate their calls for just compensation.

Professional guidebooks and trade periodicals offered many suggestions for improving estate agency expertise. Ernest undoubtedly gave the most detailed prescriptions, ranging from the best forms of practice in correspondence and advertising strategies to what he enticingly termed "mental suggestion"; the latter, he argued, constituted "one of the most important arts known and practiced by most of the successful, up-to-date Estate men of to-day."[92] Despite this insistence on the importance of telepathy in house hunting, other, more pragmatic skills and equipment were likely easier to acquire (though perhaps less effective). The two that I will focus on here are property registers and orders to view. As with an auctioneer's particulars of sale, property registers and orders to view framed property market encounters by coordinating different forms of cultural, spatial, and material practice.

The history of property registers unfolded at two very different scales, one that attempted to encompass the market as a whole and another that attempted to localize it in the material culture of an agent's office. The question of creating a universal exchange or registry for property emerged at several points over the course of the nineteenth century, including in the designs of the first London Auction Mart. In 1838, Alexander Rainy similarly called for a universal registry, though largely on the grounds of better regulating the profession by eliminating dishonest dealers. When the London Estate Exchange was founded in 1857, many heralded it as the final step necessary to bring property into the same freedom of trade as stocks or corn. The estate exchange would list all the properties available for sale and would be available for consultation to those private members invited to join. The exchange, however, remained an extremely elite institution—even by 1923, it had only 117 members—and its plans to function as an actual exchange or to create a register of property available for sale or rent never came to pass (as opposed to its plans to record sales, which did continue in the form of the weekly reports, as discussed in chapter 3). The absence of a central clearinghouse for property information—what one enterprising proposal in 1874 termed "the missing link in the property market"—had become an unending headache for the profession.[93]

Yet again, in the winter of 1903, proposals for an exchange or register of property came before the Auctioneers' Institute, first in the president's inaugural address in 1903, and then in a paper delivered to members of the institute by Sydney A. Smith in January 1904, under the title "The Estate Agency Question: A Proposal for a Central Exchange."[94] It may very well have been the case that the president chose to include his remarks in response to several letters published in the *Estates Gazette* earlier that fall, bemoaning the poor public reputation of estate agents. "There is surely 'something wrong somewhere,'" wrote one correspondent to the paper, "when members of the general public, property owners, seekers for investments, house hunters, etc., pointedly refrain from availing themselves of the services of those whose experience and opportunities should properly be of real use and benefit to them. That there is a feeling of distrust, and that the profession generally is largely discredited among the general public cannot be denied."[95] Other writers in that exchange reiterated what were by then familiar complaints about lax licensing and misdescription in property advertisements as the root causes of such low public opinion.[96]

Smith's proposal for a London-based property exchange promised to address the concerns of vendors, buyers, and agents alike. Smith's remarks were targeted at medium-size estates, but he noted that they applied equally well to other forms of property, including rental housing. Vendors and buyers, he argued, suffered from similar problems of limited market access. In the existing state of competition between agents, and between agents and other professionals (e.g., solicitors and surveyors), no one could ever be certain of having maximized the exposure of their property to the interested parties available at any given time. With property information processed through a single institution, a buyer could "see all the houses within a certain radius at one visit, and, further, with reliable registration, he would be less likely to be sent on wasted journeys through lack of information that properties are disposed of, incorrect particulars, or mis-description and mis-statements of areas and distances."[97] The advantages for agents would derive from reducing competition and inefficiency in marketing properties and from erecting barriers to professional entry by restricting access to the exchange, much as was done in the estate exchange. In sum, what Smith proposed was not unlike the multiple listing systems familiar in many parts of the world today and whose origins can be found in early post–World War I North America.

In turn-of-the-century England, however, Smith's arguments received a lukewarm reception, both immediately following the paper and over subsequent weeks and months. In his reply to Smith's talk, J. H. Townsend Green argued that the sheer size of the London market—with, in his estimation, several thousand agents and around a hundred thousand properties—would make an exchange unworkable. Green believed a register might be more practical.[98] Other respondents noted the obvious threat that would result from having an institution that could potentially be opened to the public, thereby circumventing the use of agents altogether. Another agent, writing to the *Estates Gazette*, admitted that "you could no more expect an agent to hand over his registers en bloc to any authority, than ask an opponent to expose his hand at a game of whist."[99] Later that year, at the annual meeting of the estate exchange, the chair noted in his address that the existing exchange "was already in possession of the field," but that argument was quickly denied by other correspondents to the *Gazette*, who pointed out the absence of information in the estate exchange relating to properties still on the market and to the limited territory covered by the exchange (i.e., mostly London).[100]

Both cultural depictions of house hunting and professional debates agreed on at least one thing: the multiplicity of property registers complicated access to property market information. "These multifarious registers are the very evil we wish to be rid of," complained one of the above-mentioned letters to the *Gazette*.[101] Smith had already concluded the same thing, telling his audience that if he could amass "in one colossal heap all the estate registers which exist today, and then place beside it the one register of the proposed Central Exchange, I would show you, gentlemen, a contrast far more striking and conclusive than even the famous loaves portrayed by the 'Daily News.'"[102] If securing professional power and market order could not be had through the lofty dreams of a central exchange or register, however, this did not preclude more local and pragmatic improvements in the organization of property information, advances which could in themselves bolster the framing of estate agents as holders of unique market expertise.

For Ernest, this meant approximating the ideal of a centralized register in the daily practice of an agent's office. "The equipment of an Estate office too often receives only very scant attention from the 'in-the-rut' agent," he wrote, "and yet it is a matter which should receive very close attention, for a good workman must necessarily be armed with good tools."[103] Property registers were one of these tools, and Ernest encouraged estate agents to move beyond the "grandmotherly" methods of "follow-my-leader" accounting.[104] One common alternative to bound-book registers were card index systems that combined preformatted property information sheets with vertical filing cabinets arranged according to different categories of property (see fig. 10). Such systems also permitted agents to keep track of correspondence relating to particular properties and to access that information "instantaneously." One advertisement for the Lyle dossier vertical filing cabinet offered to give an agent "the whole story in less than a minute." "No 'dead or obsolete' matter in a card index," the ad continued, "always 'live' and 'up-to-date.'"[105]

Through such improvements, the material ordering of local estate agency offices rearticulated the designs and ideals of professional expertise and the control of market information. Another guide even promoted the double-entry index system as a means for tracking claims for commissions in large offices with multiple agents (though presumably the same advantage could be had for individual agents). Arranged by either the name of the property or the name of the applicant, these systems could "enable the estate agent to tell at a glance whether he [could] claim to be a link in the chain joining vendor and purchaser, through his introduction."[106] Property registers, in other words, inscribed market relations into durable systems that evinced material claims and, by so doing, established the primacy of a particular kind of agency in the market. The links connecting transactions of land could be made visible and legitimate to a skeptical or hostile public.

Property registers offered one means for establishing claims to market expertise and for ordering disparate kinds of property (i.e., location, housing type, neighborhood, rental conditions, etc.) into a seemingly coherent and legible market space, defined within the confines of a particular agents' office and filing cabinets. They were one of the many "little tools of knowledge" whose "mundane epistemic" character made them easy to ignore as elements of the property market's everyday infrastructure.[107] The material and conceptual organization of the market, however, was only one step in the larger social relations constituted in house hunting. An equally challenging element involved the actual inspection of properties and the means by which that inspection could be made to feel appropriate in the context of

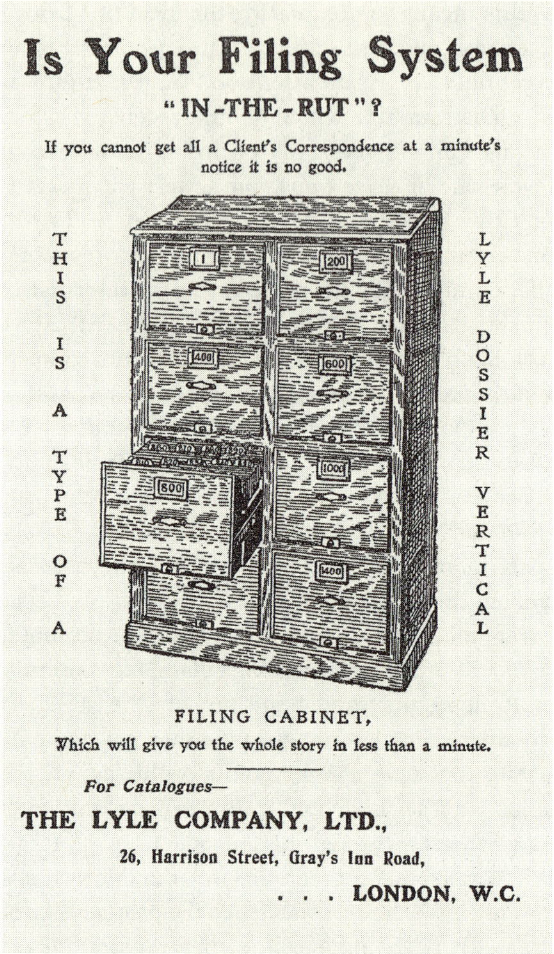

FIGURE 10. Advertisement for a Lyle vertical filing cabinet. R. Ernest, *How to Become a Successful Estate Agent* (London, 1905), back pages. Reproduced by permission of the British Library Board. 08226.b.4.

cultural norms concerning privacy and domesticity. For this more intimate task of market coordination, the use of orders to view offered a particularly common solution.

Clearly in touch with the deeper cultural anxieties of house hunting, Wells suggested that houses in the market held a similar taboo to dead bodies, complete with their disturbing vestiges of past lives: "Here, like pale ghosts upon the wall paper, are outlined the pictures of the departed tenant;

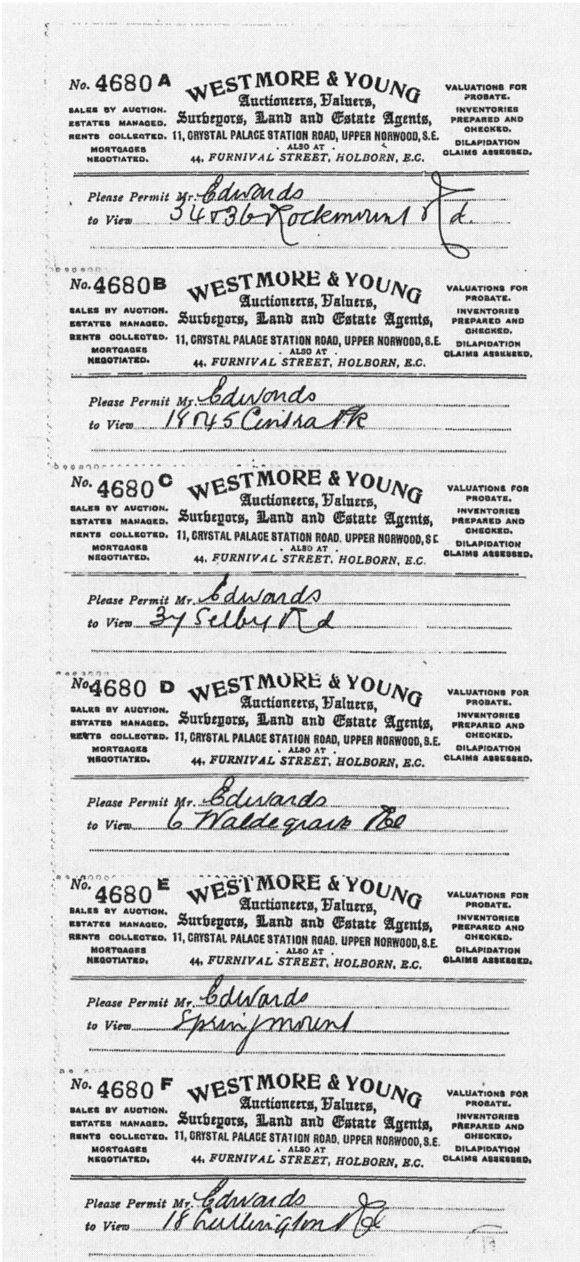

No. 4680 A
WESTMORE & YOUNG
Auctioneers, Valuers,
Surveyors, Land and Estate Agents,
11, CRYSTAL PALACE STATION ROAD, UPPER NORWOOD, S.E.
ALSO AT
44, FURNIVAL STREET, HOLBORN, E.C.
SALES BY AUCTION. ESTATES MANAGED. RENTS COLLECTED. MORTGAGES NEGOTIATED.
VALUATIONS FOR PROBATE. INVENTORIES PREPARED AND CHECKED. DILAPIDATION CLAIMS ASSESSED.
Please Permit Mr. Edwards
to View 34 & 36 Rockmount Rd

No. 4680 B
WESTMORE & YOUNG
Auctioneers, Valuers,
Surveyors, Land and Estate Agents,
11, CRYSTAL PALACE STATION ROAD, UPPER NORWOOD, S.E.
ALSO AT
44, FURNIVAL STREET, HOLBORN, E.C.
SALES BY AUCTION. ESTATES MANAGED. RENTS COLLECTED. MORTGAGES NEGOTIATED.
VALUATIONS FOR PROBATE. INVENTORIES PREPARED AND CHECKED. DILAPIDATION CLAIMS ASSESSED.
Please Permit Mr. Edwards
to View 14 & 45 Cintra Pk

No. 4680 C
WESTMORE & YOUNG
Auctioneers, Valuers,
Surveyors, Land and Estate Agents,
11, CRYSTAL PALACE STATION ROAD, UPPER NORWOOD, S.E.
ALSO AT
44, FURNIVAL STREET, HOLBORN, E.C.
SALES BY AUCTION. ESTATES MANAGED. RENTS COLLECTED. MORTGAGES NEGOTIATED.
VALUATIONS FOR PROBATE. INVENTORIES PREPARED AND CHECKED. DILAPIDATION CLAIMS ASSESSED.
Please Permit Mr. Edwards
to View 37 Selby Rd

No. 4680 D
WESTMORE & YOUNG
Auctioneers, Valuers,
Surveyors, Land and Estate Agents,
11, CRYSTAL PALACE STATION ROAD, UPPER NORWOOD, S.E.
ALSO AT
44, FURNIVAL STREET, HOLBORN, E.C.
SALES BY AUCTION. ESTATES MANAGED. RENTS COLLECTED. MORTGAGES NEGOTIATED.
VALUATIONS FOR PROBATE. INVENTORIES PREPARED AND CHECKED. DILAPIDATION CLAIMS ASSESSED.
Please Permit Mr. Edwards
to View 6 Waldegrave Rd

No. 4680 E
WESTMORE & YOUNG
Auctioneers, Valuers,
Surveyors, Land and Estate Agents,
11, CRYSTAL PALACE STATION ROAD, UPPER NORWOOD, S.E.
ALSO AT
44, FURNIVAL STREET, HOLBORN, E.C.
SALES BY AUCTION. ESTATES MANAGED. RENTS COLLECTED. MORTGAGES NEGOTIATED.
VALUATIONS FOR PROBATE. INVENTORIES PREPARED AND CHECKED. DILAPIDATION CLAIMS ASSESSED.
Please Permit Mr. Edwards
to View Springmount

No. 4680 F
WESTMORE & YOUNG
Auctioneers, Valuers,
Surveyors, Land and Estate Agents,
11, CRYSTAL PALACE STATION ROAD, UPPER NORWOOD, S.E.
ALSO AT
44, FURNIVAL STREET, HOLBORN, E.C.
SALES BY AUCTION. ESTATES MANAGED. RENTS COLLECTED. MORTGAGES NEGOTIATED.
VALUATIONS FOR PROBATE. INVENTORIES PREPARED AND CHECKED. DILAPIDATION CLAIMS ASSESSED.
Please Permit Mr. Edwards
to View 18 Cullington Rd

FIGURE 11. Orders to view from the firm of Westmore and Young, ca. 1890s. Reproduced by permission of The Bodleian Libraries, University of Oxford. Shelfmark: John Johnson Collection: Auctions 3 (171).

here are the nails of the invisible curtains, this dent in the wall is all that is sensible of a vanished piano. . . . A haunting fragrance of departed quarrels is to be found in the loose door-handles, and the broken bell-pull."[108] The analogy of house hunting to a coroner's examination was in stark contrast to other depictions of the practice as a vehicle for serendipitous romantic reunions. In one fictional account, a retired army bachelor, asked to find accommodation for a distant relative, happens upon a lost love who has hidden herself in a kitchen closet for fear of being seen by the prospective renter.[109] Between death and love, more comedic representations of house hunting played upon the confusion that could arise from false or exaggerated advertising. In one poem dedicated to the theme, a couple who has tired of their mansion decide to sell, but after many dispiriting visits to properties on the market, they settle for a home that they soon learn is their own, disguised in the puffed advertisement of their auctioneer—one Mr. Robins.[110]

Each of these accounts employed literary devices to mediate what were obviously awkward social relations of house hunting. The bonds that linked house to home could not be severed by the simple act of placing a property for rent or purchase. Mediating rituals were necessary extensions of the market, helping smooth over the social transitions between one set of owners or renters and another. By death, by love, or by farce, house hunters reconciled feelings of alienation resulting from putting houses in commodity contexts. In the world of nonfiction, however, house hunters could hardly hope to ease the estrangement of the marketplace through the fortuitous discovery of a bride hidden in the kitchen closet; more pragmatic devices were called for. One that was particularly associated with house agents and auctioneers was the ubiquitous "order to view," the pink slips with which Wells's New Adams and Eves began their suburban ramblings.

An order to view was a small slip of paper containing an agent's contact information, the name of the prospective renter or buyer, and the address of the property in question. More elaborate forms might also include details about the property pertaining to its size, layout, and contract terms. Orders could also be numbered so as to allow reference to an agents more detailed description contained in a register. In many respects, there was nothing particularly noteworthy or remarkable about these forms; they were part of the administrative ephemera generated in the daily practice of a more marginal branch of the property profession. That H. G. Wells chose these pink slips as iconic symbols of the practice of house hunting, however, suggests the degree to which they formed part of a larger cultural apparatus surrounding the search for property in the market.

More precisely, orders to view were devices empowering certain forms of market behavior that would have been otherwise unthinkable in the everyday social contexts of Victorian Britain. Thomas De Longueville, writing in the *Saturday Review* in 1879, neatly described the unusual social powers bestowed on the possessor of a house agent's order:

> Among the various conditions in life in which one feels more or less like a fish out of water is that of a man wandering about London armed with "orders to view." His powers are, for the time being, both extraordinary and embarrassing. He rings at the door-bells of people whom he does not know, provided with search warrants enabling him to inspect their homes from top to bottom. He has only to call upon a house agent in any quarter of the metropolis, and express a wish to find a house with a certain number of rooms at a reasonable rent, and he will be immediately presented with slips of paper, not unlike cheques, empowering him to invade the privacy of several of the neighbouring houses.[111]

House hunting evoked a liminal state in which each participant—"like a fish out of water"—transgressed the boundaries between public and private, market and society. Orders to view worked to normalize this precarious state by assigning discrete powers to their possessors, powers comparable in De Longueville's description to police search warrants or bank checks. Moreover, these forms linked house hunters to larger networks of market associations, which included house agents, existing tenants, owners, and the properties themselves.

In reality, of course, the powers bestowed on house hunters through their orders to view were complicated, often attenuated by a prevailing sense of unethical behavior or abuse of power. "One might imagine a being endowed with such plenary powers to be an object of dread," continued De Longueville, "but, in reality, he himself usually feels rather embarrassed and uncomfortable. He is to be observed at street corners, shyly looking over the agent's lists, and sorting his orders to view, with an unhappy and perplexed countenance."[112] In another account of house hunting, published by George Sims in 1902, the plenary powers of the pink slip were invariably constrained by the customary importance of the home.[113] His primary protagonists, Mr. and Mrs. Horace Brown, arrive at the first address provided to them by their agent and present the caretakers of the house with their order to view, only to be met with a scowl by the home's temporary caretakers, followed by a reluctant tour of the premises.

A similarly forced entry into a second home puts the Browns in direct confrontation with the family still in residence. "The members of the family," noted Sims, "try to look agreeable, but glare." As a result, "Mr. and Mrs. Brown remain on the threshold and just peer in." Moving to inspect the next room, Mr. Brown is further embarrassed when he intrudes on a young woman practicing piano, leading him to retreat to the main hall while his wife proceeds upstairs to finish the tour. He loiters, "like a man who has brought a parcel from the draper's and is waiting for the money," but even this unquestionably commercial disguise, however figurative, fails to stop the family dog from threatening him and his potentially "dishonest intentions."[114] Brought into the home via the power of an order to view, the Browns repeatedly threaten that home's domestic tranquility (see fig. 12).

The ambiguous power of orders to view in the hands of interested buyers or renters were similarly reflected in their use by house agents. As important as it was to secure an agent's expertise through the use of these forms, one had to dispense orders guardedly, since in the competitive world of house agency, the location of properties on the market was one of the most important pieces of information available to agents. One guide to the profession cautioned its readers to guard against the possible misrepresentations of competing agents. "Care should be taken when issuing orders to view to absolute strangers to ascertain the full name and address of the applicant and to write same on the counterfoil, together with the date when issued."[115] To the extent that orders to view could secure agents' expertise by linking them to properties in the market and by associating them to a potential sale (and its commission), the very same orders opened up further risk of putting the same information into the wrong hands of competing agents.

Moreover, the risks associated with brokering the market at a distance, through the agency of paper slips, could also include other encounters with local informants who might advise an agent's clients against a particular property. If, in the previous example, the problem with orders to view was the risk of them sharing information too widely with other agents, in this case the problem concerned the potential freedom that orders to view gave to clients to gather property information independently from the advice of their agents. "It is a bad policy to give any prospective customer a description and send him off alone to look at a property," advised Ernest, "as he will almost invariably find some one in the neighbourhood of the property offered who will run it down even should it be the best piece of property in existence."[116] For this reason, Ernest advised against using them altogether and suggested instead that an agent accompany a client in person, thereby

AN INSPECTION BY THE DOG.

FIGURE 12. Inspecting the home under the watch of the family dog. Reprinted from George Robert Sims, *Living London: Its Work and Its Play, Its Humour and Its Pathos, Its Sights and Its Scenes* (London, 1902), 218.

being better able to control the information that might be used to calculate an exchange.

These tools of the trade empowered and potentially destabilized the knowledge claims of auctioneers and estate agents. On the one hand, registers made the horrors of house hunting manageable by bringing order to the variable forms of property and their locations in a chaotic urban landscape. On the other hand, the same registers threatened to make information move with an efficiency that could put agents at risk of being beaten at their own game by their competitors. Similarly, orders to view could guide potential house hunters through the moral minefield of Victorian domestic morality, but could just as easily expose them to the ambiguities inherent in making the home an object of commodity exchange. The power to operate at a distance from agents could also lead clients to act independently, gathering their own information and making their own assessments of market value. In all these capacities, the sociotechnical arrangements of house hunting delineated the means by which auctioneers and estate agents asserted professional identities while facilitating Victorian property market relations.

Advertisements, particulars and conditions of sale, property registers, orders to view—these were the nuts and bolts of auctioneer and estate agency practice. Over the course of the nineteenth century, as the number of real estate auctioneers and estate agents grew, the forms of market practice they mobilized brought the commoditization of property into the public sphere of the auction room, the newspaper, the street, and even the parlor. The knowledge mobilized in this practice functioned in far less abstract or rarefied terms than did, for example, the law of property, but it remained no less powerful in terms of its capacities to orient the meaning of marketable property through a range of cultural, spatial, and material frameworks. Auctioneers and estate agents used their proximity to market transactions as a rationale for carving out an expertise of market values and patterns. The extravagance and hyperbole of figures like George Robins only reinforced this claim by emphasizing the need to connect vendors with future owners through the use of narratives and images or, as in the case of house hunting, registers and orders to view. The capacity to act in the real estate market depended on this complex web of mediating practice. Above all, this practice demonstrated the deeply contextualized and embodied nature of real estate's commodity context. Maintaining the social fabric of entangled property relations across the perceived chasm of marketability required careful attention to the details of language and gesture, of paper slips and filing cabinets.

CHAPTER THREE

Calculating the Market

Market calculation can take a variety of forms. Both the development of auctioneering and estate agency and the design of marketplaces to facilitate public sales of property entailed forms of individual and collective calculation that distinguished the marketable states of property and configured the agency of buyers and sellers.[1] Along with solicitors and other intermediaries, auctioneers and estate agents asserted their expertise as conduits of reliable information. This claim found material expression in the design of office registers, printed catalogs, and more elaborate spaces such as the London Auction Mart saloon. The vast quantity of information available through newspaper advertisements competed with the services of intermediaries while simultaneously evincing the value of arranging information in ways that could connect interested parties to a sale. Thus, most of the auction mart's features—its notice boards, schedules, and provincial registries—were meant to gather information, order it, and thereby render it legible and calculable to those seeking property. None of these forms of abstraction projected beyond the anticipated encounter between buyer and seller, however. Relatively little value was placed on information after the moment of exchange. The original prospectus for the auction mart promised to develop an archive of past sale particulars, but this was intended only as a tool for future investigations of title rather than for synoptic or retrospective analysis.[2] In short, the early nineteenth century offered few tools for imagining or calculating a more general or abstract property market.

All of this changed during the second half of the century, when the property market as a whole suddenly became the object of new forms of calculation, driven by the growth of a property trade press. Whereas newspapers had for some time published advertisements and even sporadically reported on the results of public sales, trade periodicals like the *Journal of Auctions* and the *Estates Gazette* went much further in representing the property market as a distinctly calculable object, premised on the conceptual aggregation of all property sales within a coherent market space. From the 1850s through the early twentieth century, ways of thinking about the property market were routinized through coordinated agencies of market calculation, such that by the end of this period, the "property market" had become a visible, durable, and calculable object for specialist audiences as well as for the general public.

This chapter therefore consists of two narratives, one historical and another conceptual. It charts an institutional history of how information about the property marketplace was imagined, organized, and presented, largely in the context of the nineteenth-century expansion of both the periodical and newspaper press. I begin with the rise of the property trade press in the 1850s and the subsequent innovations in property reporting during the final decades of the century. Despite efforts early on to improve the accuracy and statistical coverage of property sale results, partial information remained the norm throughout the period, and both the trade press and the dailies—who began regularly covering the property market from the 1890s onward—repeatedly devised techniques and protocols to accord legitimacy and authority to their always partial market calculations. The operation of these methods delineated some of the various conceptual techniques by which calculative agencies configured and stabilized market practices. I conclude with a discussion of the political and epistemological implications arising from this new, visible, and calculable property marketplace.

THE *JOURNAL OF AUCTIONS* AND THE MAKING OF "MARKET VALUE"

By the mid-nineteenth century, there were few precedents for coordinating property market information. Information lay scattered across a still largely invisible landscape of private and public sales. From its creation in 1808, the London Auction Mart had provided the most visible model for concentrating market information, but its achievement as a general medium for the circulation of market news was more symbolic than real. The development of financial news as a regular feature of newspapers—spearheaded in the 1820s by the *Morning Chronicle*'s City reports and the *Times*' "Money, Market and City Intelligence"[3]—gave more direct impetus, but the reports of property auction sales printed in the 1820s, '30s, and '40s showed no aspiration to be comprehensive, analytical, or regular.[4] In the 1850s, however, the development of specialized trade periodicals for property resulted in new tools and methods for ordering and mapping the market landscape.

Trade periodicals in general are one of the few species of Victorian literature not to have attracted extensive historical commentary.[5] What we do know of these sources has tended to emphasize the more prominent and general success stories rather than the early, ephemeral, and often esoteric publications that helped pave the way for their larger relations. In the realm of business and financial journals, for instance, the *Economist* has been judged to warrant more scrutiny than the *Circular to Bankers*, despite the latter having preceded the former by more than a decade.[6] Winners have likewise rewritten the history of the real estate press, with the *Estates Gazette* (1858) casting its long shadow across the early history of other property periodicals. Nor has the evanescence of these others helped. Prior to the *Gazette*, the *Freeholder* (1850) and the *Freehold Land Times* (1854) had written about land markets, though from the obvious perspective of the land movement; the *Freeholder* lasted for two years and the *Land Times* eventually transformed into the *Building News*. A similar fate befell another pioneer, the *Journal of Auctions*, which operated briefly between 1853 and 1856. These journals may have been short-lived, but their market reporting innovations nonetheless demonstrated how the organization and calculation of property market information began to take shape during the second half of the century.

Fortunately, we can piece together more of the *Journal of Auctions'* provenance than is available for many other of its contemporaries and descendants, including the *Estates Gazette*. The *Journal* was an offspring of the Cox publishing empire, headed by Edward William Cox (1809–1879), a Taunton-born solicitor and the owner and first editor of the *Law Times*. Over the course of his long career, Cox amassed a respectable fortune, founding or purchasing over a dozen periodicals, including (in addition to the *Law Times*) the *Critic* (1843–1863), the *Field* (purchased in 1854), the *Queen* (1862), and the more popularly tailored *Exchange and Mart* (1868). All of these belonged to a new genre of "class journalism" that arose out of the gradual reduction of stamp duties between the 1830s and 1850s. In a spirit of iterative entrepreneurialism, many of them also began their lives as departments in other papers, to be subsequently spun off as independent projects. This was the case for both the *Critic* and the *Journal of Auctions*. The *Critic* began as the book review department in the *Law Times*, the *Journal of Auctions* as its money market and property column. The editor of the *Journal* was another Taunton native and longtime partner of Cox's, John Crockford, who had also published and managed the *Law Times* and who had encouraged Cox to purchase the *Field*.[7] Crockford is remembered for *Crockford's Clerical Directory*, yet another spin-off, this time from the *Critic* following its shift in emphasis from general literary to ecclesiastical affairs.

Its origins as one of several marketing strategies might explain why, when the first issue of the *Journal of Auctions* appeared in August of 1853, it immediately set about soliciting the support of specific reading audiences and developing in a quite self-conscious way new formats for presenting property market information. The latter impulse is the more important one for this discussion.[8] In its original *Law Times* format (1843–1853), the "Journal of Property" consisted of two regular features, one discussing the money market and another listing the results of public auction sales. The sale results were presented much as in other papers, with a brief description of the property followed by a selling price. The *Journal of Auctions* set about improving and expanding its coverage of property sales, however, both by soliciting a more comprehensive listing of properties available for sale and by conceiving new techniques for gathering information about sale results.

Without wanting to confuse the desire to be comprehensive in collecting sales notices with the ambition to attract the most advertising revenue, it is still possible to see in the paper's developments new ways of envisioning the market. Much like the aspirations expressed at the founding of the auction mart, the *Journal* billed itself as a common medium of exchange, a veritable paper market, in which buyers and sellers could meet and treat. Conceding the predominance of the *Times* as largest source of such advertising, the *Journal* found fault with its rival on three points. The *Times* lacked the appropriate scale, focus, and efficiency. Its advertisements were not comprehensive, its pages were not properly sorted according to differing forms of property, and its frequency overwhelmed readers with too much information—too often of the wrong sort. The journal addressed these shortfalls in its own format by developing a number of new presentations, including a tabular diary of forthcoming sales, with particulars, location, and a reference to advertisements in both the *Journal* and the *Law Times*. Moreover, soon after its launch, the *Journal* moved to abandon the preference for paid advertisements in its diary and published all sales that were sent to it.[9]

Advertisements and sale notices were only the first step, however. The paper further promised to supply its readers with an analysis of the market, "similar to that which the Daily Papers publish of the Money Market, detailing generally the results of Sales of the different kinds of property—their rise or fall in value, &c."[10] Inviting one of its readers to contribute to this new field of journalism, the paper speculated that an "intelligent auctioneer" might best fill the position of a property reporter. The first issue also included a sample report, which discussed the likely impact of the Crimean War on property prices concluded with a second request, this time for the cooperation of the larger community of solicitors and auctioneers:

> As it is of great importance to buyers and sellers of land, and to all engaged as their agents, whether as auctioneers or solicitors, that this subject of the selling value of property should be fully investigated, and the facts presented to them weekly for their guidance, as is done by the newspaper with stocks, funds, and shares, we prefer an earnest request to our readers to favour us with all the facts necessary to the production of such a weekly report, as the results of their sales by auction, and any other information relating to the intrinsic value of properties, or their worth in different localities, resulting from some special circumstances, which will supply the material upon which these reports must be founded.[11]

"We have no doubt," proclaimed the editors elsewhere in the same issue, "that a wide field is open, as yet almost unexplored by journalism, for the collection of [information relating to property], and which only needs diligence on our part, and the cordial co-operation of the Auctioneers and Solicitors, to convert into a most useful, as well as a most interesting, as it will be a perfectly novel, branch of periodical literature."[12]

The success of this ambitious and "perfectly novel" project hinged on the coordination of two very different actions. In the first instance, auctioneers and solicitors were asked to submit facts, and these facts were to be provided according to specific criteria. The prevailing practice of stating the selling price of a property along with a brief general description of its particulars offered an insufficient basis for any deeper understanding of "intrinsic value." To do this, the editors called for a more sophisticated apparatus of information gathering. With the cooperation of local agents, an improved set of facts would be placed in the hands of a capable intelligence, an auctioneer/reporter, who could then transform them into reports that would track the movement of values over time and across differing localities. The ultimate goal of this proposed network of informants and analysts was spelled out several issues later. "Our purpose," stated the paper in another address to its readers, ". . . is to collect the reports of sales of property from all parts of the country, week by week; and at fixed intervals, monthly or quarterly, to present a careful review of them, exhibiting their results and showing from these what is the market value of various kinds of property, and if it be rising or falling, and how it varies in different localities."[13] Local information was to be subsumed within a larger national market framework with a set of transferable standards for the measurement of market values, and a fixed calendar transcending local variability.

Though clearly welcome in some quarters, this grand plan soon encountered difficulties. The *Journal of Auctions* was unusually frank and open about reporting both the nature of the problems and the solutions with which it proposed to address them. Without these commentaries, it would be easy to imagine the calculation of "market value" as a fairly transparent process involving the collection of known and readily available objects. Such was not the case, however. In its second issue, for example, the editor complained about the inadequacy of typical public sale reports and expanded on the need for more accuracy:

> It is not enough to know that Blackacre sold for £100 and Whiteacre for £200, unless we are informed what were the rentals, or at how many years' purchase they were bought, and if there was any peculiarity of situation to give an extrinsic value. Will the auctioneers not only favour us with the results of their sales, but do it in this form, stating in each case either the purchase price, the rental, and the acreage; or, if they object to give those details, the price, with a statement of the number of years' purchase represented by that price?"[14]

That Blackacre sold for £100 was information enough for anyone interested in whether or not the property was still available for sale or for those with inside knowledge of the property's status and with interest in its supposed public sale value. It was enough information to mark the conclusion of a public phase in the property's transfer, regardless of whether that phase concluded with an actual sale or with a more accurate determination of value for a subsequent private sale. In other words, whereas the information that had hitherto been reported in the daily press was enough to record the facts of a sale as a particular *event*, it was *not* enough to fix the result within a more generally useful, comparable and durable calculation of market value. Market value depended on a more comprehensive record of sale conditions; these conditions made it possible to extract a sale from its purely local or private context and to resituate it in a more abstract set of county or national averages.

Getting a complete record entailed a greater and more coordinated effort than could be obtained by the work of individuals alone. Another notice printed the following week hinted at the paper's skepticism that auctioneers and solicitors could be sufficiently reliable generators of data. Reiterating their request for completeness and consistency, the editors argued that "this desirable object" for more accurate and "uniform" particulars "might be secured by means of printed forms . . . for the purpose of making such a return of their sales effected, as will be required to make the report of the Property Market useful to those who are engaged in the sale or purchase of property."[15] The paper included a copy of the proposed form and invited feedback, stating that it hoped soon to make a final version available for general distribution within the auctioneering community. Arranged in several columns, the proposed template organized sale results by date, place, property (tenure, area, location, etc.), rents, sale price, and "particulars (if any) affecting value." In devising this tool, the paper sought to extend its own calculative network beyond a passive reliance on random correspondence and toward a more active disciplining of agents' own accounting. The sale results return—which became a regular accessory to the paper's operations, available by post to any interested agent—entangled local market agents in a new kind of market calculation, one that involved the collection and circulation of *useful* facts as essential inputs to a more comprehensive and universal property market report.

These reporting forms continued to be advertised in the *Journal*'s pages, and one can imagine that at least a few auctioneers took it on themselves to participate by sending in weekly reports of their sales. Later in the year, however, further developments suggest that reliance on independent correspondents had its limitations. In November, the paper again addressed its readers with news of more self-improvements, one of which involved a plan to dispatch reporters to Garraway's and the auction mart to collect sale results firsthand. The existing "meager records" published in the daily news, it argued, were "useless . . . for the purpose of illustrating the relative selling values of property in different parts of the country." Instead, the *Journal* would send its own recorders "to collect the facts and figures stated by the auctioneers, as those by which alone anything in the shape of an estimate could be formed of the actual selling values of estates."[16]

Part of the problem with both written results and even *witnessed* results had to do with routine auction room practice and the questionable reliability of what was said at the rostrum. Unlike in Scotland, where upset prices were regularly announced beforehand, English practice reserved the right of the vendor to bid on a property whose price had not passed a certain minimum threshold and to keep secret the amount of that threshold. Auctions very often had the function simply of advertising a property and of estimating a public value that could then subsequently be negotiated in private. The problem this posed for publishing sale results, however, was that properties were very often announced as sold when in fact they had been "bought in" to the vendor. Results could therefore be deceptive in showing an inflated market value. "There is no doubt," complained the *Journal*, "that many returns of sales are incorrect; that estates announced as sold are in truth 'bought in,' and that the prices at which they are knocked down are neither the prices they obtain, in fact, nor the prices at which they are intended to be sold, but fancy prices, designed to give them the appearance of a fictitious value."[17]

In order to achieve "a complete record of the Property Market of the United Kingdom," the paper pleaded with auctioneers to distinguish sold from "bought in" properties on their result forms and conceded that if auctioneers refused, they should at least omit the latter results altogether, so as not to distort the figures. The following summer a similar request asked auctioneers to clarify at the rostrum the status of properties so as to enable the paper's reporters to accurately record the results. This time editors explicitly framed their demands in terms of the need to conform to a new regime of calculation:

> Our reporters can only give to the buyers of property in these columns the intelligence of what actually transpires in the auction-room; and if the facts are misstated or concealed there, they will necessarily go to the public in the same shape, to the discredit of the Auctioneer, and to the no small damage of the interest of his client, the vendor. . . . This might have been less important, formerly, when the proceedings of Auctions passed unrecorded. But now that, by means of the JOURNAL OF AUCTIONS, they are regularly reported and widely disseminated among the buyers and sellers of property throughout the United Kingdom, and help materially to assist calculation and to guide both sales and purchasers, it has become a matter of very great importance that the information so widely diffused and so largely used should be correct."[18]

Fictitious values were just one of the many problems of deception deemed to lay within the auction room, but they posed a particularly irritating threat to the new kind of market practice initiated by the *Journal of Auctions* and continued by its successors. The distinction between fact and fiction was of course not limited to the property market; as Mary Poovey has shown, Victorians in general were consistently preoccupied by fears of commercial deception and secrecy.[19] The press was by no means a transparent window into the financial world, but for those involved in the exchange of property the public resources available for interpreting uncertainty were particularly limited, no doubt in part due to the still rather limited participation of the public in the property market. "Until we had commenced this Journal of

Property," wrote the *Journal of Auctions* self-interestedly (but not without some truth), "we had no conception how little positive information upon the subject [of property] is attainable. . . . Few facts have been gathered together out of which rules might be constructed, or from which principles may be deduced. The statistician, who has explored almost all other figures . . . has done little or nothing towards informing us of the state and conditions, rise or fall, of property."[20]

The *Journal*'s efforts achieved mixed results. Its designs for a regular property report evolved into a regular column on the "Results of Sales and Value of Property," which combined much more detailed firsthand accounts of sales with an increasingly more confident market analysis. As the format evolved, these reports would begin with a general statement of market movements, followed by a summary discussion of what the paper considered the most significant estate sales of the week. The report also began tabulating its results as a list of land values for each county in which sales had been recorded. Thus, for the first two weeks of August 1854, the paper listed the price per acre as calculated for sales in Hampshire (£25), Oxfordshire (£57), Essex (£42 and £28), Herefordshire (£34), Huntingdonshire (£42), Worcestershire (£22), and Cambridgeshire (£46).[21] Nonetheless, at no point did the paper feel confident enough to calculate more general averages. In its summary of land values for 1854, for example, the paper simply listed all the individual values calculated weekly.

Whatever strides the paper had made in making property visible and calculable, it remained a decidedly ambiguous achievement to know that in 1854 there were twenty-six different values for land in Essex, ranging from £15 to £70 per acre. Toward the end of the same year, not long before the paper ceased publication, it glumly observed (as reprinted in the *Law Times*) that "although we have been carefully preserving the results of sales for two years and a-half, sufficient facts are not yet accumulated to enable us to carry out the design, which is to present a yearly and a quinquennial statement, showing the prices obtained for land on the average of all England, and in each country, in each year, and on an average of five years."[22]

It is not clear what brought about the demise of the *Journal of Auctions*. It may have been the case that Cox and Crockford were distracted by their many other publications purchased or developed in the same period. Since the final issue of the *Journal* anticipated its division into two separate publications—one for property intelligence and another for news related to limited liability companies—a more likely possibility was that the restless movement from one theme to another, in search of a viable audience, simply overtook the *Journal* as it had other early property periodicals and swept it along to other territories. Regardless of its own fate, however, the aspirations of the *Journal*'s early property reporting survived in several other institutions founded shortly after its demise. These included, in Scotland, *McWilliam's Property Circular and West of Scotland Weekly Advertiser* (renamed the *Glasgow Property Circular* in 1877), and, in England, the *Estates Gazette.*

McWilliam's Property Circular came first, in 1856, and seems to have been closely associated with Glasgow's equivalent of the London Auction Mart, the Faculty of Procurators Hall, an engraving of which was featured on paper's masthead until the end of the century. At the end of the 1860s, the paper remained a modest one of four pages, containing a diary of forthcoming sales by public roup and reports from some sales, but no editorial content.[23] Starting in 1857, the estate exchange kept a regular record of sales results at the London Auction Mart and at Garraway's, and distributed its weekly returns to its members and to the daily papers, the latter of whom could at last count on a steady stream of facts on property sales. Finally, in 1858, the *Estates Gazette* published its first issue (see fig. 13), picking up where the *Journal of Auctions* had left off in providing more comprehensive reports and editorials on property related issues and trends. Both the *Estates Gazette* and the estate exchange managed a fairly modest business in their first decade or so of operation, lapsing into what Thompson referred to as an "interval of quiescence." Between 1864 and 1879, the *Gazette* was largely a paper of advertisements; the exchange's annual reports of auction sales disappeared after 1861, only to be continued again a decade later.[24] The next period of innovation in property market reporting had to wait until the 1880s and 1890s, when the work of specialized trade periodicals would finally make the jump into the pages of the mainstream press.

PROPERTY NEWS COMES OF AGE

The developments of the 1850s took place within a relatively small community of market agents, property vendors, and buyers. There was little evidence of wider public interest in property market reports or in the debates on how to collect and present market information. The information technology of the mid-Victorian property market was made largely by and for specialists, those whose claims to market expertise would lead to the formation of a number of professional associations later on in the century. From the 1870s onward, however, there were plenty of signs that property market news was moving to a more mainstream and general audience. The nature

THE ESTATES GAZETTE, AND INVESTMENT RECORD.

A Paper devoted to the Sale of Land, House Property, Advowsons, &c. by Public Auction or Private Contract, and Farms to Let throughout the Kingdom.

PUBLISHED ON THE 1st AND 15th OF THE MONTH AT 77, FLEET-STREET, LONDON.

VOL. I.—No. 1. | LONDON, MAY 1, 1858. | {Annual Subscription, 12s.; {Single Paper, 7d. Stamped.

NOTICE TO ADVERTISERS.

THE ESTATES GAZETTE is supplied gratuitously to the chief Hotels in the Kingdom, and the other portion of its circulation is among Solicitors, Auctioneers, Land Agents, and Capitalists interested in Land and House Property. The charges for Advertisements is 6d. a line, 6d. extra for all insertions of ten lines and under: thus, an advertisement of ten lines would be charged 5s. 6d. No advertisement taken under 2s. 6d. Advertisements should be forwarded on or before the 12th of the month for insertion in the GAZETTE of the 15th, and on or before the 27th of the month for the GAZETTE of the 1st of the following month. This intimation is necessary to prevent disappointment, as from the arrangement observed in the ESTATES GAZETTE much time is necessarily occupied in preparing for the press.

TO INTENDED PURCHASERS OF ESTATES.

Parties interested in any particular Estate are requested to communicate with the respective Auctioneers, should the day of sale not be named in an advertisement, as it is very possible a day has been appointed at the time of the ESTATES GAZETTE going to press, and under these circumstances parties might be mislead unless we cautioned them on the subject.

Rentals and particulars of any Estate can be inspected at the Office of the ESTATES GAZETTE; and should a party desire a copy to be forwarded to them, they are requested to state the county and number of the advertisement to which they refer, and remit 1s. in postage stamps, when the Rental will be transmitted without delay, postage free.

TO AUCTIONEERS.

Auctioneers, Solicitors, and Landowners are requested to forward copies of the Rental and Particulars to the office of the ESTATES GAZETTE as soon as possible for public inspection, a room being devoted to the purpose. No charge is incurred, but the Rental must be forwarded, carriage paid.

Auctioneers are also requested to have the goodness to furnish the Office with the result of their respective sales; he cannot, of course, expect it in all cases, but the information will be valued whenever it can be conveniently given.—Office, 77, Fleet-street, London.

HENRY ALLNUTT.

Bedfordshire.

Preliminary Advertisement.—Marston Mortayne, near Ampthill, Beds.

MESSRS. DANIEL SMITH, SON, & OAKLEY have received instructions from the late Jonas Atkinson Esq., to arrange for SALE, at the Mart, in one or more lots, on June 15th, the valuable FREEHOLD FARM, known as the Moat Farm, situate in the village near the church, consisting of 212 acres of capital arable and pasture land, the latter being principally sound old grazing land. The whole is under lease, for an unexpired term of four years, to Mr. William Stimpson, who has been the resident tenant for very many years. Plans, and particulars are in course of preparation; in the meantime further particulars may be obtained of Messrs. Druce and Sons, Billiter-square; or of Messrs. Daniel Smith, Son, and Oakley, land agents and surveyors, 10, Waterloo-place, Pall-mall, S.W. (A 1)

Berkshire.

Preliminary Advertisement.—The Little Titnest-park Estate, most beautifully situate at Sunning-hill, in the county of Berks, near Ascot and Windsor.

MESSRS. NORTON, HOGGART, and TRIST have received instructions to offer for SALE, at the Mart, 21st May next, the LITTLE TITNEST-PARK ESTATE, situate at Sunning-hill, in the county of Berks, about two miles from Ascot, six from Windsor, six from Staines, and eight from Reading, containing altogether about 30 acres. This exceedingly beautiful and valuable freehold property consists of a most substantial and exceedingly well built house in the most perfect order, and containing every accommodation a moderate family can require, with excellent stabling and coach houses, approached from the road by a very neat lodge entrance. It stands on the summit of a hill, and is in the midst of an elegant lawn and very nicely timbered little park; the shrubbery walks, abounding in every variety of American and other shrubs, lead to the capital walled kitchen gardens, with gardener's house, and every description of forcing-house, greenhouse, &c., all heated by hot water; in fact, no expense has been spared in contriving every luxury and comfort. Nothing can be more lovely and healthy than the neighbourhood generally; a variety of gentlemen's seats are to be found in every direction. A short distance from Titnest-park brings you to the entrance of Virginia-water, through which to Windsor-park is a most magnificent ride, and the scenery which everywhere abounds is not to be surpassed in England, particularly when it is to be taken into consideration that you are within an hour and a-half's journey by rail of any part of the metropolis. A more detailed description of the house will shortly appear. May be viewed by cards, and particulars had of Messrs. Vandercom, Cree, Law, and Comyn, solicitors, Bush-lane, Cannon-st.; and of Messrs. Norton, Hoggert, and Trist, 62, Old Broad-street, Royal Exchange, E.C. (B 2)

Berkshire.—To Capitalists, Building Societies, and Others.—Valuable Freehold Land at Wantage.

J. and E. BELCHER (late Belcher and Sons) are favoured with instruction to SELL BY AUCTION, at the Bear Inn, Wantage, on Thursday, the 6th day of May, 1858, at three o'clock in the afternoon (subject to conditions then to be produced), all that desirable FREEHOLD FARM, now in the occupation of Mr. David Robins, comprising a homestead and 3 acres, 3 roods, 8 poles of rich Meadow Land, divided into seven lots, suitable for building sites; an enclosure of rich MEADOW LAND, called "The Croft," containing 4 acres, 1 rood, 26 poles, divided into four lots, also suitable for building sites; and about 68 acres of highly productive ARABLE and MEADOW LAND, in three lots.

The Auctioneers beg to call particular attention to the foregoing truly valuable properties; the building sites are situate in the best part of Wantage, and have extensive frontages, the soil is dry and healthy, and there is an abundant supply of excellent water. Private residences are much required in the neighbourhood, and the present affords an opportunity of building, either for occupation or investment, which may not occur again for a considerable period. May be viewed on application to the tenant, and particulars, with lithographed plans, obtained of Messrs. W. and E. Ormond, solicitors, or the Auctioneers, Wantage. (B 5)

Absolute Sale.—Berkshire, on the borders of Oxfordshire.—Valuable Estate, comprising superior Farm Residence, with garden and agricultural buildings, and about 240 acres of Land, held under St. John's College on a renewal lease, and let at £320 per annum.

MESSRS. FAREBROTHER, CLARK and LYE will SELL, at Garraway's, in May, (unless an acceptable offer be previously made by private contract), a very desirable ESTATE, situate in the village and parish of Eaton, Berks, 4½ miles from the city of Oxford, and 5 from Abingdon, consisting of a superior farm residence, erected in imitation of stone, with offices, garden, and orchard, all necessary agricultural buildings, and 240 acres of meadow, pasture, and arable land, in a good state of cultivation. The estate is held under the President and Scholars of St. John's College, Oxford, on lease for a term of 20 years from 10th October, 1849, and renewable according to custom upon payment of a fine. The estate may be viewed, and particulars had of the tenant, at the Angel, Oxford; Crown and Thistle, Abingdon; of Messrs. Haines and Son, solicitors, Farringdon; at Garraway's; and at the offices of Messrs. Farebrither, Clark, & Lye, Lancaster-place, Strand. (B 8)

WINDSOR, Berks.—Building Land. About 70 acres of FREEHOLD LAND, beautifully timbered, within half a mile of the town of Windsor, and close to St. Leonard's-hill, to be SOLD, either together or in lots, by Private Contract. For particulars apply to Henry Darvill, Esq., solicitor, Windsor. None but principals or their solicitors need apply. (B 9)

Berks.—Freehold Property.

FOR SALE, STANFORD PLACE, with about 200 acres of Land, one mile from the market town of Farringdon, and four miles from the Great Western Railway, to and from which a coach passes the lodge daily. This delightful residence, in the centre of a most excellent hunt and neighbourhood, is situated on a gentle eminence, with three principal fronts, south, east, and west, containing entrance-hall, five sitting rooms, twelve bedrooms, three dressing-rooms, with servants' room, conservatory, good stabling, and every requisite office most conveniently arranged, and suitable for a nobleman or family of distinction, will be offered for SALE by AUCTION, on the premises, some time in May, by Mr. J. Dyke, auctioneer and land agent, Faringdon, unless previously disposed of by private contract. Further particulars may be obtained by letter, addressed G. C. B., "Advertiser" office, Faringdon. (B 10)

Theale, Berks.

TO BE LET, two Houses and Gardens, with 5 acres of Meadow Land, Barn, &c., near the Church, Theale. Also, for SALE, 6 acres Freehold Meadow and Arable Land, adjoining the above, which can be bought to pay 4 per cent. Apply to Mr. Bartlett, solicitor, 11, Friar-street, Reading. (B 6)

Freehold Property, Sandhurst, Berks.

MESSRS. WEEKS and SIMMONS are favoured with instructions from Major Daley, to offer for SALE by AUCTION, a compact FREEHOLD FARM, consisting of about 42 acres of Land, and convenient Farm Buildings, situate at about equal distances from the Royal Military and Wellington Colleges, and the projected Reformatory Institution. Further particulars, with day of sale, will shortly be given. (B 7)

The Winkfield-place Estate, Berks.

MESSRS. HASLAM and BUCKLAND are instructed by the Proprietor to prepare for SALE, in one or more Lots, the valuable RESIDENTAL PROPERTY, known as Winkfield-place, consisting of a well arranged and substantial Family Mansion, a compact and most convenient Villa Residence, and about 305 acres of park and arable land, well covered with thriving timber, and adjoining the Great Park and crown preserves. The whole is freehold.—Land agency Offices, 59, Cannon-street, west, City, and Reading. (B 1)

Preliminary Advertisement.—The Lovel-hill Estate, Freehold, at Winkfield, Berks, 3½ miles from Windsor.

MESSRS. DANIEL SMITH, SON & OAKLEY have received instructions from the Proprietor to offer for SALE by AUCTION, at the Mart, early in the spring (unless previously disposed of by private contract), LOVEL-HILL HOUSE, a very superior mansion, with tastefully laid out lawns and pleasure grounds, flower and kitchen gardens, plantations, &c.; also Lovel-Cottage, a comfortable villa residence, and about 125 acres of arable and pasture land, with all necessary farm buildings, several labourers' cottages, &c., the whole comprising about 142 acres. Further particulars, as soon as the survey is completed, may be had of Messrs. Jones and Arkcoll, 190, Tooley-street, Borough; and of Messrs. Daniel Smith, Son, and Oakley, land agents and surveyors, 10, Waterloo place, Pall-mall. (B 4)

Wokingham, Berks.

MESSRS. WEEKS & SIMMONS have received instructions from the owner, to offer for SALE in five lots, at the place and on a day to be named in a future advertisement, the Freehold Farm known as the WILTSHIRE FARM, situate in the parish of Wokingham, in the county of Berks, consisting of 55a. 2r. 22p. of good arable and pasture land, with a good farm-house, and all the necessary farm premises, with garden and orchard contiguous thereto, the whole being in the occupation of Mr. Andrew Sweetser, a yearly tenant, and who is under notice to quit the premises at Michaelmas next. The farm is situated near to Wokingham Church, on the road leading from Wokingham to Binfield and Maidenhead, and is within half a mile of the Wokingham Station of the South Eastern and Staines, Wokingham, and Woking Railway Company. This farm when divided into lots will offer eligible sites for building purposes. Plans and particulars may shortly be had of Messrs. Soames and Cooke, solicitors, and of the auctioneers, Wokingham. (B11)

Buckinghamshire.

BUCKS.—Freehold Residence and Land.—To be SOLD or LET furnished or unfurnished, a substantially-erected MANSION, comfortably furnished; consisting of fine entrance hall, spacious drawing and dining rooms, 10 bed rooms, three dressing rooms, capital domestic offices, &c., with 13 acres of meadow land the property of a clergyman removing. Situate 30 miles from London and six from railway station. Particulars and cards to view with Mr. Wagner, at his offices, 69, Berners-street, W. (C 5)

BUCKS, four miles from a Station.—To be LET, a capital MANSION, recently repaired and decorated, and elegantly furnished, together with the beautiful pleasure grounds, walled-in kitchen gardens, first-rate stable for 12 horses, and loose boxes, dog kennels, pheasantries, keepers' cottage, lake of 11 acres, and trout stream, exclusive sporting over 1,500a. The park is nobly timbered, magnificent avenues of approach, agricultural population adjoining proprietor's preserves. Rent moderate. Apply, for cards and terms, to Brooks and Beal, 209 Piccadilly. (C 6)

Valuable Freehold and Copyhold Estate, Langley, Bucks.

MESSRS. HASLAM and BUCKLAND are instructed to Sell by Public Auction, early in the spring (unless and acceptable offer by private treaty is previously made), one of the most valuable Estates in the county of Bucks, comprising a mansion and about 200 acres of truly productive land. It possesses some capital building frontages, and a large quantity of valuable brick earth. It is intersected by the Great Western Railway, with a station in the centre of the property. (C 1)

Bucks.—Valuable Leasehold Interest in a Landed Estate, held under Magdalen College, Oxford, and producing an improved rent of £176 per annum.

MESSRS. RUSHWORTH and JARVIS, are instructed by the Trustees, for sale under the Will of the late Rev. John Drake, to SELL by AUCTION, at the Mart, on Friday, May 21, a very desirable and compact ESTATE, situate in the parish of North Marston, between the market towns of Aylesbury and Winslow, known as the Manor Farm, comprising 222 acres, principally good sound pasture land, with a comfortable residence and convenient homestead, near to the village, and distant about one mile from the church. It is let to a most respectable yearly tenant, Mr. Joseph Ingram, whose family have occupied it for very many years, at the very moderate annual rent of £242 per annum, and is held under Magdalen College, Oxford, by a renewed lease granted in December, 1856, for a term of 20 years, subject to a yearly payment of £4, and certain corn rents, &c., hitherto received in money, and averaging for the last seven years about £66 per annum; and it has been the custom of the college to renew the lease every seven years upon payment of a moderate fine. The estate may be viewed upon application to the tenant, and printed particulars had at the principal inns at Winslow, Aylesbury, and Leighton Buzzard; and in London, at the Mart; of Messrs. Nicholl, Burnett, & Newman, solicitors, 18, Carey-street, Lincoln's-inn; of Messrs. Rushworth and Jarvis, land surveyors and auctioneers, Saville-row, Regent-street, and 19, Change-alley, Cornhill. (C 7)

FIGURE 13. Facsimile of the first edition of the *Estates Gazette*, May 1, 1858. Reproduced by permission of the British Library Board. LOU.LD78.

of these signs will be discussed below, but before doing so, it is worth noting some of the larger trends that may have helped generate greater public interest in property markets.

Three trends warrant specific mention. First, more people invested in late-Victorian property, even if direct ownership of land remained confined to a relatively small percentage of the population. Using census returns, the politician John Bright famously estimated that the total number of owners in 1861 numbered no more than thirty thousand, and even the much larger and more generous figure of a million owners calculated from government returns in 1876 still hardly breached 5 percent of the population of England.[25] However, as contemporaries often admitted and as Avner Offer has subsequently argued, these figures cast the "landed monopoly" of radical critique in rather limited terms, confined largely to rural, not urban, land and to interests in acres, not capital values. Factoring in the latter considerations, one finds that by the Edwardian period, direct and indirect interest in property transactions very likely extended to more than a million smaller owners of residential and commercial land and to those middle-class capitalists who counted themselves mortgagees to nearly a third of middle-class property tenure.[26] Second, the growth of public and institutional real estate holdings and the growing real property portfolios of insurance companies and building societies also brought movements in the property market to the attention of more than simply traditional landowners and estate managers.[27] Third and finally, interest in the property market may have grown alongside the rising tenor of debates about property in general, and the "land question" in particular, of which more will be said later.[28]

All these factors suggest that we need a more complicated model for thinking about the development of market infrastructures. If, as Thompson has argued, it was the rising tide of the 1850s real estate boom that led directly to the earlier initiatives discussed above, then the same case cannot fit for the 1880s, when another phase of development coincided with the collapse of land values. A more convincing way of framing the overall development of the press and its forms of calculation—in general and for the specific period of the nineteenth century discussed here—comes from Mary Poovey, whose work on the epistemology of financial writing suggests that periods of political, social, and economic uncertainty often fuel contingent developments in the genres used to distinguish reliable from unreliable market information. The speculative crash of the South Sea Bubble in the early eighteenth century, for instance, was associated both with a rapid adaptation and proliferation of preexisting financial genres and with the development of new analytical conventions that helped to reestablish the authority of reliable information after the crisis.[29] A similar phenomenon can be traced in the realm of property reporting in the second half of the nineteenth century, which developed its own novel conventions and technologies of value calculation during moments of uncertainty associated with both high sale prices, such as the 1850s, and with the low prices and troublesome politics associated with the late-Victorian and Edwardian decades.

What is certain is that the production of property market news did reach a new phase in these years. Between the 1880s and the 1920s the property market entered the vocabulary of a news-reading public who came to rely on regular reports and analysis of the market's movements and periodic statistical assessments of its overall size and shape. In this period, variously termed markets—for land, estates, or property—became things that people could think about on a regular basis, aided by a proliferation of new and established periodicals. The *Estates Gazette*, with its now venerable reputation as the longest operating property journal, found itself in a much more competitive news market, one that included the journals *Land: A Journal for All Interested in Landed and House Property* (1881–1883), the *Estates Journal* (1889–1894), the *Estates Chronicle* (1898–1899), and the *Property Market Review and Auction Chronicle* (1893–1913).[30] These essentially trade journals also operated within larger networks of market journalism that included both general interest periodicals, such as the *Economist*, and the national and provincial daily presses. In this section, I will trace the development in these sources of various forms of reporting about the property market.

In this later period, there arose far more extensive and reliable mechanisms for thinking about and tracking patterns of property sales. From 1871 onward, the estate exchange regularly provided weekly and annual summaries of public and some private land and building sales. It had also gained credibility as a registry of sale particulars, increasing the number collected annually from 3,262 particulars in 1871 to 5,403 in 1880.[31] In 1879 the *Estates Gazette* renewed its printing of editorials, and from 1885 onward it provided weekly summaries of public sales and annual assessments and analyses.[32] The first weekly reports remained largely sale summaries but very soon began to include more synoptic language of trends and movements. Before discussing the details of auctions in London and the provinces, for instance, the "Property Market" report for March 6, 1886, celebrated an increase in sales at the auction mart over an equivalent period in the previous year, from £325,822 to £528,403.[33] Conversely, later that year, in June, it informed readers that "yesterday the market was in a very depressed state, only seven out of the fifty-three lots of property offered, changing hands."[34]

These kinds of statements began a process that would establish the paper's authority as not just a record of sales, but also an interpreter of market trends and behavior.

The *Gazette*'s first annual market assessment, printed in January 1886 but with a retrospective look at the previous year's developments, demonstrated a similar analytical framework that would become common in property reports and which combined an apparently objective quantitative description of property sales with the qualitative impressions gained through close familiarity with market practice. Thus, while the estate exchange figures had shown another slight fall in overall sales (from £5,976,931 sold at the auction mart in 1884 to £4,453,878 in the following year), the *Gazette* warned that these figures could be deceptive to an amateur audience. It suggested that for "professional readers" the green shoots of recovery were readily discernible: "These straws which show how the wind is blowing, may not be so clearly visible to the general public as to those who are professionally concerned in the transfer of land. The great body of the public accepts the results of auction sales as the real criterion of the condition of the land market. It needs but little professional experience, however, to know that this idea is to a great extent illusory."[35] The editorial went on to note that public sales, representing only a fraction of overall sales, could never hope to capture every nuance of the market's movements. That being the case, in the following year's report the same warning of the deception of public sale figures was offered without any admission that the paper's own earlier predictions of recovery had failed to materialize, Estate Exchange figures presenting yet another decline, of around £180,000.

Numbers rarely speak for themselves, but this was particularly the case for property market figures, which did not have the benefit of comprehensiveness associated with other exchanges or commodities. The estate exchange could record the public transactions carried out at the auction mart; and it could add to these figures the private transactions submitted to its registry by its largely London-based membership, but it did not enjoy the exclusive institutional authority of, say, the stock exchange, with its rule barring members from outside trading. As a result, the total figures distributed weekly and annually invariably contained a large degree of uncertainty, one of which contemporaries were deeply conscious and for which they tried through various means to overcome or compensate. This is a feature of the market that has often been underappreciated in subsequent histories of property prices or transactions. At the time, however, one very important way of grappling with the problem of framing the market statistically was to present numbers alongside other genres of qualitative description.

The result was a pervasive tension between two very different but complementary and codependent conventions for describing and calculating the market for property.

Though the estate exchange figures had achieved widespread recognition as the most authoritative measure of the relative size of the market, and by comparison year-over-year of its general trends, in the 1890s the *Estates Gazette* revisited the ambitions of the *Journal of Auctions* and began developing new tools for calculating market values. In 1891, for example, a contributor to the paper prepared a summary of both private and public land sales recorded in the *Gazette* over the previous year. The journal presented these results alongside its other annual assessments. Contrary to the *Journal of Auctions'* earlier reticence in actually calculating averages, the *Gazette*'s analysis aggregated the price and acres of total sales by each county for England, Scotland, and Wales. It then accompanied its table of figures with descriptions of the more significant sales in each case.

Thus, whereas an acre of land in Middlesex could be had for £280 on average, an equivalent Wiltshire acre cost £18. The average price for an acre of land in England as a whole was £45, compared to £31 for Wales; a British acre (excluding Ireland) sold for £43.[36] Speaking to the authority and significance of the effort, the paper argued that it represented as good a sample as could be had from any newspaper and that the calculation allowed them "to strike a series of averages which may be depended upon as thoroughly representative of the prices that are being obtained for landed property from one end of the country to the other." It concluded that, though the figures were "necessarily partial and incomplete," they nonetheless confirmed the inherent marketability of land despite the pains of agricultural depression.[37] It is unclear just how useful average land prices might have been to local agents as measures of comparative value, but this was beside the point when judged by the value of understanding the health of the market overall. It was the conceptualization of property value as scalable to regional or even national levels that was the pertinent point for the paper, which could then offer to the public its generalized assessments as evidence of professional competence and optimism.

The publication of annual average land values was just one of the many innovations developed under the leadership of Frank Wilson, who had purchased the *Gazette* from its founder, Henry Allnutt, in 1884.[38] Under Wilson's ownership, the *Gazette* grew, and by the turn of the century it had diversified to include the publication of professional manuals, stationery, and a diary containing useful reference material for various property practitioners. Its numerous projects elevated it as an institution and reinforced its central place in a developing network of property expertise and market calculation (see figs. 14 and 15). As part of this expansion, Wilson introduced, from 1893 onward, the *Land and House Property Yearbook: A Guide to Investments in Real Estate.* If, as one historian has argued, the estate exchange register operated essentially as a restriction on market information, making its summaries available for general publication but keeping the details of transactions for the exclusive use of its limited membership, the *Gazette*'s yearbook served as a direct challenge to a such an information monopoly.

The yearbook was available to the public at a price of five shillings and referenced all the sales carried out at the auction mart, arranged alphabetically and by category according to London and suburbs, ground rents (i.e., improved but undeveloped urban land), country properties, and the like. Published annually between 1893 and 1923, the yearbook provided its readers with yet another tool for analyzing the market value of properties at an unprecedented level of detail. "If a would-be buyer wishes to ascertain the value of property in a certain locality," boasted the *Gazette*, "he has only to turn to that district." The yearbook "shows at a glance the results of sales at the London Auction Mart during the past year. . . . Buyers are thus put in possession of important facts as to the value of property at auction in any district in London or the suburbs, as well as the country." The guide was also directed to property professionals and investors, for whom it would be a "*vade mecum* to the Auction Mart."[39]

It is not clear how Wilson developed the idea for the *Yearbook*, but he most likely was familiar with a Scottish equivalent that had been in existence since the mid-1880s. As early as the 1870s, the *Glasgow Property Circular* had been offering its readers historical comparisons of weekly sales at the Faculty of Procurators Hall in Glasgow, and in 1885 it published its first index of all public auctions held at the hall during the previous year.[40] The index provided very similar information to that which would eventually be reported in the yearbook, arranging properties according to those that were actually sold and those that were unsold ("adjournments," in Scottish terminology), and providing information as to the reserve price for a property, its selling price, and an reference to information advertised in the *Glasgow Property Circular*'s pages. In the preface to the first volume, the publisher, John C. King, specifically noted that the index would be of value to anyone interested in following the "Property Market." "Considering that so much of the Nation's wealth rests in Land and Heritable Investments," he wrote, "it is astonishing how few methods there are by which the general public can note the fluctuations therein."[41]

Figure 14. Photograph of the *Estates Gazette* linotype and case room, ca. 1908. *Estates Gazette*, Fiftieth Birthday Supplement, June 20, 1908, 15. Reproduced by permission of the British Library Board. LOU.LD78.

Figure 15. Photograph of the *Estates Gazette* publishing office, ca. 1908. *Estates Gazette*, Fiftieth Birthday Supplement, June 20, 1908, 15. Reproduced by permission of the British Library Board. LOU.LD78.

These various forms of market quantification—weekly and annual statistical descriptions, annual analysis of sale volumes and average unit prices, and guidebooks to detailed local market values—provided insights to the property market and lent weight and legitimacy to the idea of a market as a single coherent national space, a thing with its own internal ebbs and flows that could be captured, however imperfectly, in average prices per acre or annual sale figures. What figures could not do, though, was convey the meaning of it all. As we have seen, total annual sales at the auction mart could dip and rise from one year to the next; but if the figures represented only a small and uncertain sample of a larger market, the reliability of general calculations based on these figures inevitably lay open to interpretation. A gap of uncertainty plagued property market news.

That gap was filled by the consolidation of market expertise. Expert analysis appeared in a number of forms, the simplest of which could be identified in the initial market reports of the *Journal of Auctions*, where the sales of a given week were ordered according to those most indicative of a general market value. Estate sales usually headed the list, as these were deemed to be untainted from the distortions of "town value." The *Journal of Auctions* had also made efforts to educate general readers on the basics of property market investment, such as in differentiating between intrinsic value and market value in relation to the rise and fall of interest rates.[42]

The *Estates Gazette* analyses discussed above were another form of market expertise, in which the experience of the auction room channeled through the pen of the editors helped interpret estate exchange figures. In 1889, the same paper set about developing another ambitious annual review, this one based on the collective expertise of its readership. It invited correspondents from around the country and from leading London auction firms to send to it their own assessments of the past year's market performance along with forecasts for the upcoming year, including the prospects of anticipated legislation effecting property ownership and trade. This feature became a staple of the January editions of the *Gazette*, running to multiple pages over several issues, and involving the participation of dozens—if not over the course of many years, hundreds—of auctioneers and agents.[43]

In 1893, for example, the *Gazette*'s annual correspondents' review encompassed eight full pages of print in five issues and reproduced the opinions of fifty-seven different individuals or firms. The content of the reports presented a huge range of opinion, some directed strictly toward trends in sales, others sliding into political commentary. A number mimicked the format of newspaper results, with initial general overviews of the market followed by examples of specific sales used to illustrate critical value assessments. For instance, before detailing several sales that showed an average value of between twenty and twenty-two years' purchase (a measure of yield on investment), the correspondent from Thompson, Rippon and Co., in Exeter, offered more general remarks: "House property in Devonshire has been very difficult to get rid of. There seems to be very little demand and we have never known so little competition. Land has not sold readily, and farms, especially if large, have been quite a drug in the market."[44] In contrast, "A. V." wrote from Wycombe, Buckinghamshire, to report "a fair demand during the year both for land and house property, and prices have been maintained much as in 1891."[45] Several others were willing to share their own aggregate figures in addition to their written analyses. For instance, J. W. Stride and Sons, in Brighton, reported a slight decrease in sales by public auction, from £144,608 sold in 1891 to £140,712 sold in the current report year.[46] Generally speaking, most reports shared the view of one Shropshire writer's opinion that the outlook for the coming year's market was "exceedingly gloomy."[47]

Expert opinion, however, could often diverge in dramatic fashion, as seen in the opening reports of the 1891 review. The first, by the eminent firm of Farebrothers, Ellis, Clark and Co., congratulated the *Estates Gazette* on a sound prediction made in the previous year for an improved market and wrote, "We have no hesitation in making the assertion that things are much brighter than they have been for years past. We confidently anticipate for the year 1891 a solid revival in the demand for real property." In the next column, however, "E. H. B." shattered that confidence: "How then does the property market look from that standpoint [the present]? Flat! Unquestionably flat! And not without reason—uncertainty reigns all around." That uncertainty was blamed partly on the state of trade, which had made "filthy lucre in the guize [*sic*] of 10 per cent. dividend" more attractive than landed securities, but also partly on anti-property legislation—in particular, a disproportionate burden of taxation levied on property through local rates.Presented adjacent to each other, the market reports by Farebrother, Ellis and Clark and E. H. B. offered drastically different assessments. What the *Gazette* called the "great practical value" of these reports clearly depended on the authority one assigned to differing accounts.[48]

Uniformity of opinion, however, was not necessarily what these annual reviews were really about. The journal never spelled out in detail how one might have used them to practical effect, but at least one function emerged from their very existence as form of legitimacy for the *Gazette*'s efforts at composing market analyses. The reports did not need to concur in order to contribute to a general framing of the project as a collective inquiry into a common national property market. By participating in the annual reviews, local correspondents consolidated their own expertise while at the same time lending authority to the *Estate Gazette* as the leading voice of property market opinion. Each local report became an extension of a general calculative project whose results could be used to shape understandings of both national and local property markets. A network of associations linking local market agents to elite London firms and the provincial and daily press to specialized trade periodicals collectively made both the property market and its calculation visible and durable across time and space.

Some of the impact of these innovations can be judged from their reverberation in the local press, which began using *Estates Gazette* reviews to report on local market conditions. The *Cheshire Observer*, for example, used the "Land Sales of 1890" statistics to inform its readers of property values in that county.[49] Over the course of the decade, correspondent reports were likewise reprinted in Leicester, Derby, Oxford, and Bristol.[50] Summarizing the *Gazette*'s submissions in 1892, the *Manchester Weekly Times* affirmed that "a number of the most experienced land agents and keenest men of business in the country agree in regarding the prospects of the land market as much more encouraging than they have been of late."[51] It went on to paraphrase one report from a Midland firm. "That opinion is not speculative," concluded the paper, "but is largely based upon the experience of the year that has just closed. . . . in most parts of the country there seems to be a general belief that the market is looking up."[52]

Written property market reports and assessments proliferated more generally throughout the 1890s, with many daily papers standardizing their coverage. One early and particularly consistent example was the *Financial Times*, which in June 1894 published a "Property Market" column—initially as a special feature, but then continuing as a regular daily report of tabulated forthcoming auction sales, sale results, and written news and analyses.[53] The conservative *Morning Post* likewise started regular reporting on the property market in the fall of 1894. Unlike these two papers, the *Daily News* chose to keep its reports on estate, land, and property sales in its "Money Market" column, and though there was a greater deal of inconsistency in terminology (it variously referred to land and property markets, City and house property), it eventually settled on reporting under "Auction Mart" or "Tokenhouse Yard." The *Times*' coverage of property sales established a more fixed pattern after 1897, when it regularly reprint weekly market assessments from the *Estates Gazette* under the heading of either a "Property Market" or "Estate Market" report.

Indeed, by this moment in time the *Estates Gazette* had consolidated its position as the leading professional journal of property and of market news related to property, and it made a concentrated effort to organize its market intelligence in formats that could be readily transferred to other general circulation papers. Periodically at first but with more regularity as the decade progressed, the paper would print a one-paragraph summary—either on its editorial page or in its "Occasional Notes" section—of the dominant market trends for the previous week and of the most indicative or notable properties put up for sale. These were similar to the summaries offered several decades earlier in the *Journal of Auctions*, with the exception that the *Estates Gazette* could now depend on its market briefs being more widely disseminated through the large dailies and general weekly papers. On February 5, 1898, for example, both the *Times* and the *Daily Mail* reprinted the *Gazette*'s weekly summary of "The Estate Market," which appeared on that periodical's editorial page:

> Business at the Tokenhouse-yard Mart during the past week has not been very active, owing to the short supply of properties. Freehold securities, however, found a ready market. The chief of these comprised business premises in the main Boro' High-street, producing £300 per annum, which sold at £5,590, and freehold licensed premises at Broadway, Westminster, and Westgate-on-Sea, producing £100 and £140 respectively, with possession in about three years, which realised £8,560 and £4,040 each. There was no demand whatever for ground rents, but a few small brick and mortar investments were disposed of.[54]

The *Financial Times* and *Morning Post* also borrowed analysis from the *Estates Gazette* in their early property market reports, but they quickly limited the practice in favor of developing independent reports written by their own correspondents. The *Times* did the same in 1906 and used its weekly reports to compile annual market assessments, which also began that year. The proliferation of property market journalism thus coincided with an increasingly crowded auction salesroom, filled not just with bidders, auctioneers, and vendors but also with journalists able to record and to print firsthand the happenings and outcomes of sales. Reacting to this development in a comment copied in the *Financial Times*, the *Estates Gazette*'s anonymous opinion editor, "Onlooker," suggested that firms selling at the London Auction Mart should be obliged to leave copies of their particulars of sales for reference by the daily press, in order to reduce the "vast amount of struggling and pushing from room to room, 'à la Rugby football,'" commonly observed in the salesrooms. The same author had earlier recommended that orders of sale be printed and distributed in each room for a similar purpose. The *Financial Times* agreed with the recommendations, concluding that they "would be a considerable assistance to members of the Press."[55]

Following these related trends in England, the *Glasgow Property Circular*, which had changed its name yet again in 1898 to the *Glasgow Advertiser and Property Circular*, issued its own annual property market reports and analyses, the first in 1906. These were based on its existing annual index of sales but included breakdowns of sales according to month, district, and type of property. For its review in 1906, it noted a decline in overall sales from the previous two years and acknowledged the recent election of a Liberal government, "the complicated and far-reaching effect of which baffles prophecy."[56] In many of its earliest annual assessments, the paper had also tried to situate the importance of the property market in relation to other aspects of the economy, as if attempting to justify its targeted focus on the exchange of property. In 1909, however, its yearly affirmation of the market's importance tried to link the calculation of the market with an even broader understanding of property's value:

> The "Property Market" is an accepted commercial barometer, alike sensitive and accurate in its indications as to local trade conditions. It is one of the rare economies that affect concurrently both the domestic and the commercial life. Indeed, the former, perhaps, is the more susceptible of the two. The cot, the cottage, and the castle, in a comparative sense, are equal necessities; for he is poor indeed who possesseth not a home.[57]

The end result of these various innovations was that by the time of the First World War, an extensive flow of property market intelligence was available and in general circulation throughout Britain. A capstone of sorts for this discussion was the annual property market assessments published in the *Economist*, the first of which appeared for the year 1911.[58] The 1913 report (for the year 1912) drew together information from all the various sources discussed so far. For instance, it combined the published annual and quarterly statistics from the estate exchange and set these in the context of the district correspondence compiled in the *Estates Gazette*. It likewise referenced the *Financial Times* and quoted from other local reports in the *Manchester Guardian* and *Yorkshire Post*. Even if the overall movement of the market remained, as the *Economist* put it, "enigmatical" and, despite the obvious need to account for geographical conditions, "bound to vary widely as between town and country, or between different towns and different rural districts, according to the vicissitudes of trade and fashion" the ability to describe, calculate, and analyze the property market had dramatically changed over the course of half a century.[59] A novel toolkit now existed with which one could think about property and its market.

THE POWER AND POLITICS OF PROPERTY MARKET CALCULATION

The development of new tools and practices for property market information gathering and reporting underlined the importance for contemporaries of late nineteenth-century Britain in thinking coherently and accurately about the space of real property exchange. The property market became a thing to which one could refer with growing confidence using the weekly reports published from the registers of the estate exchange or the analytical tools developed in the press. But knowing more about the shape of a portion of the market and some of its movements did not solve the inherent ambiguity that plagued a commodity deeply obscured in private worlds of ownership. The representation of the property market was in some ways made more difficult through the development of new diagnostic tools, since the growing divide between calculable and incalculable markets only highlighted problems of uncertainty.[60] The reporting of market information also shifted discussions of uncertainty to more public contexts, where the sanctity of professional expert opinion encountered greater skepticism. I want to conclude with two examples of the politics of market uncertainty. The first looks at the issue of representation taken from the perspective of the press itself. The second examines the relationship between representations of the market and the parliamentary politics of Edwardian Britain.

The extension of real estate news to more general audiences in the 1890s did not come without resistance. Whereas the *Journal of Auctions* had earlier encountered most of its difficulties in collecting accurate information about the market and in overcoming the obstructionism of auctioneers and solicitors, the problem of supply was less apparent by the 1890s, when readers could count on a steady stream of estate exchange figures and firsthand auction sale reports. More problematic were concerns about the appropriate use of such information in depicting and interpreting the nature and movement of the market. Those seeking to exercise for themselves the authority of professional expertise found it increasingly frustrating to have their analyses circulated widely in daily papers, and often without the contextual background deemed necessary for a proper interpretation of the facts. In one of its early salvos against the daily press in 1893, for example, the *Estates Gazette* complained bitterly that "the daily newspapers have of late developed an imitating habit of commenting upon the nature and extent of the real property which comes into the market during the auction season. It is imitating because it is ill-informed."[61]

The problem was not simply one of insufficient facts, but rather of too many facts distorting the representations of the market offered to the public. This was particularly the case with the sale of large estates, which were very often difficult to sell in pressed markets but which drew the attention of a public accustomed to seeing estates as the epitome of landed status and authority.[62] On several occasions, the *Gazette* tried to counter arguments that poor estate sales demonstrated the collapse of the real property market, instead pointing to the robust market for urban household property as a sign that the market as a whole was no worse off than any other security. Despite its assurances, however, the *Gazette* concluded that the daily papers were seemingly only interested in writing "nimble paragraphs" communicating "intelligence of disaster" over "glad tidings of great joy":

> Arguing from the particular to the general they not unnaturally suppose that these stray reports, carefully picked to prove depression are a fair representation of the condition of the market for real estate. Of the vast number of private sales that are taking place all over the country every day nothing is heard; and the man in the street might be pardoned for supposing that the English land was as unsaleable as Argentine bonds.[63]

Scaling information up was important, as was delivering such insights to the general public; the question was who should perform such functions and how.

Safer ground, however, was no more easily found in the territory of statistics, where in theory one could have at least avoided the problem of generalizing from individual sales. But, in fact, the same argument about the distorting effects of a single property sale were applied to complaints over the use of the weekly statistics produced in the estate exchange and published widely in other papers. The leading critic of this practice was "Expertus," the (likely male) opinion editor in the *Property Market Review*. In his regular "Week at the Mart" commentary, he had already complained on an earlier occasion about the use of weekly sale totals from the auction mart. In 1897, he began another series of attacks on the practice. Observing that he had "never on any occasion made comparisons of the totals of one week's or one year's transactions with another, or made any pretense at ascertaining the rise or fall of market values from averages deduced from such totals," he argued that the absence of a complete inventory of transactions inevitably meant that single sales could distort the results of a given week. Indeed, the very idea of a comprehensive and complete set of market figures, despite the "very copious tables to which considerable publicity has recently been given," was "scarcely less than chimerical" and could easily "show that the market has a downward tendency, when, as a fact, the very opposite is the case."[64]

Some of this criticism reflected the evident competition between the *Property Market Review* and the *Estates Gazette*, but Expertus nonetheless tried to set his complaints in a larger context, pointing to the obfuscation and mischaracterization that could result from dependency on a now well-established network of news circulation. In one instance he cited, for the week ending February 5, 1898, the *Gazette*'s abridged market analysis concluded with the claim that there was "no demand whatever for ground rents."[65] In typical fashion, copies of the analysis had appeared on the same day in the *Times*, the *Daily Mail*, and the *Daily Telegraph*. Expertus railed against "such a nonsensical, blundering yet mischievous report" and reprinted a letter of complaint sent to the *Daily Mail* by a firm of London auctioneers, who stated that the rents put up for auction that week were of "doubtful quality" and had been given unrealistic reserve prices.[66] It had been a "perfect farce and entirely useless," said the same authors in a follow-up letter to the *Property Market Review*, "to make comparisons between one week . . . and another, with regard to the 'demand' for any particular class of property, unless the comparison is between property which are in every way identical . . . while even then one property may, for special reasons, quite independent of its market value, be more in 'demand' and fetch a higher price than an identically similar property."[67] They further argued that the *Estates Gazette* report had confused very differently valued rents in the form of those associated with apartment development compared to "ordinary ground rents."[68]

Central to each of these exchanges was a concern about the power of the press to frame the property market in more coherent terms than was considered by some to be accurate or legitimate. The growth of property news reporting gave specific inflection to the very familiar and longstanding question of whether or not real property truly was just like any other article of commerce. For those who saw such property in distinct and local terms, the reports in the daily press—and the complicity of the leading trade journals in feeding the demand for market information—were well-meaning but misguided attempts to create an abstract market where none existed.

Expertus sarcastically pushed the logic of his opponents to its furthest by lampooning the marketing of London neighborhoods as though they were species of stock or merchandise:

> Obviously it is an easy way of "making copy" to report that there has been "a quiet demand this week for brick and mortar investments, and that the market for landed estates has been characterised by a good deal of briskness." But why not carry this line of reporting a little further? Why not go just a little more into detail and tell us that there has been a keen demand for Camberwells, that the long-continued activity in Peckhams shows some signs of sagging; that a good deal of in-and-out buying is to be shortly expected in Kensingtons, and that while Islingtons, Balhams, and Anerleys are coming more and more into favour, Lambeths and the Dials are for the moment off colour? As in this progressive age nothing stands still, I am looking forward to an early development of property-market reporting in this direction.[69]

The sarcastic juxtaposition of Camberwells for sale alongside Anerleys made a mockery of the whole enterprise of property market news. Such humor, however, betrayed significant tensions arising from taking private information and translating it to a public marketplace. And no matter how confidently one might speak of the movement of averages or total sales in real property, the question of its status as a freely tradable commodity was only heightened by the regular analysis of sales in the press. The important point is not that this analysis was more or less accurate (though this clearly mattered to some), but rather that the very existence of the market in print reconfigured the politics of uncertainty surrounding marketable land and brought forth a host of new agencies empowered to negotiate that uncertainty.

The above examples demonstrate the contestability of property market information within the relatively small community of property professionals during the 1890s, but there were occasions when market news entered larger debates. Not surprisingly, one prominent instance of this involved the land politics of the late Edwardian period. When David Lloyd George, then chancellor of the exchequer to Prime Minister H. H. Asquith's Liberal government, introduced his finance bill in the spring of 1909, he provided an immediate and visceral example of the political consequences that could arise from different perspectives on how to understand and represent property market information. There had been earlier occasions when politics and real estate markets were seen to overlap, but the land taxation clauses of the 1909 "People's Budget" gave particularly stark definition to the problem of relating the two realms.

Lloyd George's budget proposed a number of new property-related taxes, including taxation on stamp duties for conveyances, on leasehold reversions, on capital values, on licensed properties, and, most contentious of all, on the "unearned increment" of land values, the last to be determined through a comprehensive and unprecedented—at least since the Domesday Book—land survey.[70] The *Estates Gazette* immediately characterized the budget as a penal one directed toward real property and a week later noted that "some idea of the disorganization of the market which has been produced by the Budget proposals may be obtained from a perusal of our reports of the business done at the Mart this week."[71] The *Times* reported the weekly sales figures at the auction mart as £41,464, compared to £148,255 in transactions carried out over the equivalent week in 1908.[72] The estate exchange report for the month of April likewise showed the first monthly decrease from the previous year's returns. Later that summer, in a follow-up discussion to a speech delivered before the Incorporated Society of Property Owners, Edwin Evans, one of the delegates who had been sent to a meeting with the chancellor, offered another calculation of market performance using figures from the mart: "He [Evans] had taken out the results of suburban building estates within ten miles of London since May 29 from the columns of *The Estates Gazette*, and found that not a single building estate had been sold since the Bill was published."[73] The market, it appeared, had conclusively rejected the bill.

August saw further debates, one in which the prime minister made the following observations in regard to the bill's effect on the market:

> I do not believe that, within recent years at any rate, there has ever been a time when there was so large a demand for land, when such good prices were being realised, when land changed hands so quickly, and when the market was so brisk and vigorous as has been the case during the few weeks which have elapsed since my right hon. friend introduced his proposals. Be it observed that land is being sold at an enhanced, and not at a diminished, price.[74]

Asquith's comments could not have posed more stark a contrast to the gloomy accounts offered by Evans and others, and though his were not the first words to offer a more sanguine market assessment, they nonetheless prompted an immediate response. Speaking for the opposition later in the same debate, Andrew Bonar Law countered Asquith's views with familiar-sounding statistics from the London Auction Mart. Bonar Law reiterated Evans's observation on unsold building estates, calling it a fact "any one could verify." Moreover, he added the case of another estate in Richmond, previously sold for £25,000 but which had failed to even reach a reserve bid of £21,000 at a recent auction. For its part, the *Estates Gazette* stood "amazed and aghast" at the prime minister's comments. "Any casual reader of *The Estates Gazette*," stated an editorial, "is better informed upon the position of the land market than the Prime Minister of England. It is notorious that the market is very far indeed from being brisk and vigorous."[75]

The authority of the leading property journal may have stood firm against the prime minister's speculations had there not appeared further signs of dissent from within the professional ranks. Throughout the spring and summer, the major professional institutions had sent delegations and several memorials to the chancellor in opposition to the budget's land clauses, and in these they had claimed to represent the view of all their members. Responding in the *Daily Telegraph* to one memorial sent by the Auctioneers' Institute, a disgruntled member writing under the pen name "Thirty-five years' experience" argued that "notwithstanding the wholesale denunciation of the Budget by interested persons, and the immense quantity of talking and writing about the land clauses . . . the fact remains that, generally speaking, auctioneers and estate agents are doing much better business now than twelve months ago."[76] The *Estates Gazette* duly reprinted this letter along with a rebuttal from "Thirty-six years' experience," who thought that the professions were "doing practically no business at all."[77] Even more senior opinions came the following week from "Forty-five years' experience" and "Fifty years' experience."[78] Outnumbered, "Thirty-five years'" held to his views and replied with further evidence of successful auctions held throughout the month of August—"notwithstanding the fact that this is commonly called the dull month for sales"—and promised "there is every probability of a splendid boom in property during the next few months."[79]

The most determined effort to gauge the market, however, came from Evans, who challenged "Thirty-five years' experience" to identify himself publicly and who offered to underwrite a survey of the Auctioneers' Institute's membership in order to gather an accurate sense of professional opinion. Evans duly prepared and circulated a letter containing some of the correspondence, the original statement by the prime minister and two simply worded questions asking recipients to indicated whether they approved of the institute's memorial and whether they felt the market in their areas had improved over the previous twelve months.[80] The *Estates Gazette* offered to verify the results of the survey, and it subsequently published many of the responses in what must surely have seemed an uncanny resemblance to its annual correspondents' market reports. Only 67 members who replied felt that the market had improved; 1,192 disagreed. Responses from London topped the list. "Absolutely no sale for property," wrote an agent in the north of the city; "market lifeless," offered another in the southwest. A Staffordshire writer "cannot give property away," and in Lancashire another correspondent concluded that "the property market here is absolutely dead."[81] Professional consensus here underlined an assessment that figures had once again failed to make conclusive.

As many writers understood only too well in 1909 (and as they likewise had in the 1890s), market judgments often depended on how one framed the market and, in particular, what kinds of properties one deemed to be a part of it. This was a point raised in the *Estates Gazette*'s own editorial on the prime minister's statement. Presuming that Asquith's conclusions had been based on the recorded sale of several very large estates, the paper argued that these properties were invariably unreliable indicators whose movements through the auction room depended more on private family circumstances than they did on purely "fiscal changes": "Transfers of such properties do not constitute 'the market.' They are quite beside the market, and it is conceivable that they might take place even in the midst of revolution or invasion."[82] Howard Frank, a leading West End auctioneer, had similarly argued, "The market lives not upon transactions involving £100,000 or more, but upon small sales, where the amount involved ranges anything between a few hundreds and a few thousands."[83] Such discernments, however, remained needlessly arbitrary to critics such as "Thirty-five years' experience," who continued to point to aggregate figures as the best source for objective assessments. In one of his last letters on the issue, for instance, he returned to the published records of the estate exchange, which, for equivalent periods in 1908 and 1909, demonstrated a growth in sales of £4,633,906 as against £4,264,404.[84]

Ultimately, these debates about the likely impacts of the 1909 budget on the real property market revealed the continuing challenge for both professionals and the public in describing and understanding the market in single and coherent terms. No one could deny the significance of the problem, but few could offer any definitive answers in light of the different ways of characterizing where the market began or ended. The political implications of such uncertainty, however, were far more evident when discussion moved from the backrooms of Tokenhouse Yard to the debating chambers of Parliament. In light of the intense public attention brought about by politicians' statements, Evans's survey of auctioneers may have helped to reinforce professional market knowledge and authority, but his use of unorthodox methodology—even if communicated with the sanction of the leading trade journal—undoubtedly unsettled the confidence of many who were used to more traditional sources of information. Perhaps it was this feeling that motivated the *Times* to argue that "there is no use in denying the fact that the state of the property market has been elevated, or degraded, to the level of a party question, and that in itself tends to destroy the utility of statements furnished in answer to special appeals, from whatever quarter they may arise." "The only reliable index of the condition of the market," it continued, "is the information which comes through the ordinary channels, and is eventually deemed worth insertion in the regular reports of the Estate Exchange and in these columns and elsewhere."[85]

It is clear that the attempt to direct the public gaze away from the embarrassing spectacle of professional disagreement and back toward the "ordinary channels" risked running against the longstanding project to make the property market more visible to the man in the street. Indeed, one could argue that the profession had met with some success in the latter. It was not insignificant, for example, that the prime minister had chosen to frame the implications of his government's budget in terms of its impact on the health of the property market. This was not the only way that the budget was discussed, but the very acting of granting authority to the market as a measure of policy underscored the success that had been achieved in making such assessments viable in the first place. The politicization of professional opinion was thus a mark of some success in having assembled the property market as an object of knowledge.

Real estate news and analysis was well established by the Edwardian years, but the clearest statement of this Victorian achievement came after the First World War, when a glut of property kept out of the market during the war years suddenly came up for sale and generated intense media scrutiny. The *Estates Gazette* noticed the uptick in sales in March 1919 and wrote that even professionals had been "taken by surprise by the unprecedented rush of land into the market."[86] Then, on May 10, under the headline "England Changing Hands," the *Times* printed a notice to its readers alerting them to the many property sales advertised in its pages.[87] At the end of June, the paper wrote that the amount of land sold so far that year was "an area equivalent to that of THE WHOLE COUNTY OF DORSET."[88] Such ads and images were soon followed by mention in the paper's property market column, in an editorial, and in a special five-part series on the state of landownership printed under the same "England Changing Hands" banner, with the first issue adding the subtitle "A Silent Revolution."[89]

Media interest in the postwar land market also included the publication and presentation of figures and calculations of aggregate sales. Individual geographical comparisons such as the above-mentioned reference to Dorset were popular. The *Estates Gazette* offered its own historical comparison by referring to the legendary career of George Robins, who was reputed to have sold more than seven hundred thousand acres over the course of twenty-seven years spent behind the rostrum. Current turnover easily eclipsed Robins's illustrious record, however, with some individual firms having placed similar amounts of property in the market within the most active weeks of the 1919 summer season alone. By 1921 the numbers had climbed still higher. The *Estates Gazette* offered the case of one firm that had sold 1,776,727 acres of property over the course of the season, equivalent to the area of Middlesex, Hertfordshire, Bedfordshire, Buckinghamshire, and Berkshire combined, and well surpassing earlier comparisons to Dorset. Official figures produced by the estate exchange—the only supposedly comprehensive recorder of market transactions—suggested that total sales in 1919 and 1920 were £21,542,134 and £18,275,839, respectively, or nearly double the size of any prior year. Sales at Winchester House and the London Auction Mart for the same years had likewise significantly exceeded any previously recorded amount. Indeed, the paper argued that, based on a reasonable extrapolation of the official figures, "a quarter of England . . . must have changed in four years [1918–1921]."[90]

Beyond the dramatic headlines announcing a revolution in landownership, however, the *Times* noted another important revolution in the role that the press had come to play in calculating, framing, and reporting on the property market. With a hint of immodesty, the paper observed that

> for the first time in the history of English journalism the Estate Market has become, in the columns of *The Times*, a regular daily feature, and instead of an article once a week, the progress of business has been noted from day to day. The official summary of auction results in the London sale rooms has also been given daily, with the chief country totals, and, in addition, hardly a day has passed without a mass of supplementary information, based partly on communications from correspondents, as to private and other transactions.

"The public has learned to look critically at the operation [of the market]," continued the report, and "this awakening of general interest in the property market has a definite value, for it has concentrated attention upon the investment possibilities of what had been too long regarded as concerning only a limited class."[91]

It should be apparent by now that when the *Times* in 1919 assumed for itself a reputation as the most innovative voice in property market news, its boast rang hollow amid a sea of competing developments, all of them originating over the preceding half century. Upon learning of the *Times'* claim to have been the first to institute daily property market reports, the *Financial Times*, which had carried its own daily reports since 1894, quipped that there was in fact "nothing new under the sun."[92] In asserting its claim, however, the *Times* did point to the evident transformation that had taken place in the representation of real property. A sophisticated and elaborate apparatus had arisen for gathering, analyzing, and presenting to the public the market transactions associated with properties passing through public auctions (and some private sales) in London and in other leading provincial businesses.

The idea for greater coordination of property market information had been expressed earlier in the century, but it was only from the 1850s onward that a true infrastructure for market intelligence was assembled through institutions like the estate exchange and the early property trade periodicals. Moreover, the property press emerged out of very specific calculative practices. From the ordering of market value in a series of formulated criteria to the disciplining of respondents and auction room participants, the fabrication of property news depended as much on the agencies of countless disparate individuals as it did on the leadership of metropolitan professional institutions. When, from the 1880s, the politics of real property erupted across a range of issues and interests, property market news jumped from the pages of specialist trade periodicals to the columns of the daily press.

The development of market intelligence succeeded by accommodating the inherent uncertainties of marketable property. At no point were there the institutions or practices that could guarantee universal transparency and accountability for fluctuations in the value of real estate, and this inherent uncertainty produced different representational strategies that were often combined to effect greater authority and legitimacy for those donning the cloak of professional property market expertise. Both statistical and qualitative methods were used in this endeavor. Over time, these different strategies succeeded in giving greater shape and durability to the property market, and by the 1890s and early 1900s property news was mainstream. It could be found in all the daily papers of the period as well as in more general interest economic periodicals such as the *Economist*. Many dailies still depended on the circulation of prepackaged analyses provided by periodicals such as the *Estates Gazette*, but metropolitan auction rooms also increasingly welcomed journalists reporting directly to their editors and producing reports independent from specialized input.

The institutional history of press development, however, was only part of the story. This chapter has put forth that property markets, like all markets, were embedded in specific practices and that both the material devices of forms, investment handbooks, and newspapers as well as the agencies of correspondents, auctioneers, estate agents, and journalists were necessary to perform the "marketization" of property. The social and material relations necessary to sustain market relations were perhaps most apparent in the controversies associated with building and maintaining institutional expertise, such as through the negotiation of the criteria that would be used to determine and record market value or in the use of local property market correspondence to bolster the authority and legitimacy of metropolitan intelligence. The end result was a system that engendered new ways of thinking and acting in relation to marketable property. Those who participated in this collective calculation of market value (as readers, correspondents, journalists, or politicians) gave more coherent form to the property relations that were so much a part of Victorian and Edwardian politics and culture.

CHAPTER FOUR

States of Marketability

What did it mean to speak of legally "marketable" real estate, and how did the marketability of property change over the course of the nineteenth century? In 1838 Solomon Atkinson published one of the earliest treatises on the doctrine of marketable titles for property. This term, he observed, had emerged during the previous century in courts of equity, and it referred to a more nuanced definition of property ownership than was typically recognized in courts of common law, wherein title to property was judged in stark categories of good or bad, legal ownership or its absence. The principle of equity instead assessed titles by degrees of doubt in the certainty of a title's legal and factual evidence. A marketable title was one for which a court would force the performance of a contract on an unwilling purchaser, but this would only be possible in cases where evidence of ownership precluded any possible uncertainty.[1] The odds of holding such a perfect title of ownership were slim, so much so that one witness to an 1846 House of Lords select committee testified that most titles to landed property were technically "unmarketable."[2]

The way of getting around this obstacle was through a different understanding of marketability—one that both admitted to the reality of land sales among even the most stable of landed families and served to accommodate this reality within the endless flexibility of contractual agreement. The goal of perfect legal marketability could never hope to mesh perfectly with actual sales of land, and so a proliferation of "special conditions" emerged to limit a buyers' right to inquire into the more questionable or uncertain aspects of a property's history, those aspects that were best ignored for the sake of a sale.[3] A buyer who agreed to limit inquiry into the terms given by the conditions of contract effectively consented to more pragmatic definitions of marketability. By midcentury, special conditions had become a common feature of property auction contracts and had even spread to private sales, driven by increased skepticism on the part of buyers as well as a more general emphasis on increasing the speed between contract and conveyance.[4]

During the second quarter of the nineteenth century, land-law reformers mooted another idea of marketability. This one promised to merge theory and practice by removing the assessment of legal marketability from the world of private conveyancing and instead placing it in the hands of the state, using the mechanism of a registry. A bureaucratic calculation would replace a contractual one, combining the certainty of formal law with the efficiency of the market in the rules governing the exchange of land. The question of whether to adopt title registration began a debate over how best to balance the need for marketability along with the need for legal security, and this debate lasted well into the twentieth century, when title registration finally secured a permanent place in England's property regime.

The history of land transfer reform has been well documented, but with a tendency to emphasize the self-interest of solicitors seeking rents from conveyancing fees or the internal story of legal professionalization.[5] This chapter instead explores the broader cultural context of reform. The attenuated evolution of title registration—and its subsequent interpretation as a failed project of reform—has obscured the broader effects it had on the conceptualization and practice of property exchange. What matters here is less the time to reform or the specific path of jurisprudential thought than the way in which reform framed marketable property within a broader world of British imperial and commercial culture. This story is told through three examples of commercial discourse, colonial economy, and material culture.

TITLE REGISTRATION AND THE DISCOURSE OF COMMERCE

From the 1840s, title registration attracted the attention of legislators, law professionals, land reformers, and the general public. One feature of these discussions was the ubiquitous use of commercial analogies to explain what title registration was meant to do for real property and how it could be made to work. Title registration, said its proponents, would render the sale of land as easy, fast, and convenient as the sale of ships, stocks, or railway shares.[6] The property of the feudal age, in other words, would at last be unfettered through the same market mechanisms used to circulate the quintessential commodities of the commercial age. "Free trade in land," adapted from the contemporaneous radical politics of the anti–corn law league, epitomized this principle of assimilation between real and personal property, but the principle was in fact far less novel than the specificity of envisioning land as stocks in both practical and theoretical terms. Title registration advanced slowly and unevenly during the nineteenth century, much to the frustration of its supporters. The pace of reform, however, obscured an important cultural transformation between the 1820s and 1870s concerning what that reform was meant to achieve and what the transfer of land should mean for the conceptual understanding of real property.

The debate on registration in England developed under very different conditions from those that existed elsewhere in Britain. The starkest contrast was between England and Scotland, where the latter had largely retained its own distinct legal and commercial traditions following the Acts of Union. Unlike in England, Scots land law recognized a perpetual right for superior landowners to collect duties on earlier grants of land to legal vassals. This meant that from a very early period there was a strong incentive in Scotland to record transfers of property, and so the Scottish Parliament had created a General Register of Sasines in 1617. In addition to the Scottish system of title registration, other jurisdictions in Britain operated forms of deed registration (the recording of documents used to prove ownership claims, as opposed to the claims themselves). A voluntary deeds registry operated in Ireland from 1707, for example, though this would not prevent later calls for the registration of title (see below). Deeds registries were also created for Yorkshire, in 1703, and for Middlesex, in 1735.[7] For the most part, however, England was an outlier in having no nation-wide system of registration, and so the reform debate initially focused there.

The royal commission appointed to inquire into the laws of real property summed up best the pre-reform view on land transfer. Its second report, published in 1830, concerned the creation of a general registry for title deeds, which, it wrote, "has appeared to us to exceed in magnitude and importance all the other subjects within the scope of our Commission."[8] The point of such a registry was to improve the transparency of retrospective investigation of title (investigation of past conveyances and other legal burdens related to a property). Since real property operated under a theory of legal estates, ownership of land was very often distinct from possession and could be divided into a number of separate interests, each with its own history of transfer proved using separate written instruments. Mortgage interests and the interests of future beneficiaries of strict settlements encumbered estates in layers of arcane legal deeds, drafted under the often-maligned expertise of conveyancers and solicitors. Whereas possession of real property could be proved "on the ground," legal ownership was another matter altogether, since no amount of expertise could avoid the inherent uncertainty of potentially undisclosed evidence of outstanding interests.

At its best, then, the ownership of land was a question of legal interpretation and confidence in the practice of retrospection, and the difficulties associated with both convinced the real property commissioners that insecurity existed to an extent "which would alarm the holders and purchasers of lands, if they were aware of the risk to which they are exposed."[9] The commissioners readily admitted that evidence of this risk was typically anecdotal, or recorded in case law, but they further supposed that even the costs of lengthy investigations added unnecessary expense and depreciated the value of land in England. Other supporters of deeds registration similarly concluded that the higher value of land in Belgium, Prussia, or France could in part be attributed to lower legal costs.[10] Hence the value of a deeds registry that would protect the security of transactions by guaranteeing that all relevant documents were available for consultation. At its simplest—and the details of the debates were anything but simple—the registration of deeds perpetuated traditional conveyancing practice by reinforcing the principle of retrospective title investigation. The problem implied in such a design was not the nature of ownership but rather the degree of sophistication by which ownership was established. For the commissioners, then, the substance of the problem rested in the delays, difficulties, and unnecessary expenses associated with traditional conveyancing.[11]

Buried within the evidence of the royal commission report, however, was another proposal to reform the transfer of property by abandoning altogether the need for retrospection. Two respondents—having evidently made their recommendations independently of each other—suggested that the cost and delay in investigating title might better be addressed by borrowing from the world of commerce.[12] The transfer of stocks, for example, required no examination of the history of ownership at all. Instead, a person wishing to sell simply visited the Bank of England to have their ownership transferred in the bound registers held there. Only the name of the current owner entitled to receive dividends was recorded in the register. A similarly modeled register of land titles would rid itself of the elaborate apparatus of deeds registration by focusing on the current facts of possession alone. In the words of one historian, title registration "was a register of conclusions, not of information from which conclusions might be drawn."[13]

The need for a title registry for land was best expressed in evocative comparisons between the transfer of land and the transfer of other modern financial instruments. "There are few persons," wrote Thomas Jefferson

Hogg, one of the two abovementioned respondents and a practicing Temple barrister,

> who have bought stock for the first time without being agreeably surprised at the rapidity and facility of the transaction: the purchaser pays the price and in a few minutes a receipt is handed to him; he is entitled to receive the interest when it becomes due, and to transfer the principal; he is, in short, instantly put into possession of all the rights of the seller: whether the sum be large or small the proceedings are equally simple and summary, as they are also in the case of a sale of stock.[14]

The contrast with the sale of landed property could not have been starker, he continued. "It is natural, therefore, that persons who have experienced the convenience of the one kind of transactions and the inconvenience of the other, should compare them together and wish the latter were as commodious as the former; that they should wonder and inquire why it is not."[15]

The other respondent, Thomas George Fonnereau, referred to the already existing deeds registries in Middlesex and Yorkshire and rejected them as "worse than useless," having contributed nothing more than additional expense and delay.[16] He too suggested the model of public funds and astutely acknowledged the political implications of the comparison, but argued that, while stocks might not compare well with land in terms of stability and influence, they surely held their own in terms of security of ownership. A family living off the proceeds of a landed investment endured no greater risk than one benefiting from funded property. For both Hogg and Fonnereau, everyday commercial practice offered an obvious path to reforming real property law.

Had it depended only on Hogg's and Fonnereau's suggestions to the real property commissioners, title registration may have remained a fringe concept, the royal commission report neither making mention of their comments nor offering any endorsement of title registration. Deeds registration enjoyed the support of most reform-minded jurists until well into the 1840s, when title registration reappeared in several more publications, once again buttressed with comparisons to personal property. One of the more persistent law reformers and designers of title registration was Robert Wilson, a solicitor and early member of the Law Amendment Society. He published his first plan for a title registration scheme in 1844, and in 1863 offered a revised and expanded book on the subject.[17] Throughout this time, he remained a staunch advocate of title reform, including as a correspondent and witness to the 1850 Royal Commission on Registration and Conveyancing and as a member of the 1857 Royal Commission on Registration of Title, which laid the groundwork for both the Transfer of Land Act of 1862 and Land Transfer Act of 1875.[18] Indeed, the basic principles of Wilson's plan were still visible in the Land Registration Act of 1925, and historians have often credited his first essay as the earliest detailed plan for implementing title registration reform.[19]

Like Hogg and Fonnereau, Wilson critiqued the problem of retrospective investigation of title, but recognized the legitimacy of protecting derivative interests in property, which retrospection was intended to address. His solution was to situate retrospection in theoretical terms and then propose an alternative theory from which to carry out reform. Retrospection derived from what he called a "theory of estates," a theory particular to real property that had developed over the course of English legal history. Where once leases had been treated as terms of years under a single fee simple, courts of equity had gradually designated them and other interests as separate estates integral to the right of property. As a result, the theory of estates transformed property into a kind of legal bricolage, where past terms remained latent and therefore attached to the present ownership. Modern property ownership, Wilson complained, was "cemented together, but the marks of the previous fracture remain[ed]."[20]

Wilson's alternate theory, the "theory of representation," offered a return of sorts to an older and simpler model of property ownership based in possession. Here he turned to analogies with personal property, where possession was routinely presumed to coincide with ownership. When buying a watch (to use the example offered in his revised treatise), a buyer rarely questioned the vendor's right to sell; possession alone sufficed as evidence of ownership. Conveyancing practice held to the opposite assumption that possession of land only rarely coincided with legal ownership, but Wilson argued that at least in theory this distinction between real and personal property, between the ownership of land and the possession of watches, was false.[21] Title to land, after all, was nothing more than a conclusion drawn from documentary evidence of continuous possession, and instances could be found when possession of personal property did not coincide with full ownership, as was the case with artwork or heirlooms held under family settlement.

The law of personal property, however, allowed possession to stand in for ownership—to represent it in theory, even if in practice exceptions could be found to disprove it. There was no reason, Wilson claimed, that the same could not be done for real estate: "Simplicity might be made the rule, and complication the exception. . . . It is this disentanglement of the general property from the mass of inferior interests in which it is involved, which constitutes what we have called the 'theory of representation'; . . . and which it is now proposed to apply, with improved machinery, to facilitate the transfer of land."[22] Improving the machinery of transfer was critical to Wilson's proposal, and here again the operation of public funds and other commercial instruments provided the model. He credited the earlier ideas of Hogg and Fonnereau in drawing the comparison with the registers held in the Bank of England, but he went further in suggesting mechanisms leading to even greater visibility and mobility for property titles, with an obvious eye on the value of mobility to mortgage lending.[23]

Wilson proposed that title should be represented symbolically in the form of a certificate held by the registered owner, who would be able to transfer ownership through a simple process of endorsement. He likened these certificates to the dock warrants used to trade bulk goods held in London ports, though he also made reference to bills of exchange. All these instruments shared in common a second order of abstract representation that created an artificial simplicity in order to improve the convenience of transferring property. "If the title to goods can be manifested by transferable symbols, though occasionally complicated so as to suspend their usefulness," he asked, "can the title to land be similarly manifested, notwithstanding its similar, but more frequent, complication?"[24] Wilson believed so, and he demonstrated the practicability of the idea by reproducing several examples of dock warrants, share certificates, and his proposed "land certificates" (see figs. 16 and 17).

If the theory of representation could be made to operate in the law of real property, why register estates at all? What was the purpose of registering a title if one accepted the premise that possession alone was sufficient evidence of ownership? Anticipating these questions, Wilson argued that registration, through its various abstractions, benefited both the security and the mobility of ownership. Again, in his revised argument, he likened the register of title to an estate map. The latter was not inherently more reliable than the "hedges and ditches" it purported to represent in ink lines; rather, it offered mobility to that which was immobile: "In the symbol the fixed becomes movable, and the inert active. The map transmits the land by post for inspection, and compounds it with other matter in the particulars and conditions of sale." Similarly, a register of title, like a map, "represents an outwards appearance—the surface of the title, if I may so call it—not to make it visible, but to mobilise its visibility, and to facilitate an exhibition of its relations and conditions."[25]

Northumberland, No. 1, *House and Garden.*

10A. 2R. 5P.

Proposed symbols of the property in land.

Official Seal.

This is to certify that John Smith of Percy House, in the county of Northumberland, Esq. is the owner of the house and garden, being No. 1 on the map of Northumberland.

A. B. Registrar.

London, 1st January, 1845.

FIGURE 16. Sample land certificate for proposed title registration. From Robert Wilson, *Outlines of a Plan for Adapting the Machinery of the Public Funds to the Transfer of Real Property* (London, 1844), 26. Reproduced by permission of the British Library Board. 1390.k.19.

East and West India Dock Warrant.

EAST AND WEST INDIA DOCK COMPANY.

Mark of Goods. W. I. Dock Warehouse 2.

Ship's rotation, No. 751.

Warrant for the following ten bales of Jute, imported in the Ship Nelson, from Calcutta, Capt. Thompson, entered by A. B. & Co. on the 14th November, 1843. Rent payable from* the 15th of November, 1843. [*Here follow the particulars of the Goods.*]

Examined and entered, Cargo Ledger 58, fol. 21.

(Signed) O. READING, Clerk. H. DIXON.

LONDON, 12th December, 1843.

No. 66,827.

Deliver the abovementioned goods to A. B. & Co. or assigns by indorsement hereon. (Signed) S. G. TULLOCK.

FIGURE 17. Sample East and West India Dock Company warrant. From Robert Wilson, *Outlines of a Plan for Adapting the Machinery of the Public Funds to the Transfer of Real Property* (London, 1844), 63. Reproduced by permission of the British Library Board. 1390.k.19.

In terms of security, however, a map and a title register were quite different, since a register was still fixed in place, albeit at a distance from the land itself. Only its related certificate could circulate freely; together, the two elements maximized the marketability of land with its equitable security. "The fixed record supplies a local support or centre for non-possessory titles to cluster on: the movable extract—certifying possession in coincidence with ownership, or possession and its appendages, as the case may be—preserves to the possessor's title the quality of ubiquitous transferability."[26] Mobility and security, in other words, would both be served by new forms of abstract representation, borrowed from the worlds of finance and commerce, disentangling land from its local conditions, and resituating its ownership in a new legal geography and a material order of fixed title registries and transferable title certificates.

Both the fixed registry and mobile certificates offered mechanisms for protecting derivative interests. The two most common and important of these interests related to mortgages and to family settlements. Wilson proposed two mechanisms for dealing with the former. The first copied what was already a common means of raising credit by depositing title deeds with lenders. So-called equitable mortgages, however, would be faster and more reliable with the use of land certificates, since mortgagers would be secure in knowing that land certificates were backed by the state registry.[27] Moreover, so long as any transfers of title depended on presenting title certificates to the registrar, mortgages based on deposited certificates could take place in private, thereby avoiding the public scrutiny of financial records common to continental registration models.

Alternatively, the registry of title would permit legal mortgages by transferring title to the mortgager, conditional upon repayment arranged with the mortgagee. These arrangements would be further protected through the use of caveats in the register to ensure appropriate notice to all interested parties. The model, once again, came from the Bank of England, which routinely attached a caveat, known as a *distringas*, on the transfer of stocks.[28] These caveats acted to delay any transfer until notice could be given to the party registering them. Distringases became important mechanisms for protecting other equitable interests, particularly those associated with family settlements, which Wilson proposed restructuring under a single legal ownership held by trustees but administered on behalf of the associated estates (e.g., life estates, entails, and remainders).

Finally, the register itself—what Wilson referred to as a "book of reference"— would record each transaction and its associated caveats, providing a current record for the state of a given property's ownership.[29] As transfers took place or caveats were removed from the register, the registrar would modify the account by crossing out past transactions. The analogy with business accounting was not lost on Wilson, who noted that changes in the assignment of leases under a title could be added up and carried forward with each new transaction, much like the daily reconciliations of a cash book. Each issue of a new set of title certificates "would thus become the virtual opening of a new account."[30]

In both its theory and its practical details, Wilson's plan registered more than just property; it also registered the tone of a new commercial discourse shaping public understandings of real estate. As one historian has recently noted, the real challenge of Wilson's scheme came less from the idea of registering title than from the "aggressive middle-class understanding of property it embodied"; according to this view, it was on this basis that Wilson suggested replacing aristocratic conventions of strict settlement based on legal estates with the concept of registered trustees and caveats.[31] Regardless of whether Wilson's ideas can or should be reduced to strictly class terms, there is no doubt that part of the power of the stock analogy came from the concrete prescriptions it evoked from the everyday experience of metropolitan commercial life, and this may explain why reformers like Wilson dedicated so much space to explain the details—the forms, maps, indices, registers, protocols and buildings needed to make the registry work. Even without these specifics, however (and despite the undoubtedly cool reception it received from some corners of landed society, of which more will be said in a moment), the image of land as stock transcended its origins by capturing the intuitive sense of an even larger public than those familiar with commercial practices.

For example, the analogy quickly found its way into debates over "free trade in land," the neglected intellectual sibling of the anti–corn law movement.[32] Early versions of the free trade argument gave only the slightest nod to deeds reform, but in a series of letters to the *Times* in 1846, another eager law reformer, James Stewart, announced his conversion to title registration by including it in his appeal to the landed community. "We are to have free trade in the produce of the land,—let us also have free trade in the land itself," he wrote, adding:

> the laws relating to property should be few and simple. Intricate and difficult questions will no doubt arise in civilized states; but the familiar transactions, the sale and the mortgage, should be easily understood and

> easily performed. We know they are so in personalty, in produce, in stock, in the funds.[33]

Stewart called for several specific measures, including the creation of a cadastral map for the whole country and a "general registry of titles." His letters produced a sizeable outcry, and of those correspondents who wrote in his defense, several reiterated the principle of assimilation with consols and company shares, and one even directly referenced Wilson's plan.[34]

The idea quickly implanted itself into the legal consciousness of radical liberalism. John Stuart Mill, for one, inserted an endorsement for the analogy in his *Principles of Political Economy* (1848). "To make land as easily transferable as stock," he argued, "would be one of the greatest economical improvements which could be bestowed on a country; and has been shown, again and again, to have no insuperable difficulty attending it."[35] Another early historian of the free trade movement firmly believed that the same principles that had liberated corn would ultimately exert themselves on land, all according to the model of shares and bank notes.[36] The failure of the Chartist land campaign and the takeover of the freehold land movement by suburban building societies dimmed hopes for any immediate conquest of aristocratic privilege, but free land reformers like James Beal, an auctioneer, held to the belief that "our laws will never be commercial until land may be transferred with as much ease as stocks, railway or bank shares."[37] Overall, title registration played a relatively minor role in free land reform campaigns. It certainly never garnered the same interest as the abolition of entails or primogeniture. But whenever it was mentioned, reformers rarely failed to entice their audiences to imagine in their minds the ease with which a land market might work if only it could work more like the sale of those things that epitomize modern market efficiency.[38]

Even opponents of the stock analogy conceded its persuasive powers. In a paper read to the Juridical Society in 1859, J. M. Ludlow admitted that the questions of land transfer and registration were "discussed from a totally different point of view to that of five-and-twenty or thirty years ago—of the days of the Real Property Commission." With a nod to Wilson's pamphlet, Ludlow noted that the idea of title registration had"taken hold of the public mind to a great extent" and that stocks and the model of their registration at the Bank of England constituted the reformers' ideal. In his opinion, this ideal and its popularity fit perfectly with the prevailing culture of the times:

> There is none of us who is not familiar with the comparison, who at least has not heard some of the arguments founded on it, from legal lips

> or lay; and, from the point of view of which offers itself so naturally to our mercantile age, that of the cheapening of land in the market, I suppose there is no one to whom those arguments have not sounded now and then irrestistible.[39]

It is worth pausing to consider Ludlow's criticisms, if only to emphasize what was considered to be at stake in the debate and to outline some fairly typical attacks on the principles of assimilation. Overarching all his arguments was a belief in land's specificity, both in terms of its physical characteristics and in terms of its legal and social complexity. Unlike stock, land did not exist in the abstract. It could not be divided into equal units but was instead embedded in differing parcels, each with their own characteristics of value. The right to sell land was itself only one particular incident of property's many unique features, and elevating that right—by way of a fictional owner in possession with complete powers of alienation, as Wilson had proposed—distorted entirely the reality of landownership. "Its alienable quality is entirely subordinate to the question of its beneficial use," concluded Ludlow, "and I can conceive of no more frightful and anti-social state of things, than that which our original comparison between land and stock implies as desirable—that in which every estate in England could be daily quoted at the Stock Exchange."[40]

Another critic of title registration, Edward P. Wolstenholme, similarly used the comparison with the sale of stock to frame his own counterproposals for legal reform. Preferring the "known evils of the existing system" over the "unknown evils of any substituted system," Wolstenholme rejected the utility of title registration by carefully dissecting the principles of the stock-as-land equation.[41] He began by identifying the four "specialities" on which depended the simplicity and efficiency of transfers of stock: 1) the fact that the Bank of England was not liable to consider the interests of anyone other than the person named in their registers; 2) no interests other than the absolute owner (fee simple) were required to be registered; 3) the bank took on the risk of having to compensate legitimate owners in the case of fraud; and 4) compensation of stock was as simple as replacing an identical amount of stock purchased from the available funds in the market.[42]

Of these four supposed advantages, only the first two appeared to Wolstenholme to have any legitimate comparison with real property, since the unique characteristics of each parcel of land made it impossible to simply swap one unit for another. Wolstenholme therefore proposed to simplify the ownership and transfer of property by adopting the principles of a single legal owner in possession and the subordination of all other derivative interests.[43]

His plan would incorporate these principles into the law of property itself, rather than via a new and untried state bureaucracy. Wolstenholme's paper was significant to the present discussion for two reasons. First, it represented the germ of what would become the reform of real property in the legislation of 1925 and the perpetuation of a private system for land transfer.[44] Second, it demonstrated the degree to which the commodity discourse of stocks determined the early reform of both public and private conveyancing practice.

As influential as Wolstenholme would later become, his ideas appeared anachronistic to many in the mercantile age evoked by Ludlow. This was certainly true for the authors of the Royal Commission on Registration of Title report, who in 1857 issued the penultimate articulation of the stock analogy in mainstream legal opinion. Appointed in 1854 following the recommendation of a select committee on deeds registration, the registration commissioners subsequently took the benefits of title registration over deeds registration as a given.[45] The latter, in their view, could provide for the security of title, but would not improve simplicity or the efficiency of transfer. Only a system for registering ownership could achieve these last goals, and the commissioners took the comparison with stock and other commercial property as a perfectly acceptable one: "No one doubts that it would be a great benefit to the proprietors of land if they were able to convey it with the same facility as the owners of ships, or of stock, or of railway shares, can now assign their property in any of them. But the question is, Can this be accomplished?—and, if so, how?"[46] The commission answered with a plan for title registration that looked very similar to Wilson's original proposal and to the revised version he outlined in his reply to the commission's final report—an unfortunate irony, given that he was the only member of that commission not to sign it.[47] The registry, based in London but with branch offices in provincial districts, would allow the owners of land in fee simple to register their titles voluntarily. At the time of registering, titles could be recorded either as statutory titles—free from all encumbrances save those recorded in the registry—or as possessory titles that would gradually become statutory once they had been registered up to the statute of limitations on adverse possession. Statutory titles would be guaranteed by the state.

Those registering titles would receive a certificate of title listing the name of the registered owner, the lands registered, any caveats inhibiting transfer, and references to various indexes stored in the registry. Once registered, "the title to the property, for the purposes of transfer, [would] be manifested by the register, and by that alone; and so eventually the only title to land which a purchaser need examine [would] be the last transfer as the same [was] recorded in the registrar's books."[48] In other words, the register would replace parchment deeds as evidence of title and the certificate of title would operate with the same security in terms of equitable mortgages as deeds deposited at a bank. The report also included the use of caveats, but left their variety and exact nature open so as to accommodate flexibility in securing settlements and other derivative interests. Unlike with Wilson's revised plan, the commissioners rejected compulsory registration and the need for a completed cadastral map as a basis for identifying properties. In summing up the advantages of the absolute title that would ultimately emerge from the registry, the report argued that it would "increase the value of land as a marketable commodity" and offer the same security "as stock which is purchased in open market."[49]

The 1857 royal commission report provided a benchmark for nearly twenty years of legislative effort. Throughout this time, politicians and legal observers invariably promoted or opposed reforms based on precedents in the sale of stocks, ships or company shares and on perceptions of the relevancy of these examples. In 1859, for example, the royal commission's plan for a registry of title informed a bill introduced to the House of Commons that just missed being enacted due to the fall of the government. The solicitor general, Hugh Cairns, introduced his bill with an encomium to the facilities through which one could buy stock or shares in mere hours, ships in only five minutes.[50] Nearly every speaker on the bill felt obliged to address similar comparisons and even those who rejected it did so on the familiar grounds that the unique qualities of land made it unsuitable to similar market relations.

Three years later, a new Liberal government rehearsed a very different bill with nearly identical scripts. "I want only to introduce alterations in the mode of perfecting and manifesting titles," stated the new lord chancellor, Lord Westbury, upon introducing the new legislation in 1862, "to facilitate the disposition of estates, and to bring them as near as possible into a condition of easy alienation, so that land may be dealt with almost the same facility as ships or railway property, or shares in public companies, or the enormous amount of wealth invested in Government securities."[51] This time, with the help of government pressure, the bill passed, establishing the first registry of title in England and Wales.

The registry's design caused problems from the start, but that did not stop some estate marketers from using the new system to sell land under the aegis of improved efficiency and security. The *Estates Gazette* made a point of alerting its readers to the very first advertisement for land sold with a registered title. The auctioneering firm responsible for the sale of the Kent estate, Debenham and Tewson, clearly felt that the public would recognize and appreciate the value of a registered, indefeasible title. They purposefully reminded buyers that the lots developed on the estate would sell with as much ease as "a ship or money in the funds."[52] The advertisement proved that at least one firm had recognized the advantages to urban builders touted by the law's promoters.

It is unclear if the public responded with similar enthusiasm, but critics of the legislation did not. The problem with Westbury's act, as it would later be determined, was that his emphasis on perfecting and manifesting titles led him down routes very similar to a deeds registration, since he rejected the idea of a single registered owner and instead insisted that all encumbrances be registered separately from the title and charges.[53] The act further rejected earlier suggestions for an insurance fund to warranty titles, and, as a result, it required extremely strict conditions for establishing statutory title and identifying property boundaries. The so-called marketable titles demanded by the act were those that a court of equity would force a buyer to accept in an open contract; additionally, the criteria for meeting this standard far exceeded those commonly found in special conditions of sale. The three separate registers prescribed by the legislation—for titles, encumbrances and charges, each cross referenced and each involving their own forms of investigation—hardly mimicked the simplicity of a stock register. More to the point, Westbury himself was more intent on replicating the "condition of easy alienation" associated with stocks than the actual mechanism used to transfer them. Only 507 applications for title were received between 1862 and 1868, the latter the year in which another royal commission was tasked with examining the failure of the Westbury Act.[54]

That commission reported in 1870, and it specifically addressed the usefulness of the analogy between stocks, ships, and land. It did so by comparing the strict criteria for indefeasible title with registered interests as set out in the 1862 act, with what the commissioners believed to be a popular understanding of what a registry was for. "Ours is a commercial country," they concluded, "and we desire all property, even land, to pass readily from hand to hand." The point of a registry, according to this logic, was not the security of interests but rather "cheapness and speed"; thus the real question was how to achieve these things without undermining the security that already existed. "The nearest analogies that we have for our guidance," wrote the commissioners, "are the Registries of stock and ships."[55]

Their comparison went as follows: As with the ownership of land, the ownership of ships was often separate from actual possession, not least because ships were often at sea when bought or sold, but also because the legal ownership of ships was divided into sixty-four shares. Ships, therefore, depended on documentary titles and the registration of those titles proved that the uniqueness of documentary title in land offered no inherent obstacle to registration. The commissioners then admitted the common distinction between the abstract identification of stocks and the shares in ships, but then argued that the specificity of land actually increased its advantages in registration. So long as land remained fixed in its locally embedded associations, its derivative interests would be protected by the inherent need to reference local conditions when purchasing land. The abstract nature of stocks meant that purchasers rarely questioned the identity of the vendor, but most purchasers of land would be unable to avoid some kind of inquiry into the local relations of possession. Confident that derivative interests would look after themselves without the help of registration, the commissioners returned to the direct analogy with stocks expressed earlier in the 1857 royal commission report, and recommended that only the absolute owner of land be registered and that the register of mortgages be replaced with a system of caveats, as was done in the Bank of England registers.[56]

The strong assertion on the part of the commissioners of both the commercial spirit of the stock market and the administrative letter of its practice eventually found its way into the Land Transfer Act of 1875, which restored many of the principles recommended in 1857. The act permitted the registration of three forms of ownership: an absolute title, a qualified title, and a possessory title. Various forms of restrictions and caveats placed on the title certificate would protect all other encumbrances. The most debated point in the lead up to the act's passage was the question of compulsion, which had come to be seen as an essential step in achieving widespread registration. The previous Liberal government had included compulsory clauses in 1874, but Lord Cairns dropped these in his 1875 bill in response to strong lobbying from solicitors. The dismal figures for newly registered land in the years immediately following the legislation undoubtedly reassured critics of the need for compulsion, but it was not until 1897 that a supplemental act extended it to London, ostensibly on a trial basis. Registration was then gradually extended to other counties following the consolidating Law of Property Act of 1925 (full compulsory registration in all counties, however, came about only in 1991).

Both at the time of the passage of the 1875 act and in subsequent years, commentators believed it to have articulated within its legal mechanisms the principles common to markets for personal property.[57] Historians have generally concurred. For J. Stuart Anderson, the acceptance by the 1870 commissioners of a division between a single absolute owner and all other interests in real property (the "curtain principle," as it became defined in jurisprudence) effectively demonstrated that "a middle-class conception of land as merely a form of wealth had become unexceptionable, to the extent that the state should provide simple mechanisms for landowners who themselves saw land that way."[58]

The expression of this new conception through analogies with stock and ship markets persisted in the decades after 1875, though with perhaps less intensity and enthusiasm than before. One of the reasons for this was the changing political context for the land question after the 1870s. In the aftermath of Henry George's campaign for the taxation of land values or Alfred Russel Wallace's call for land nationalization, the idea of free trade in land with a reformed system of land transfer lost its radical appeal. Conservatives viewed the idea more positively, but, at both ends of the political spectrum, as for the public in general, the old liberal exuberance of the stock analogy to land transfer fell away toward the end of the century. "We believe that a thorough and workable system of registration of title would increase the stability and consequently the value of land and houses," wrote one *Estates Gazette* editorial in 1888, "but it is idle to expect that belongings of this kind can be made to pass from hand to hand with the cheapness and expedition that shares and such-like securities pass."[59] That being the case, the allusion to stocks was still being debated twenty years later during a royal commission inquiry into the 1897 Land Transfer Act.

Regardless of how long the analogy found purchase in public debates, the more important point is the role that it undoubtedly played in framing the early history of title registration. The mechanisms for title registration and the conception of what they should aim to do for real property emerged out of a new commodity discourse that placed land in a very direct analogy with some of the most abstract and celebrated commodities in Britain's commercial empire. Joint stock companies and merchant shipping epitomized the universal market principles whose application to land promised to liberate the last remaining impediment to social and economic modernity. Comparisons between stocks and land did more than simply demonstrate the end benefits of a reformed market, however—they also presented land law reformers with replicable technology for building a new kind of market infrastructure, one enshrined in the 1875 Land Transfer Act (38 & 39 Vict., c. 87). Even alternative and less statist proposals, such as Wolstenholme's simplified regime of private deed conveyancing, looked to the model of personal property in stocks as the ideal from which to orientate future changes to the law. Insofar as title registration concerned the legal framework governing the identity and exchange of marketable property, the influence of stock and ship analogies offers compelling evidence for a new market culture shaping the parameters of the property market in nineteenth-century Britain.

THE COLONIAL CONTEXT OF LAND TRANSFER REFORM

The analogy of stocks and ships with land title registration was meaningful in more ways than just similarities in modes of registration. Like stocks and like ships, title registration circulated widely, moving between territories and crossing seas and oceans to connect disparate market cultures and their property law regimes. It is impossible to discuss the histories of title registration and property market culture in England without situating them in a larger imperial and transnational context. Historians of land politics have recognized the necessity for a comparative perspective far more readily than have historians of land transfer reform, the latter of whom have written the history of title registration within very specific contexts of national political economy and legal professionalization.[60] Only recently have scholars challenged such isolationism by pointing to the influence of colonial legal innovations on British title registration debates, most notably the enactment of Torrens registration in South Australia four years before the first registry was established in England.[61]

The life of Robert Torrens, the champion of that colony's early title reforms, aptly demonstrates the complicated international social and cultural networks that shaped the debate on title registration in Britain. Torrens, after all, was born in Ireland, the second son of Robert Torrens senior.[62] At the age of twenty-eight, he emigrated to South Australia to take up a position as a customs collector for the colonial government. It was there that he learned of the method of registering ships that he would later claim inspired his model for land registration. His own lucrative and questionable land dealings gave particular significance to the law that he helped enact in 1858, though recent research has demonstrated that Torrens also borrowed heavily from a draft bill modeled on title registration in Hanseatic towns and written by another immigrant, Ulrich Hübbe.[63] Torrens did eventually return to England as an MP for Cambridge, where he lobbied for his own system of registration, but not before first landing in Dublin, where he lectured widely on his South Australian experience, helped found the Registration of Title

Association, and codrafted a bill for title registration that was introduced to Parliament in 1864, one year before the passage of the Record of Title Act (Ireland).

Torrens's journey from Ireland to South Australia, and his ultimate return to promote registration in England are significant for several reasons. First, it underscores the role of migration in stitching together the nineteenth-century British world and in linking the development of similar property regimes throughout that world.[64] Second, whereas many accounts of property law and empire emphasize the export of English legal customs to settler societies, or the adaptation of shared English perceptions in new world environments, Torrens's biography shows the importance of reimports to metropolitan debates.[65] Indeed, as the following discussion will demonstrate, debates about title registration and the different kinds of market cultures best suited to registration actually reinforced conceptual divisions between colonial and metropolitan experience. Finally, Torrens's involvement with title registration linked him to both Ireland and South Australia, the two most frequently discussed comparisons made in midcentury English debates on land transfer reform.

It is perhaps not surprising that title registration appeared as early as it did in discussions of Irish land reform. Perceptions of Irish land tenure, after all, were largely dominated by the prejudices of English political economy until well after midcentury. Up until then, most reformers—even those based in nascent Irish academies—held to the view that the point of reform was to instill universal commercial principles in a supposedly primitive Irish culture, the British response to famine in Ireland being the most tragic example.[66] With the additional pressure throughout the 1840s of mounting public interest in the Irish land question, it took very little time for free trade in land slogans to traverse the Irish Sea. Title registration, promoted with the same commercial analogies as those being used by Wilson and others, was likewise included in prescriptions for the Irish land question.[67]

The perceived need for free trade in land varied somewhat in each country—in England the emphasis was on security, cost and speed of transfer; in Ireland the main concern was a lack of investment in heavily encumbered estates—but both shared a general sense of land markets clogged by sclerotic systems of transfer. The application of free trade principles to Irish land, however, proved far more radical than anything achieved in England at the time. Many hoped that free trade would revitalize Irish society through the influx of a completely new class of English-styled owners, variously described as either middle-class or even yeoman farmers.[68] If, in England, the still trendy calls for deeds registration amounted to an improved regimen of diet and monitoring for the health of land titles, legislation passed for Ireland in the late 1840s—much of it in response to the politics of famine—promised nothing less than full bypass surgery.

The 1849 Encumbered Estates (Ireland) Act (12 & 13 Vict., c. 77) revised an act passed the previous year that had tried to push sales of encumbered estates through chancery courts. The new act, passed by a Whig government but with strong Peelite support, instead created a fully independent commission with powers to force estates into the market and launder their titles of any outstanding encumbrances, leaving the new owners with what amounted to parliamentary titles. Indebted estate owners so heavily used the commission—to the extent that owners of unencumbered estates were known to have created fictitious encumbrances in order to gain access to the commission—that its functions were transferred to a permanent Landed Estates Court in 1858. The point of the commission, as the solicitor general directly stated when introducing the 1848 version, was "to make land in Ireland a marketable commodity, which it was not now, or only to a very small extent."[69] The contradictions of coercive force applied in the name of a providentially ordained free market were, of course, not unique to land. As W. L. Burn noted long ago (and with particular respect to Irish land): "The task of the early Victorians was not primarily that of working a free economy: theirs was the preliminary task of bringing about the conditions in which a free economy could work . . . [even when this required] measures so radical as to be almost revolutionary."[70]

As effective as the commission was at manufacturing marketable land—though not with the desired effect of transferring land to new, more enterprising owners[71]—many were skeptical that that marketability would last very long, since the commission did not have the means to register the titles it was creating. It could clear titles in order to sell them, but there was nothing stopping titles from quickly accumulating new legal burdens. To many observers, this remained a major deficiency of the commission, particularly so for any intentions to model it in England, where transfers were considered far more problematic than the need to remove encumbrances. It was not surprising, then, to see another reformer, Vincent Scully, propose a reformed land system for Ireland that included the basic principles of the Encumbered Estates Commission combined with a model for title registration.[72]

Not long after publishing his proposals, Scully arrived in Westminster as the elected MP for Cork, bringing with him his ideas for land reform. Claiming to have sought election in order to promote title registration, Scully tried to convince English reformers that his own proposals for Ireland could easily be adapted for English needs. In 1853, his first bill for title registration was referred to a select committee already considering proposed legislation for deeds registration—the same committee, in fact, that would soon recommend a royal commission inquiry for title registration. Scully served as a member of both.[73]

The royal commission carefully considered Scully's proposals and those of other Irish witnesses—thirty in all—who were asked to testify before it. These included the attorney general for Ireland, the master of the rolls, and two of the three members of the Encumbered Estates Commission. In the end, the commission rejected Scully's recommendation for a land tribunal modeled on the judicial powers given to the Encumbered Estates Commission in Ireland, preferring instead the lesser ministerial powers of a registry office. The commission also rejected the idea of allowing a land tribunal or registry office to issue land debentures, or fixed-amount securities that Scully argued would function similarly to railway shares, with the same ease of transferability and relative security.[74] It did, however, suggest that all its recommendations with respect to establishing a registry of title were more than applicable to the problem of reforming the transfer of land in Ireland. The need for registration was as acute in Ireland as in England, and the facilities for implementing it were already in place to a far more developed extent.[75]

The commissioners listed three reasons why title registration should be extended to Ireland. First, they argued that the "almost universal use" of Ordnance Survey maps for estate management, land sales, and valuations made it far easier to identify and value Irish land. Second, they believed that the Irish deeds registry, in existence from the early eighteenth century, would offer better access to information for proving title. Finally, they pointed to the success of the Encumbered Estates Commission in creating more marketable titles. In all, the commissioners concluded that these facilities—many of them the products of England's colonial rule in Ireland—"furnish[ed] materials and machinery for effecting the transition from the existing system to the new one much more readily and speedily than [could] be anticipated in England."[76]

The traffic in ideas moved both ways, and one way to improve the pace of change in England was to import machinery from Ireland. This was first attempted in 1859, when Cairns's Registry of Landed Estates Bill was paired with a second bill that would have created an Encumbered Estates Court for England. Introducing both bills, Cairns suggested "that the House should look to the case of Ireland" for guidance on how to rid English property of its conveyancing evils.[77] He calculated that since its inception in 1848 the Irish Encumbered Estates Court had transacted over twenty million pounds' worth of property, numbering 8,500 separate conveyances and amounting to a seventh of the total land area of the country.[78] The supposed advantages in Ireland, moreover, could easily be found in England. Tithe maps, for example, and the recently completed twenty-five-inch Ordnance Survey maps for the northernmost counties in England, were more than sufficient for the purposes of identifying properties. Cairns stressed, however, that the importation would be specific and that there would be no need to recreate the compulsory sales associated with the Irish Court.[79] The fall of the government ended the progress of both bills, but Cairns's preference for an English estates court continued even after his reform of the title registry in 1875.[80] Defeated, proponents of the Irish estates court model had to settle for having directly inspired the West Indian Encumbered Estates Court, set up at the request of landowners in 1854.[81]

Much to the chagrin of Irish reformers, the legislation that ultimately brought title registration to Ireland carried with it many of the problems associated with England's first attempt in 1862. That legislation had not been extended to Ireland, but three years later in response to significant public agitation for title registration—organized in part by the Dublin Registration of Title Association—the government passed the Record of Title Act (Ireland) (28 & 29 Vict., c. 88).[82] This act placed responsibility for the registry in the existing Landed Estates Court that was now empowered to register the parliamentary titles generated from its deliberations. Unlike an earlier bill introduced by supporters of Torrens's system, the final act adopted many of the leading principles of the English system, including the rights for landowners to opt out of registration, to choose traditional deeds conveyancing over registered transfers, and to have settlements registered separately from the fee simple. Not surprisingly, the Irish act fared as poorly as its English equivalent; only after the extension of partial compulsory registration in 1891 did any widespread adoption of its provisions take place.[83]

Thanks in no small measure to Torrens's advocacy, public debate on the question of title registration in Ireland for the first time included extensive comparisons between Ireland, England, and Australia. In addition to his involvement with the Registration of Title Association in Dublin, Torrens toured throughout Britain, presenting his evidence of antipodean experience to, among others, the Law Amendment Society and the annual meeting of the National Association for the Promotion of Social Science, held in Edinburgh in 1863.[84] Torrens's Law Amendment Society paper caught the eye of Robert Wilson, who quickly added extensive quotes from it in a footnote to his revised plan for English title registration, published in the same year. When he opened the second reading of the 1865 bill for registration in Ireland, the attorney general gave credit to "the zeal and ability with which he [Torrens] had promoted the cause of public improvement on this subject." "The Bill," observed a more sardonic MP, "had been born in Australia; so that from that happy colony they were to derive not only reforms in their Constitution, but in the law of real property."[85]

The same MP went on to foreshadow the kind of comparisons that would become routine among opponents of title registration and that captured a major cultural prejudice of nineteenth-century British imperialism. "The doctrine applicable to a country where the settlers cleared away the trees and the natives, and then laid out the land for each other according to their own plans," he noted, "was to be introduced into a country where the laws of real property were, fortunately or unfortunately, rather complicated."[86] The distinction made was between the facility for crafting law in a relatively "new" country compared to the complexity involved in reforming the legal regime of an "old" country. As Edmund Rogers has recently demonstrated, the dichotomy between new settler societies and old metropolitan ones, while often serving to legitimize aspects of British imperialism abroad, equally shaped social and economic debates at home, including those relating to land reform.[87]

According to Rogers, historians of title registration have marginalized Torrens's impact on English debates by underestimating the significance of Australian legislation as a source of experimental evidence used by both supporters and opponents of reform. Opponents of reform, for example, complained that one of the reasons title registration had been so successful in Australia was that Australian titles exhibited far greater simplicity than did English ones.[88] Australian titles derived from Crown grants of relatively recent origin and were encumbered with far fewer and more recent settlements. English estates, in contrast, could theoretically trace their root titles back through several centuries of continuous occupation, with settlements extending across multiple generations and through elaborate family networks. Caveats might well be used to protect the rarity and simplicity of colonial settlements, but they could never be relied on to protect the frequent complexity of English ones. Complexity, moreover, was patterned on the ground, in the form of poorly defined and irregular boundaries, fences, and hedgerows. The attorney general for Scotland, John Douglas, testifying before a select committee in 1878 contrasted this English landscape with the more "geometrical" one found in colonies. "If you have seen the title-deeds of property in the colonies," he stated, "you will have seen that it is a very simple thing . . . like describing the squares upon a chess-board."[89]

Torrens argued vociferously against such objections. He pointed out that many titles could be found in colonies dating back several decades and that the frequency of transfer, combined with the poorer quality of conveyancing expertise, could quickly complicate titles to similar degrees as in England. The idea that settler families did not favor settlements was likewise based on the "distorted vision" that "assumes that Englishmen and Germans when they emigrate beyond the seas . . . leave behind them all sense of duty as regards making provision for their families." The immediate need for liquidity did prevent families from encumbering lands initially, but very soon "the old-country instinct to make provision for their families prevails, and settlements and entails become less rare." Finally, in terms of maps, Torrens reversed the logic of his opponents to argue that the longevity of English settlement actually made identification of property easier, even without modern Ordnance Survey maps, since "ancient hedge-rows and parish bound-stones afford ready means of identification." Colonial surveys, he noted, were known for their serious inaccuracies.[90]

Ireland clearly offered a middle ground in these debates, since the existence of the Landed Estates Court and the completion of a six-inch Ordnance Survey map for the whole island demonstrated that new institutions in an "old" country could create similar conditions for the registration of title as existed in supposedly "new" country. In 1863, Torrens sought to build on these achievements when he wrote regarding the Landed Estates Court that "the Legislature having thus achieved all that is really difficult or hazardous in the task, as if paralyzed by the greatness of the effort, have stopped short of thorough law reform, and omitted to provide means by which future dealings may be conducted without inducing fresh accumulations [of encumbrances]."[91] Later, in 1882, he similarly argued that colonial Crown grants were really not that different from other forms of title generated in England and Ireland through such institutions as the Copyhold Commission, Irish Church commissioners, or the courts of equity.

Beneath all these other distinctions, however, operated a more fundamental perception of different colonial and metropolitan market cultures that also brings us back to the analogies with stocks and shares. For opponents of registration, the dangerous idea that land should be traded as easily as stock belonged not to the social and economic conditions of England, but rather to those of its colonies, whose market cultures were naturally disposed to more extreme forms of commoditization. Basing his comments on the direct experience of his son, who had served as head of New Zealand's title registry (yet another example of the role of migration in facilitating the exchange of ideas), the barrister and author of a textbook on property law, Joshua Williams, told the Select Committee on Land Titles and Transfer (1878) that colonial settlers

> buy land not to settle it on their wives and children, as they do in England, but they buy land as a speculation, and sell it again directly there is a little rise in the market. There it is a commodity in which people, as they call it in England, job; they buy it to sell again, and that is all that they do; whereas in England, when a man buys land, it very often is at the end of a successful mercantile career; and he buys a large estate with the intention of making a family.[92]

Liberal land reformers did not so much disagree with Williams's characterization so much as believe that the same universal principles of commerce should apply equally well in England as abroad. "For Liberal Radicals," concluded Rogers, "this very different character of land in new countries embodied the transformation they wished to engineer in Britain: a post-feudal modernity which archaic land laws prevented the Mother Country from reaching."[93]

Both sides of the debate on title registration in England thus drew on the colonial experience of Ireland and Australia to clarify their positions and demonstrate the practicality or impracticality of further legal reforms. In addition, the commodity discourse that shaped the evolution of title reform in Britain had its concomitant in an imagined imperial geography of property regimes defined in relation to their embrace of market culture. As is evident from the fact that commercial analogies had figured in English land debates long before discussions of Irish or Australian reforms, the correlation between commodity and imperial discourses was historically contingent, not fixed, and should therefore not be accepted with the equivalence that their proponents often attributed to them. Both discourses, however, framed land within legal and cultural contexts that increasingly emphasized the importance of supposedly universal principles of market exchange.

As a final point in this discussion of legal, imperial, and market discourse, it is worth mentioning that all these discourses depended on the stability and perceived legitimacy of various legal fictions. The most obvious of these fictions was the principle of *terra nullius* that underpinned the Crown grants in South Australia and that made title to them appear so simple to English conveyancers. As Torrens implicitly recognized in his allusion to the effects of English parliamentary titles and the Irish Landed Estates Court in making possible the equivalent of Crown grants in the form of secure marketable titles, similar acts of fiction sustained the marketability of British landed property. Indeed, the common practice in courts of equity in limiting the root of marketable titles to sixty years—reduced to forty in 1874—represented another legal fiction operating to limit the burdens of retrospective investigation. No one at the time appears to have mentioned the fact that the everyday acceptance in English property contracts of titles with roots as short as thirty years muddied even further their supposed distinctiveness from colonial titles. As Timothy Mitchell has demonstrated, for the creation of Egypt's nineteenth-century colonial property regime, these and similar fictions were in fact essential to the task of making both law and economics appear to consist of axiomatic and universal principles.[94] That they might equally hold true in England was something that many opponents of title registration were unwilling to admit.

THE "TYRANNY OF PARCHMENT DEEDS" AND THE MATTER OF MARKETABILITY

The evolution of title reform depended on, and fed into, larger cultural debates about ideas of commodities, markets, and market cultures. If we return to Wilson's proposals for reforming the practice of the law through the construction of new models of bureaucratic statecraft, however, there is also a clear emphasis on linking ideas of property with very material practices, embedded in countless "little tools of knowledge" similar to those we have already discussed in estate agency practice or property reporting: indices and registers, certificates and forms.[95] The states of marketability implied in abstract analogies to stocks or colonial cultures were premised on new states of materiality that could translate and transport ideas of title through the conduits of legal and commercial practice.

The spatial and material practices connected with land title registration warrant closer examination for three reasons. First, even in the absence of significant numbers of registered titles, these practices established the basic protocols and machinery that would eventually process much greater numbers following the introduction of compulsory registration in 1897. Second, like the discursive construction of title registration, the bureaucratic assemblage of registration reveals many of the subtleties and contingencies through which were communicated larger ideas about the state, property markets, and the law. Third, attention to the materiality of property law reflects a growing recognition of its importance to larger questions of state formation and jurisprudence. As historians and historical sociologists have moved to study the material infrastructure of state formation and governance more closely in recent years, so too have legal scholars and anthropologists interrogated how the law defines and constitutes relations and distinctions between people and things.[96] In considering what a material and spatial history of property law might look like, this final section explores two forms of practice that embodied the transformation of perception associated with title registration: title certificates and property maps.

Nineteenth-century writers and speakers on land transfer reform were fond of evoking medieval conveyancing practice, which was said to have involved the cutting up of a portion of turf using a ceremonial blade, followed by its physical transfer to the new tenant.[97] This "livery of seisin" was gradually replaced, possibly in the seventeenth century, with the use of written documents to provide evidence of title; Alain Pottage has evocatively suggested that both the turf and the parchment shared a similar function as tools for reconstituting the local memory on which the legitimacy and trustworthiness of ownership depended: "The fact of a conveyance lived on, marked in memory by its association with the symbolic object, which also served as the agent of recall."[98] However, trust in writing also entailed an often underappreciated coordination of labor and materials, which in the seventeenth century would have been carried out by scriveners, but which by the late nineteenth century consisted of innumerable law stationers' offices employing both skilled and casual labor in the task of copying legal documents by hand. Given the resources and expense invested in these "law factories," it is no wonder that when Jeremy Bentham first wrote about deeds registration in the 1820s, he saved his greatest excitement for a technology that he thought could revolutionize the labor of conveyancing: manifold writing (i.e., carbon copying).[99]

Land transfer reformers repeatedly stressed the material transformations that would be necessary to bring about registration. When Lord Westbury introduced his transfer of land bill in 1862, for example, he railed against the orthodoxy of hand engrossing, a system he denigrated as a "tyranny of parchment deeds." If printing on paper had been introduced to conveyancing practice earlier, he argued, a great deal of confusion, uncertainty, and expense would have been saved. And the single piece of paper that best captured the essence of title registration was the simple certificate of title. "I want to construct a legal instrument that shall not only enable a man to obtain a statutory title at the present time," stated Westbury,

> but which shall enable him to give from time to time entries of the results of all future transactions and dealings with the land. . . . He can then go into the market with that certificate, and a purchaser may safely deal with the estate, the simple certificate obviating the necessity for the difficult and cumbrous and expensive investigations that are now required.[100]

In the subsequent act, any registered owner was entitled to apply for a certificate of title, and in rules issued in 1864, presentation of a certificate was made mandatory for any transfer of the fee simple.[101] In the same year, Lord Campbell underscored the symbolic importance of certificates when he responded in the House of Lords to criticism of the registry by producing the first registered certificate for the inspection of his fellow members. The certificate, he announced, "is a piece of parchment written on one side only, and is the result of the investigation of an abstract of title extending over 150 sheets."[102] Lord Overstone was so impressed that he requested that the certificate be printed, believing that it "would produce a great effect on the public mind, and would do more than anything else to make the measure intelligible to the public."[103]

The intelligibility of title certificates, however, was never as easily comprehended as reformers wished. Take, for example, Robert Wilson's earlier proposals for land certificates, which suggested many of the same features found in later official certificates. We have already seen how he emphasized the mobility a land certificate afforded to title alongside the protection and reliability that would come from a title register fixed in either local or metropolitan public offices. In 1850, however, when Wilson submitted his plan to the Registration and Conveyancing Commission, the problem of capturing the complexity of ownership on a single form dominated his presentation. Of the more than forty sample forms he appended to his evidence, eighteen consisted of variations to the now renamed "Certificate of Ownership," not including several other draft certificates used to record derivative interests, such as rights of redemption on a mortgage.[104] To critics like J. M. Ludlow, such variation within a single species undermined any claims for the assimilation of real and personal property and prophesied the extinction of the plan in general.[105]

What made such adaptation possible was a careful delineation of space on the certificate into sections pertaining to all the possible circumstances associated with the exchange of real property. The form itself consisted of four pages, and—in a telling concession to the problem of trust in writing—Wilson noted that the document should be made out of "large and strong demy paper . . . so that when folded up into four parts, it would make a respectable substitute for a title deed."[106] The first page identified the nature of the certificate, provided a summary of the charges registered to the land, and indexed it to its equivalent plan and record held at the registry. A written description of the property was found on page 2, to provide a check against forgery similar to the written sums on a bank check. The third page included forms for various actions that could be taken in regard to the property, such as transfers, mortgages, and surrenders. The fourth page contained a simple endorsement, "in order that the certificate, when folded up into four parts, might be kept conveniently and look respectable." The entire form, he concluded, "may be considered as containing the elements of every legal interest, and of every possible dealing with that interest."[107]

Wilson's certificate was a far more complicated instrument than the one sketched out in his initial proposal a decade earlier. As he carefully led the commissioners through each variation on the form, specifying how certificates could be produced for fee simple owners, transferees of a mortgage, owners subject to a mortgage or those subject to a lease, the intricacy of the system revealed itself. "I am sorry to have to explain these things so particularly," he said at one point, "but I am afraid if I do not do so the plan will not be intelligible."[108] Here he was specifically referring to the system of indexing devised to protect certificates holders from fraud, but the commissioners could undoubtedly have been forgiven for attributing the comment to the system as a whole.

Wilson's efforts to mobilize the visibility of a single fictitious fee ownership constantly confronted what his critics saw as an intractable feature of land compared with other property. Ludlow argued that the only reason stock registers were able to appear so mobile was because they ignored the reality of complication, and that as soon as a settlement was needed, holders of stock very often resorted to traditional deeds to secure their interests. "*The instant the stock becomes specific the system ceases to work* and the one adopted is modeled upon the poor old despised one of land titles."[109] Wilson's struggle to contain the specificity of land within the universality of a simple bureaucratic form demonstrated the highly contentious question of trust and authority in the public registration of ownership. Granting all its simplicity and "ubiquitous transferability," could a certificate of ownership be made to embody the authority of parchment deeds?

Not surprisingly, the conservatism of the Land Registry Act of 1862 (25 & 26 Vict., c. 53) assigned a great deal of security to certificates of title by insisting that they mirror a complete record of the information held at the registry. As a result, the certificate proffered in the House of Lords was the equivalent in law to title deeds—all the evidence one would need to prove title—and therefore easily deposited as collateral in equitable loans. That authority made title certificates valuable to bankers but once again restricted the movement of certificates in other cases, such as when an owner sought a second mortgage but could only deposit the certificate with a single lender. In 1875 the rule was reversed and certificates lost their equivalence with deeds, their new status being "not much more than an office copy of a superior kind."[110] Owners could still request a certificate for a fee. Finally, in 1897, under pressure from bankers to return to the gold standard of 1862, the registry once again mandated that any registered transactions require presentation of certificates, such that they would now contain a complete and current record of the ownership status. Certificates could once again be trusted as accurate reflections of the register, though they remained subordinate to it.[111]

The practice of designing, printing, circulating, and holding certificates of title shifted in these ways and according to the need for trust and security among competing users. The authority of certificates, however, also depended on less formal effects. For some, the tyranny of parchment deeds offered a tangible comfort particular to English habits. When Cairns testified before a select committee in 1878, for example, he offered this surprising speculation for why the 1875 act had up to that time failed to significantly increase the number of registered titles:

> In the English mind, although there is a great readiness to complain of title deeds, and of their length and their cumbersomeness, there is at the bottom a most profound respect for title deeds, and that when the supreme moment comes at which a man is told that he must part with all his title deeds, and leave them in a registry office, and accept in lieu a little piece of paper which is to be evidence of his title for the land, the sacrifice is too great for human nature to make, and he declines to make it.[112]

Witnesses to the royal commission set up in 1908 to investigate the working of the Land Transfer Act similarly complained of confusion on the part of the public over the status of certificates. Their handling at the registry did not help matters, since, as the registrar, Charles Fortescue-Brickdale, admitted to the commissioners, it was common practice to refurbish old certificates by appending new transactions under the crossed-out lines of earlier ones. This led to some certificates becoming cluttered with technically irrelevant information—one was said to have held the crossed-out records of as many as three hundred transactions—that could occasionally lead to suspicions of outstanding derivative interests in a title. Conversely, several witnesses compared this treatment of land certificates to the practice of stock and share certificates, both of which were routinely issued as "clean" documents. The dilapidated, flimsy state of many land certificates underscored the fact that, as one witness noted, they did not garner "the same sacred regard as title deeds."[113]

Even attempts to fabricate certificates that *looked* sacred could not satisfy critics. Toward the end of the century, presumably after his promotion to chief registrar, Brickdale ordered a new front cover for title certificates—no doubt in an effort to improve by aesthetic means the fragile authority of this "little piece of paper." Designed by his sister, Eleanor Fortescue-Brickdale, the cover featured a new scrollwork border in pre-Raphaelite style, framed with the coats of arms of six lord chancellors associated with the registry's creation (fig. 18).[114] The cover came under attack by an MP from Fifeshire, who complained in 1900 that property owners would now be forced "to keep an inartistic document" with the names of "irrelevant and extraneous gentlemen . . . to be substituted for the old pigskins to which we were wont to attach so much importance."[115] No amount of effort seem capable of satisfying old English habits. The inertia of old pigskins and habits was a force to be reckoned with and underscores the "mangle of practice" that wove the discursive construction of title registration with its equivalent ontology of legal and administrative objects.[116] Forms have a history, and that history can reveal important aspects of the dynamics often thought to exist independently from them. The transition from parchment deeds to paper certificates—the latter moving with the same security and effortlessness of stocks or shares—was never as straightforward as reformers or legislators might have wished. Trust in the law of property was as much about the feel of a document as it was about its contents or origins.

A similar process was at work in terms of the evidence used to prove identity in real property.[117] Ownership depended on both proof of devolution—based on the theory of legal descent from an original owner—and identity, or the ability to define that which was owned. In private conveyancing, retrospection of title served both purposes in that it embedded proof of ownership in local networks of memory, social expectations, and everyday land use. The narrative embodied in title deeds and abstracted in the conveyance worked in conjunction with various stated and unstated assumptions about local knowledge. The framework of legal contracts, in which the conditions of sale defined the acceptable limits of uncertainty (e.g., where retrospection would end for the purposes of sale), related the ambiguities existing between theories of ownership and local practice.

As a part of this process, the use of narrative descriptions of property worked in conjunction with other forms of evidence, such as parole evidence from local informants or the possessory evidence available from onsite inspection by buyers' agents. Thus, in 1882, when Robert Torrens—the peripatetic advocate of title registration whose journeys to Ireland and South Australia had inspired him to devise his own system of title registration—

FIGURE 18. Land certificate issued to the Great Northern Railway Company, 1902. Reproduced by permission of HM Land Registry. HMLR 128.

celebrated the fact that in England mapped property boundaries could be checked against the durability of hedges and walls, his effort to bolster the cause of cartographic knowledge underscored the practical knowledge of those who maintained and perambulated the local landscape. "The question of identity," writes Alain Pottage, "could be addressed only by someone who was sufficiently familiar with this local sense of place."[118]

The shift that moved "the measure of land" from sites of local calculation to the more abstract domain of a public archive, ordered and maintained according to bureaucratic techniques, did not come suddenly, though it was certainly well under way by the time Torrens made his observation about hedges. Pottage proposes a number of more immediate and longer-term forces. The development and visibility of cartographic technology, for example, had been brought to public notice through such state projects as the Tithe Redemption Commission and the Ordnance Survey, and these served both to identify local misidentification as a problem and to provide a ready solution for improved precision. A host of other social and economic currents—the breakup of landed estates, large-scale urban and suburban estate development, and the standardization and professionalization of land transfer services—also combined to make topographic plans desirable alternatives to traditional modes of proof. Finally, one has to acknowledge even longer-term transformations in ideas of calculation in relation to land, such as those arising from the centuries-long growth of estate mapping and related practices of estate management and calculation.[119]

All these forces served to make cadastral mapping a relatively "normal" function of conveyancing practice by the end of the nineteenth century. This was particularly true for advocates of title registration, for whom a "paper landscape" served as the essential complement to a fictitious registered owner. Proof of devolution and identity were both addressed according to a similar process: "Having reduced the dimensions of juridical ownership to paper, [title registration] effectively did the same with topography."[120] One of the turning points in the association of topography with registration came in 1850, when the Registration and Conveyancing Commission recommended the production of a general public map for the purpose of indexing registered deeds.[121] Interestingly enough, Wilson's plan for the registration of title included a map index, and his description of it foreshadowed the epistemological order that was to come—but not without also hinting at the obstacles faced by a public archive of property. The map, as he explained to the commissioners, "would be nothing more than a Government picture of the country. The Government would say to the public, Here is a certain field having a boundary there, another there, another there. I should think the Government could be trusted to make a picture of that kind."[122]

Trust in the state's "picture of the country" was about as easily achieved as trust in the authority of certificates of ownership. For instance, when the 1862 Transfer of Land Act stipulated that registered titles should have precisely defined boundaries associated with them, one might have thought this a victory for topographical calculation. As it turned out, however, the stringency of the act toward proof of identity became one of its leading flaws. This was because in seeking to define property lines for registration, owners were force to give notice of their intention to each of the adjacent property owners, and, since most boundaries contained at least some degree of uncertainty based on local knowledge and practice, they invariably led to disputes and further legal action required to settle them. Whereas private conveyancing by contract could accommodate the uncertainty of localism by leaving buyers to "[contract] into this network of assumptions, relying on it as the ground of marketability and validity," the 1862 registry could not.[123] The result was a system in which topographic states of marketability could not easily be reconciled with local ones, and so, when the 1870 commission submitted its report, it recommended that boundaries be left undefined, and that the assertions of owners in possession be taken as a reference for future determinations of indefeasibility based on the passage of time.[124]

Ultimately, trust in a paper landscape prevailed over narrative descriptions of property; this change in practice transformed the idea of marketable property, shifting its parameters from private contract and a "lived and remembered medium" to the "calculable and finite surface" of a registered plan.[125] As with the material practice of title certificates, the spatial practice of cadastral mapping traced some of the many intersections between the nineteenth-century property market and the forms of statecraft that tried to regulate it.

In 1925, the registration of title was consolidated with other changes to the laws of real property in a combined Law of Property Act. The act implemented a regime of reformed property law that was, in many respects, unique to any other common law property tradition.[126] In particular, the act drastically simplified the number of legal estates in land to only two: an absolute possession in fee simple (freehold property), and a term of years (leasehold property). All other previously legal interests were shifted to equitable interests, hidden behind a so-called curtain that gave to real property the attributes of legal simplicity similar to personal property. These changes essentially implemented the principles of legal assimilation proposed by Wolstenholme in 1863 and tentatively articulated in the conveyancing reforms of the early 1880s. Furthermore, they contributed to another unique aspect of the British system, which was the structural recognition of two completely different systems of land transfer. On the one hand, solicitors could continue to transfer land through a modern system of simplified private law; on the other hand, the registration of title with the state enabled transfers to take place through a publicly administered bureaucracy. Both systems emerged out of political debates that had framed the need for real property reform in comparison with the ideal model of personal property transactions—specifically, the transfer of stocks and shares; and both systems contributed to a shift in the emphasis of property law toward what one modern interpreter has termed "dynamic security," or the interests of "the market" over the protection afforded to owners.[127] Both the ideas and the practices of British commercial culture gradually reworked a new understanding of marketable land.

The year 1925 thus marked a watershed in the history of property law reform, but it did not in any way mark the end of debate over the place of title registration. For Avner Offer, the act was less of a compromise between a private and a public system than it was a defeat for the latter at the hands of the same entrenched legal monopoly that had long fought to keep conveyancing in the hands of solicitors.[128] The fact that title registration has very gradually come to predominate as the standard mode of transfer does little to assuage this criticism, particularly given that the extension of compulsory registration was still incomplete by the turn of the twenty-first century.

What is often missed in this long history of legal reform, however, is the conceptual break that the bureaucratic calculation of ownership portended. Pottage underscores this point in his discussion of further administrative rules that followed from the 1925 act. If solicitors had succeeded in making the registry an adjunct to private practice, the registry's gradual enforcement of its own rule-based bureaucratic practices had nonetheless redefined what proof of ownership meant and had lodged the marketability of land in an institutional and material regime entirely different from a deeds-based system. "The presuppositions which governed traditional conveyancing techniques," observes Pottage, "which even committed advocates of registration often seemed to take for granted, had been undermined by the discreet consolidation of the bureaucratic process of registration."[129] The marketability of property, long held to be an uncertainty best left to the interpretation of contract, could now be trusted through the institutional and material practices of the state.

CHAPTER FIVE

The Limits of Marketability

A recurring theme of the previous four chapters is that the marketability of property—which is to say, the social, political, cultural, and material conditions under which the disinterested exchange of land and houses was considered normal by those actors involved in the exchange—was rarely taken for granted in the everyday practice of buying and selling property in nineteenth-century Britain. The idea of marketability was instead a driving animus for the various agencies and arrangements that emerged to organize the property market. Marketability offered both a representation of how the exchange of property could or should function and a practical framework for organizing the everyday life of the market. This duality was made meaningful at every site and stage of the transaction process, from auction sales, handbills, catalogs, verbal descriptions, professional etiquette, correspondence, and marketplace settings to newspapers, filing cabinets, forms, law treatises, maps, registries, and titles. Each of these reflected, to varying degrees, a deeper ambivalence—a mixture of celebration, acceptance, and denial—found throughout Victorian culture as to the nature and virtues of a rapidly expanding commercial economy and culture. To conclude with a chapter on the limits of marketability, then, might seem to present a contradiction. If the characteristics of marketability were so often and everywhere contested, what did it mean to speak of further limits? In other words, were not the limits of marketability defined with each new transaction, each attempt to market an estate or house, or every new proposal for arranging property information or reforming property law? Certainly this was the case; but in each of these examples, and in the others discussed so far, the status of property was debated in the context of securing a more marketable condition. This chapter reverses direction to examine instead the work of securing a less marketable condition, viewed from the perspective of the Victorian land preservation movement and its efforts to shelter land from urban and commercial development.

Viewed from the wider lens of late-Victorian land politics, the preservation movement was hardly alone in questioning the limits of an open land market. As discussed in the introduction, the shift in liberal opinion away from earlier calls for free trade in land resulted in a growing sense, from the 1870s onward, that the unearned increment—the value of land that was derived from its naturally and socially endowed qualities, rather than the labor applied to it—justified some degree of public claim. The more radical step of rejecting entirely the legitimacy of a land market came soon after, with calls to nationalize the land outright or for full taxation of unimproved land values. Then, from elsewhere in Britain and its empire, Irish and Scottish and South Asian reformers finally gained footholds in their efforts to have customary tenure rights acknowledged and protected by law—moves that had the similar effect of closing down any further inclination to generalize an English-style property regime. The idea that there should be some accommodation on the part of landowners to a public need for open space was thus well within the horizon of late-Victorian politics, though as we shall see, it was still far from inevitable that any such concessions would emerge.

In still other ways, however, law and public policy had already carved out important precedents for interfering in private property. The late-eighteenth and early-nineteenth century development of highways, canals, and railways are the more obvious examples. In particular, the consolidation of compulsory purchase powers under the Land Clauses Consolidation Act of 1845 (8 & 9 Vict., c. 18) gave much greater leeway for railway corporations to force sales of land in the name of development, albeit with prices that were seen to be more than favorable to landowners.[1] Newly created municipal authorities were also given powers to purchase land for gas and water infrastructure, and the passage of slum-clearance laws in the 1870s permitted the demolition of overcrowded housing in the name of further urban improvement.[2] There were limits on how far such powers could extend, however. This was famously demonstrated in the case of *Bradford v. Pickles*, which was decided by the House of Lords in 1895 and established the modern precedent for protecting a property owners right to act against the public interest (in this case, over a disputed water supply).[3] Both in theory and in practice, the limits of land marketability were widely considered up for debate. Land preservationists thus competed in a crowded field of public opinion.

The land preservation movement began as a campaign to resist the enclosure of urban and metropolitan commons and grew to encompass the protection of rural commons, town gardens, footpaths and open spaces, and other places of natural or historic value.[4] Its legislative achievements included the passing of several acts for the regulation and protection of common land and ancient buildings, as well as the National Trust Act of 1907 (7 Edw. 7, c. 136), which gave statutory authority to an association established twelve years earlier as a private nonprofit corporation. As part of the 1907 legislation, the National Trust, through its board of trustees, was granted the power to declare "that such lands or tenements or such portions thereof as may be specified . . . are proper to be held for the benefit of the nation and . . . shall thereupon be held so . . . and shall be inalienable."[5] The first schedule of the act granted inalienable status to twenty-eight properties, a designation reversible only through the will of Parliament. For all the political and theoretical discussion concerning the appropriate limits of marketable land, no other action in modern British history came closer to creating actually unmarketable property. Today, the National Trust is the largest conservation organization in Europe and the largest private landowner in the United Kingdom, possessing more than six hundred thousand acres of land, most of it deemed inalienable.

Though the principle of inalienability expressed in clause 21 of the National Trust Act passed with little commentary at the time, historians have noted just how unprecedented it was.[6] No other organization aside from the trust's Scottish equivalent (founded in 1931) has been given a comparable power, and the principle of inalienability later proved sound enough to resist even state attempts at compulsory purchase for town planning and improvement schemes. It is tempting, therefore, to think of inalienability and the broader movement of land preservation as a decisive statement against urbanization and the commoditization of property and as a fitting epilogue for a history on the making of a nineteenth-century property market. Tempting, in other words, to agree with Karl Polanyi, who saw such measures as inevitable forms of "social defense" against an unleashing of the land market by earlier Bentham-inspired legal reforms and the "subordination of land to the needs of a swiftly expanding urban population."[7] Where economic ideology swept forward a tide of disinterested and contractual exchange, society pushed back, employing the bulwarks of national heritage and public use to create territorial islands elevated above the turbulent waters of modern capitalism.

In fact, and as we see throughout this book, the boundary between market and nonmarket was rarely so self-evident. The limits to marketability were produced through social and cultural contestations over language, law, and practice that shifted over time, continually reframing where, when, and how the property market was to be found. The principle of inalienability and the larger preservation movement that helped to secure it were the outcomes of a series of particular and often local entanglements of shifting ideas and practices of land marketability. The consolidation of general enclosure practices under the Inclosure Act of 1845 (8 & 9 Vict., c. 118) and the continued growth of London renewed pressure to bring metropolitan commons under development and forced local landowners, commoners, and other interested parties to reconfigure complex tapestries of legal and customary rights. Early reformers tried to resist metropolitan enclosures by using the established principles of common right, but this strategy appeared vulnerable to costly court battles, struggles to define the value of common land, and landowners who were willing to purchase rights to enclose without the approval of Parliament. Organizations like the Commons Preservation Society (CPS) supported the legal defense of commoners against enclosure efforts, but also campaigned for reforms that would allow local authorities the power to purchase and hold rights themselves. Preservation advocates ultimately concluded that a new corporate model would be required, not to defend traditional common rights, but to purchase land rights outright and secure them in perpetuity for the use and benefit of the public. Within the span of a few decades, the campaign for land preservation had shifted from defending traditional common rights to the direct purchase of land rights by public and private corporations. The solution to the problem of reframing common land as marketable was to enter the land market as a purchaser in the public interest, thereby reinforcing a generalized condition of marketability.

THE ENCLOSURE OF METROPOLITAN COMMONS

The loss and degradation of commons and open spaces in Victorian cities was part of a larger, centuries-old process of land enclosure that was nearly complete by the mid-nineteenth century. Whereas earlier phases of enclosure relied on local agreements or private acts of Parliament to convert common land to individual ownership, the final phase of enclosure was marked by the passing of the Inclosure Act, which consolidated a statutory process of parliamentary enclosure administered through a permanent bureaucracy of enclosure commissioners.[8] Appointed commissioners could now investigate applications for enclosure and prepare provisional orders independent of Parliament, subject only to an annual requirement to submit all enclosure proposals to Parliament in a single bill. This made the process both cheaper and less time consuming, but resulted in a perfunctory oversight from parliamentarians that was not seriously challenged until the late 1860s. However, compared with earlier phases of enclosure—when far more of the common land of England was enclosed—the efficiency of the Inclosure Act was expended on a relatively small area of common land, amounting to 570,000 acres enclosed between 1845 and 1914, or around 2 percent of the country's total land area. Nonetheless, this amount represented nearly a quarter of the estimated 2.5 million acres of common land remaining in 1845.[9]

Aside from making enclosure easier, however, the Inclosure Act also set out some minimal considerations for parishioners lacking specific rights of common and for the general public. For example, the act required that any land within fifteen miles of London or within two to four miles of other large towns (depending on their size) be enclosed only with the approval of Parliament. It also blocked any enclosure of village greens and provided that enclosure acts include allotments for the poor and "for the Purposes of Exercise and Recreation for the Inhabitants of the Neighbourhood." The actual amount of land required to be set aside was small, however, up to a maximum of ten acres for a town of ten thousand inhabitants. Finally, the act included a more general consideration that any provisional order to enclose be issued with "regard as well to the Health, Comfort, and Convenience of the Inhabitants of any Cities, Towns, Villages, or populous Places in or near any Parish in which the Land proposed to be inclosed or any Part thereof shall be situate."[10] These relatively small concessions to the public helped set a precedent for a public right of recreation that would later be promoted by commons supporters.

Enclosure in the formal and legal sense was thus a far more efficient process, and one that was marginally more considerate of broader public need; but this applied only in cases where application was made for the full enclosure of common land. In the absence of such schemes, commons were vulnerable to more piecemeal encroachments and degradation from a variety of sanctioned and unsanctioned uses. One example from London that later figured in debates on how to protect commons was the case of Wandsworth Common, located in the southwest of London. In the fall of 1863, the *Times* reported that a group of two hundred petitioners had complained to the lord of the manor, the 5th Earl Spencer, of encroachments by private individuals and the Brighton Railway Company, the latter having cut a line through the middle of the common.[11] "What the railway company has done on a grand scale others imitate in a humbler degree. A heap of decaying cabbage stumps or mud is very carefully protected with a little trench, and a few sticks or bushes. This trench has a marvellous power of widening and deepening; the heaps increase in area, the bushes grow, and in the course of time these rubbish heaps become the eligible site of a detached cowshed."[12] For the same author, wealthier neighbors engaged in similar activity, using the local court leet to approve informal encroachments that gradually transformed into legal ownership: "In the course of time the rich man dies, and his executors advertise and sell as eligible building land which 15 years ago was common land upon which I played a game of cricket."[13] Other complaints, at Wandsworth and elsewhere, included the disfigurement of commons from excessive gravel digging for roads and building, unlawful grazing of cattle, and the presence of travelers and others illegally living and working in the commons. The story of a dead body being pulled from a flooded gravel pit on Wandsworth Common only added to the menacing tone used by many in describing the state of open spaces throughout the city. There was also a class dimension to these complaints, expressed when a later witness compared the state of Wandsworth Common to the more socially upscale and better regulated Clapham Common.[14]

Wandsworth Common came to mind again in 1865, when the same Earl Spencer, as Lord of Wimbledon Manor, submitted a private bill to Parliament aimed at enclosing Wimbledon Common for use as a public park. As he emphasized in later testimony, Spencer was sympathetic to public concern about diminishing access to open spaces but felt that the existing ambiguity with respect to his and others' rights to the common made it difficult to manage the growing number of demands on it. He therefore proposed to transfer most of his rights as lord of the manor to the public, reserving only the income derived from gravel digging and the right to build for himself on a dedicated portion of the common. Seven hundred acres would be set aside and fenced for public use. Both the sale and the maintenance of this land would be paid for through the sale of other outlaying portions of the original common. Spencer estimated that £14,000 would be required for such improvements, and he identified 170 acres from the common that might be profitably sold to cover these costs, depending on the actual realized prices.[15]

Despite the earl's declared intentions of acting for the public good by improving the deteriorating state of the common, many local inhabitants rejected the sale of any portion of the common and the claim on the part of the earl that no common rights other than his own existed with sufficient power to challenge his plans. Local opposition led to calls within the House of Commons for a select committee to examine the legislation as well as the larger issue of "preserving for the public use the Forests, Commons, and Open spaces in and around the metropolis."[16] In seconding the motion to form the committee, Alderman Rose reminded his colleagues of the fate of

Wandsworth Common, wherein "there was not a public right which had not been sacrificed, and contrary as he thought, to law"; the same fate, he implied, might befall Wimbledon and many other other open spaces throughout the city in the absence of any investigation.[17] The select committee thus embraced a broad scope of inquiry, examining more than sixty witnesses and investigating the condition and prospects of open spaces throughout the metropolitan area, including at Banstead Downs, Blackheath, Epping Forest, Epsom, Hampstead Heath, Tooting, Wandsworth, and Wimbledon.

What the committee found in repeated instances was great variety, uncertainty and ambiguity in the laws and customs of common rights that in turn invited very different estimations of marketable value. Generally speaking, the rights associated with common land fell into two categories: those of the lord of the manor and those of the commoners. The lord of the manor owned the rights to the soil, subject to various use rights held by commoners for pasturing animals, or gathering fuel from peat or forests. Commoners could hold rights either by copyhold tenure or by previous grant of freehold (i.e., an enfranchised copyhold).[18] A final category of right was that for customary or prescriptive use rights, based on a documented history of local practice—though, as Alun Howkins has shown, this last category of rights was by far the most neglected in cases of enclosure as well as in the debates on preservation, despite the ongoing importance of such commoning to the lives of many urban and rural inhabitants.[19] In terms of commoners, the challenge came in trying to identify who held various rights and to what degree. In several notable cases, lords of the manor and their stewards insisted on a complete absence of common rights, suggesting that historic rights had either expired through a lack of use, or were held as fictions on the part of locals. This was the case for Wimbledon Common, for example, where the steward for Lord Spencer, William S. Forster, insisted on the full autonomy to inclose as the lord of the manor wished.[20] Elsewhere, when questioned by the committee on his understanding of common rights for the manor in Tooting Graveney, the lord of the manor, William James Thompson, recognized only a single copyhold tenant with rights to the common and dismissed all other claims as "imaginary rights."[21] For landowners like Spencer and Thompson, the absence of widespread common right meant that the market value of common land should therefore reflect prevailing rates for nearby building land. Thus, whereas Thompson had purchased the manorial rights to Tooting Common at auction in 1861 for the small sum of £3,650, he would later claim before the select committee in 1865 that the discovered absence of significant commoners placed the true market value of the Common at nearly ten times that amount. When pressed to explain the serendipitous change in value, Thompson said only, "If certain persons were wrong in their opinion [that the land was a waste with common rights], and if these rights do not exist, and if there are very few commoners, as we believe, it becomes my actual freehold property."[22]

Others disagreed, both on the number and nature of common rights and the implied value of the land that was subject to them. According to Thompson's own solicitor and steward, when the assistant commissioner held a meeting in Tooting to investigate Thompson's enclosure application, "almost every one in the parish" showed up to declare themselves decidedly nonfictional commoners.[23] At Wimbledon, several local tenants also testified before the committee to assert common rights based on their freehold or copyhold properties. William Williams, a solicitor living near Wimbledon, even admitted that he had purchased a cottage with right of common for the explicit purpose of protecting against enclosure, despite him not even having a horse with which to exercise his right of pasture. He felt confident that the right was active all the same. During his testimony, he also revealingly suggested that the best protection for common land may well have been the uncertainty associated with commoner rights: "I look upon [commoner rights] as a great protection to the public," said Williams, ". . . because the very fact of their being unascertained protects the public . . . The fact of the common being maintained in that condition, with undefined and undefinable common rights, has had the effect from time immemorial of preserving it as an open space."[24] "It is the uncertainty as to who are the commoners which keeps it [the common] safe," concurred another Wimbledon resident and barrister, Joseph Burrell. Earlier in his testimony, Burrell warned that "when you ventilate the subject, you will find more rights than anyone imagines; when once you have ascertained the rights, you will find you will have to pay a very large amount of compensation."[25] The complexity of overlapping rights both protected commons and substantially depressed their real market value, and though this was true of common land everywhere (and was in fact one of the driving forces behind the history of enclosure), the ever rising values of urban land made the contrast even more apparent. As the steward for the lord of the manor of Banstead Downs conceded when asked to compare land values in and outside the common, "as a common, the property of the commoners is worth next to nothing."[26]

Who, then, held rights over common land? What relation did one category of right bear to another, and how did different rights to common land shape the market value of open spaces? These questions had definite implications for how one might go about protecting a public right to commons. A principle element of the Wimbledon Common scheme, for example, was that the lord of the manor had the inherent authority as part of his ownership of the common to sell off portions of it in order to help pay for the improvement of the remainder that would be dedicated to the public. This would keep the costs of improvement from burdening the local rates or the purse of the lord. Thomas Alcock, lord of the manor for Banstead, put forth a similar idea in his proposal to convey his rights to a body of trustees who would in turn sell portions of Banstead Downs to help fund improvements.[27] The legal argument for these plans was based on the Statute of Merton (20 Hen. 3, c. 4), a fourteenth-century law that empowered the lord of the manor to enclose portions of the common up to the minimum amount required to support the claims of any commoners.[28] Where commoner rights were seen to be extensive, their claims to a common could be so great as to render little leeway for a lord of the manor to act. Private preservation initiatives thus depended on the presumption of wide latitude for lords of the manor and higher market values for those portions of a common that would be sold to help pay for the rest.

The idea of selling parts of a common to help pay for improvement and preservation was also the principle at work behind the controversial plan put forward by the Metropolitan Board of Works (MBW). The chair of the MBW, John Thwaites, presented the select committee with a resolution passed by the board on May 5, 1865, calling on Parliament to grant it the power to purchase and hold rights of common to open spaces in London.[29] Thwaites was quick to point out, however, that this proposal could work only if common rights were purchased at their nominal value rather than as building land, citing Thompson's purchase of manor rights at Tooting Graveney as an ideal example of the kind of prices that would be required to make a public scheme viable. The MBW resolution for protecting open spaces in London was thus similar to the proposals of more philanthropic-minded landowners, except in how it treated the marketability of common land at the point of initial public purchase. "Commons," Thwaites insisted, "must be looked upon as distinct from freeholds. It is a great mistake to suppose that the lord of the manor is a freeholder pure and simple."[30] This was a particularly pertinent point for the MBW to make, given that it was considering the purchase of Hampstead Heath amid rumors that the lord of the manor, Sir Thomas Maryon Wilson, was willing to bargain only on the basis of full building land valuation.[31]

Ultimately, however, the select committee recommended against the MBW plan and the strategy of purchasing common rights or selling parts of commons in order to fund their protection and maintenance. Instead, the committee sided with the view that the competing interests of commoners and lords would provide sufficient protection against further enclosure: "The existence of those undefined rights [of common] are virtually the safeguard of the public in preventing inclosure."[32] In its two reports, issued in April and June of 1865, the committee also called for the repeal of the Statute of Merton, rejected the Wimbledon enclosure scheme, recommended the extension of metropolitan police authority to commons, and suggested that a board of trustees be established to register and hold any common rights that it might acquire through grants from the Crown or private owners. Finally, the committee grappled with the general question of public rights over common land, and though it conceded the opinion of expert legal witnesses—that there was, in fact, no precedent for a strict legal right to public access beyond rights of way or those rights granted to individuals or a local parish—it found such conclusions "to rest upon no very intelligible principle. Your Committee are at a loss to conceive why, upon general principles, a right of enjoyment which may be acquired by the inhabitants of a small hamlet should be denied to the inhabitants of the Metropolis, or even to the general public." Indeed, the report cited the 1845 Inclosure Act as evidence of an earlier implicit recognition of a general public right and suggested that Parliament might formally declare such a right as the courts had thus far refused to sanction.[33]

Though the legislation that followed the select committee report did not include any direct reference to public rights over commons, it did embody many of the committee's other recommendations and kept alive the debate over how best to frame, value, and protect common spaces. Introduced to the House of Commons in March 1866, the Metropolitan Commons Bill banned the Inclosure Commission from acting within the fifteen-mile limit and created a process whereby the lord of the manor, commoners, or local town authorities could propose plans for regulating commons and paying for improvement through a levy on the local rates. The bill also allowed the MBW to contribute to regulation schemes, but it did not grant the board power to purchase or sell common rights. In defending the government's approach, William Cowper argued that the public could not afford to compensate rights on the same basis as railways, and that "it was an awkward way of preserving a common to begin by selling and alienating the portion most adapted for building purposes."[34] Conservative MPs disagreed, however; one called any plan without provisions to purchase commons "a complete confiscation of the rights of lords of manors" based on the principle that the lord of the manor's right of ownership was all but absolute.[35] Defenders of the bill reiterated the view that, in fact, the legal case was far from self-evident, and that public compensation for unproven rights would be misguided. Though this question was again left unresolved, the bill passed into law in August (Metropolitan Commons Act, 29 & 30 Vict., c. 122), the first legislation aimed explicitly at checking any further enclosure of common land in the region of London.

THE DEFENSE OF COMMON RIGHTS

It was left to forces outside Parliament to resolve the status of commoner rights. Only weeks after the select committee had tabled its final report in 1865, one of the committee's members, George Shaw Lefevre (later Lord Eversley), hosted a meeting to organize a movement on behalf of the preservation of commons. The CPS was born, as M. J. D. Roberts has shown, with a decidedly Liberal-leaning makeup. In addition to Lefevre, five other MPs from the Select Committee on Open Spaces (Metropolis) were founding members, and others came from a sampling of Gladstonian radical, metropolitan, and Whig liberals.[36] As an organization, the CPS quickly established its willingness to campaign aggressively against any further enclosure of common land. For example, though the society had decided against a direct campaign to repeal the Statute of Merton, it did call for the ban on any further enclosure that became the basis of the Metropolitan Commons Act of 1866, and it advocated contesting enclosure efforts wherever the means to do so could be found.[37] One of its earliest and most notable opportunities occurred just weeks before the introduction of the Metropolitan Commons Bill, when trustees acting on behalf of John William Spencer, the second Earl Brownlow, ordered the erection of iron fences on Berkhamsted Common, Hertfordshire. Seeking an opportunity to test the claims of commoner rights in court, Lefevre reached out to Augustus Smith, a local estate owner who arranged for a nighttime raid on the fences by a gang of 120 hired laborers, who in turn torn down the fence and induced the trustees to charge Smith with trespass.[38] Smith countersued, and the court decided his case in 1870, vindicating the rights of Smith and other commoners and contributing to a carefully planned strategy on the part of the CPS to shift legal opinion on the legitimacy of commoner rights in cases of present-day enclosures. As Ben Cowell has argued, these direct-action tactics evoked an older tradition of fence breaking on common land with a decidedly modern aim, to establish a legal public right to common land.[39]

The battle over Berkhamsted Common was one of a number of early court cases that convinced the CPS of the soundness of its legal approach.[40] So long as local residents could be found with verifiable rights of common and the resources to endure a potentially lengthy court battle, the CPS could target courts of equity to contest any effort on the part of a lord of the manor to encroach on open spaces. Having asserted the legal rights of commoners and demonstrated that those rights were sufficient to block any further enclosure of commons, there would be no need to consider purchasing the rights of manor lords or selling portions of a common. The passage of the Metropolitan Commons Act provoked many manor lords to test what they believed were absolute property rights; within a relatively short time, the CPS was advising legal challenges at Berkhamsted Common, Hampstead Heath, Plumstead Common, Bostall Heath, Wimbledon Common, and Epping Forest. In the first published report of its activities, the CPS acknowledged the difficulty of pursuing so many court battles, but insisted that the end result would be preferable to purchasing commons: "Onerous as is the prosecution of these suits in the way in which alone they can be successful, yet the questions involved in them are vital to the cause which this Society advocates, the only alternative being to purchase at a cost which is beyond any existing resources the whole of the common land which they are designed to protect from inclosure."[41] The protection of public access to common land, in other words, hinged on limiting any concession to its marketability.

However successful commons advocates were in their early courtroom victories, the rights-based strategy of preservation faced two longer-term hurdles. The first was the willingness of other public bodies—the MBW in particular—to negotiate the purchase of common land. At the end of 1866, despite having been stonewalled by the select committee on open spaces and Parliament, the MBW authorized the reopening of talks with Sir Thomas Wilson for the purchase of Hampstead Heath. These discussions were delayed by litigation over the status of commoner rights but resumed in 1869 after Wilson died, his manor rights having passed to the inheritors of his estate. A year later, the MBW agreed to purchase Hampstead Heath for £45,000, plus legal costs—a sum admittedly lower than the £1 million to £2 million originally proposed by Wilson's agents, but significant all the same.[42] Nonetheless, any amount was bound to upset those set against the purchase of rights. The CPS had long been critical of the MBW and its proposals, with one anonymous pamphlet in 1867 flatly stating that "much of the Commons has been filched from the people bit by bit, and the Metropolitan Board of Works are ambitious to be the last trespassers."[43] Another memorandum published the same year as the Hampstead Heath agreement adopted a less provocative but equally firm stance. "It has never been shown to be necessary to pay away large sums of money in the compensation of rights," argued the Society, "and a body having the custody of public moneys, such as the Metropolitan Board of Works, in proposing to do so [in the Hampstead Heath case], undertakes a grave responsibility towards its ratepayers" and "prejudice[s] the interests of the public in others."[44] The fear in this case was that a strategy of purchasing common rights would very likely increase the value of those rights and put added pressure on public authorities with fewer resources than, say, railways companies, whose compensation for acquired land was generally pegged to market values.

The MBW was not the only authority to undermine the CPS's position, however, and the practice of other public authorities purchasing common rights eventually pushed the CPS toward greater accommodation. An important turning point was the 1876 Commons Act (39 & 40 Vict., c. 56), passed under the second Disraeli government, which gave urban sanitary authorities the power to buy commoner rights using local funds. Similar powers were also employed by the Corporation of London, which had been a close ally of the CPS and had led the legal challenge against the lords of the manor in the Epping Forest dispute. The corporation won its suit in 1874, securing a definitive legal vindication for commoner rights; but it went ahead with plans to purchase the manor rights to approximately three thousand acres of forest, largely on the grounds that doing so would give it greater authority to manage the land.[45] Though the CPS had worked closely with the City in its suit—Robert Hunter, the CPS's solicitor, advised the corporation's lawyers throughout the process—Lefevre would later maintain that the additional purchase of manor rights had been entirely unnecessary.[46] This did not stop the CPS and another open space organization, the Kyrle Society, from returning to the corporation in 1879 to request its assistance in purchasing the manor rights to Burnham Beeches (fig. 19), a common located outside London that had been advertised for sale by auction and marketed as a site ripe for enclosure and development. Under the powers of the 1876 act, the City agreed to purchase the common rights for £6,000.[47] These purchases marked an important shift in attitude toward the preservation of common land, one that would contribute directly to the later conceptualization of the National Trust.

The second challenge to the strategy of defending commoner rights as a means of protecting open spaces was the risk that commoners might themselves be willing to negotiate with lords of the manor. When the 1865 select committee first asked George Cooke (an enclosure commissioner) about this possibility, he admitted that the purchase of all outstanding commoner rights would have effectively enclosed a common through private means, without any opportunity for public input.[48] Cooke initially thought the practice was rare, but in later testimony he conceded that he likely did

FIGURE 19. Transparency photograph of Burnham Beeches, taken from a collection of slides used by the National Trust in its campaigns, undated. Reproduced by permission of The Museum of English Rural Life, University of Reading. SR OSS PH5/E/2.

not know of its true extent. In any case, he argued, curbing the practice represented an unreasonable restriction on the individual right to deal with one's own property.[49] As it turned out, the tactic was far more widespread, though the difficulty in settling with commoners often precipitated stronger approaches, like the erection of fenced enclosures. This was the case at Berkhamsted Common, for example, where the fence torn down by laborers in 1866 had been build out of frustration at the slow pace of negotiations with local commoners.

Another infamous case was that of Banstead Common.[50] Recall that in 1865, Thomas Alcock had unsuccessfully attempted to enclose the common for the purpose of entrusting the land to the public. Alcock died the following year, before he was able to implement a regulation order under the Metropolitan Commons Act. The manor rights passed to his inheritors and were subsequently sold, in 1873, to Sir John Hartopp. Rather than favor preservation, Hartopp endeavored to enclose and develop the land. Unlike Alcock, however, who confessed to the 1865 select committee that he had no specific knowledge of the commoner rights tied to the land, Hartopp was better informed. In 1866, the London and Brighton Railway had surveyed the common and produced a detailed list of rights holders to facilitate the acquisition of land under the Land Clauses Consolidation Act of 1845. The protection of ambiguity that had made earlier enclosure so contested and difficult was now lost, and Hartopp used the information gained from the survey to target the remaining commoners, investing thousands of pounds to buy up rights from twenty-seven local residents. "One by one the Commoners were so dealt with," Lefevre later wrote. "To some the temptation offered was the enfranchisement of their copyholds free of charge; to others, money payments. . . . In none of the other Commons cases had there been such an assiduous and well-devised effort to clear away the rights of Commoners, with the object of converting the wastes into private property."[51] In 1876, Hartopp began construction on the common but was stopped by a concerted effort from the remaining commoners, who brought a suit that was settled thirteen years later, in 1889. Four years after that, Banstead Common was placed under a regulation scheme of the Metropolitan Commons Act. Prior to this settlement and throughout the period of contested court battles, its status underscored the practical limitations of a strategy based on the defense of traditional rights alone, and pushed advocates for commons and other open spaces in new directions and toward new frameworks for understanding and securing a public right of access to common land.

Indeed, by the early 1880s, the land preservation movement had evolved and diversified in more ways than one. For one thing, the CPS was no longer the lone organization working on behalf of open space preservation. The founding of the Kyrle Society (1876), the Society for the Preservation of Ancient Buildings (1877), and the National Footpaths Preservation Society (1884) brought new attention to the protection of such places as town gardens, burial grounds, historical monuments, and rights of way.[52] Moreover, for the Kyrle Society in particular, open spaces were reframed as being important not just for middle-class urbanites but for the working classes as well, and for reasons beyond supplementing livelihoods (as had been the argument for allotment, or community, gardens). Octavia Hill,[53] sister of Miranda, the Kyrle Society's founder, penned several essays on the importance of commons and other open spaces for working- and lower-middle-class families and argued that the preservation of commons should look beyond their "money value" to the benefit of such spaces for the nation as a whole. Hill also argued against allowing manor lords to purchase the rights of commoners, which she saw as the shortsighted sacrifice of "our common birthright in the soil."[54] It was Hill's own experience in trying to purchase fields in the London district of Swiss Cottage that introduced her to the work of the CPS and further convinced her of the need to broaden the campaign to include land not held in common.[55] Through her work and the work of others, preservation thus evolved to integrate the new inflections of a broader political franchise and more collectivist reform politics.

PRESERVATION BY PURCHASE

The limitations inherent in mounting repeated individual legal challenges to enclosure, the complications of multiple authorities and organizations involved in preservation, the pressure of private negotiations undermining protection schemes, and the evolution of attitudes toward commons and open spaces all came together in the idea for a new organization that Robert Hunter first proposed in the summer of 1884. The idea came in response to a request from Octavia Hill, for help in finding a means to preserve Sayes Court, the private estate of seventeenth-century author John Evelyn, located in southeast London.[56] Evelyn's descendants wished to secure the estate in perpetuity for the public, but after researching a number of legal options, Hunter wrote to say that no convenient method existed.[57] He speculated, however, that some new association—perhaps incorporated under the Charitable Trustees Incorporation Act or the Joint Stock Companies Act—might satisfy the need for a body that could receive gifts of land and buildings without contravening laws designed to limit the possession by charities of property held in perpetuity. Hill approved of the suggestion but concluded that there would not be time to implement it for Sayes Court.[58]

Convinced that the idea warranted further thought, Hunter revised his initial thoughts and presented them the following autumn at the annual congress of the National Association for the Promotion of Social Science, held in Birmingham.[59] Hunter opened his remarks by highlighting how quickly public opinion had shifted from generally supporting enclosure to appreciating the health and recreational benefits of common land for a nation of city dwellers. He cautioned, however, that "in a country like England, where land is a limited commodity and has a high value, there will be an ever present danger that space which should be left for the public enjoyment may be reduced into private ownership, or turned to some money-getting purpose." Whereas some enclosure pressures, such as from parliamentary schemes or from railways and other utility corporations, had in place effective mechanisms for public scrutiny by organizations like the CPS, Hunter admitted that the strategy of contesting private enclosure through court battles was unsustainable. It was costly; it was time consuming; it required "considerable public spirit" and the willingness of local commoners to fight long legal battles; and, finally, it depended on funding third-party suits for which it was difficult to mobilize public support. On the last point, Hunter also warned that "certain somewhat musty provisions of English law" made it difficult to rely on third-parties suits as a long-term legal strategy.[60] The solution was obvious: protect common land by acquiring common rights, thereby eliminating the need for courts and intermediaries.

At this point, Hunter invoked an image that underscored the ongoing threat to commons while simultaneously offering a new avenue for acquiring common rights and a subtle reframing of the very mechanism that had once been viewed with such trepidation: the disinterested marketplace. "A Common is never in greater danger than when it is put up for sale," he observed, "while, at the same time, an exceptional opportunity of preserving it is offered."[61] The danger he imagined came from the severing of the social bonds represented by an established manor lord and the speculative forces unleashed in the mind of an alien investor. The specific investor Hunter had in mind was Sir John Hartropp—"a Yorkshire Baronet, who had no family connection with the place [Banstead Common]"—and the dynamic Hunter described is worth quoting in full:

> When a Manor has been in a family for generations the owner is usually slow to disturb the status quo. He probably has old acquaintances amongst the farmers and cottagers, and knows how they would be affected by an attack upon their Common rights. He is not therefore very likely to inclose the Common to any serious extent. But, if the Manor is sold, the purchaser is probably told by the Auctioneer in express terms, or by implication, that he can make money out of the Common. On this supposition he, perhaps, pays a larger price for the Manor. He has no knowledge of the place and its customs or of his neighbours. Perhaps his lawyer gives some off-hand statement as to his rights which leads him to despise those of his neighbours, or perhaps he does not consult his lawyer at all, but merely jumps to the conclusion that there is too much unproductive land, and that he cannot be blamed for turning some of it to account. These are the conditions under which large inclosures are made, or the high-handed action with regard to Common rights which paves the way for inclosure taken.[62]

Such an outcome could be avoided, Hunter argued, if the manor was instead sold to an entity willing to see the "money value" of commons as simply a means to a greater end, one with the preservation of open space for the public as its primary goal, a company like the CPS. As a voluntary association, however, the CPS had no corporate legal identity permitting it to enter the market and acquire common rights, and so a new company was needed.

"The central idea is that of a Land Company," Hunter concluded, "formed, not for the promotion of thrift or the spread of political principles, and not primarily for profit, but with a view to the protection of the public interests in the open spaces of the country."[63] This company would be empowered to purchase common rights as well as rights to other open spaces, such as town gardens and burial grounds; and it could fund its programs by leasing or selling copyhold property within the manor, as well as sporting or pasturage rights, or by charging fees for the use of public gardens. It could also cooperate with local authorities, using its powers to assist in the purchase of schemes like Burnham Beeches, which had been complicated by limits on the rights of local authorities to possess both land and common rights. Rather than extinguish commoner rights, as earlier purchase schemes had envisioned, Hunter's land company would retain them as part of the manor, reestablishing the abovementioned status quo, by entwining the relations and customs of local commoners with the needs and values of the public as lord of the manor. Through the agency of a joint-stock company, Hunter's proposal thus transcended the division that had evolved up to that point between the right of commons and the purchase of them, using the market itself as a resource to establish, on behalf of the public, the limits of marketability. Finding the association with market practice still too close, Hill wrote to Hunter and suggested he call it a trust rather than a company; "you will do better, I believe to bring forward its benevolent than its commercial character."[64]

It would be another decade before Hunter's proposal was realized, but in the meantime both he and Hill experimented with other versions of the same concept. One opportunity to test the idea came with the passage of the City of London Parochial Charities Act (46 & 47 Vict., c. 36) in 1883, which directed the Charity Commission to consolidate thousands of locally endowed charities into ecclesiastical and general funds, the latter to be put toward education, libraries, social improvement schemes, and open spaces.[65] Thanks to successful lobbying from open space advocates, the commissioners agreed to contribute funds to a number of individual projects—most notably, the purchase of the Parliament Hill estate adjacent to Hampstead Heath. In 1887 and 1888, however, a delegation from the Kyrle Society, the CPS, and the Metropolitan Public Gardens Association lobbied for more and called on the commissioners to create a permanent fund administered by an existing "trust body."[66] Hill suggested that lawyers for the Kyrle Society investigate as one possibility the Society for Improving the Condition of the Labouring Classes (SICLC), an association founded in 1844 and given a royal charter in 1850. A memo subsequently sent to Hunter noted that, under its charter, the SICLC could buy, sell, exchange, or hold property in perpetuity (i.e., notwithstanding legislation against mortmain) so long as its activities were in support of its stated purposes.[67] Since petitioning the Charity Commission required an entity capable of holding land, the authors of the memo recommended that members of the three societies join the SICLC to steer it in support of open space preservation. The commissioners ultimately chose a fund for polytechnic education over a permanent fund for open spaces,[68] but the possibility of using a royal charter to empower a new trust was considered again, five years later, during a meeting held at the CPS offices to discuss the formation of the National Trust for Places of Historic Interest or Natural Beauty.

At that meeting, held on November 16, 1893, and in the resolutions that led up to the incorporation of the National Trust in January 1895, the founding members established a basic framework that borrowed from Hunter's earlier proposal and anticipated the principles later articulated in the National Trust Act of 1907. Overlapping membership certainly played a role in this.[69] Both Hunter and Hill sat on the executive committee of the new organization, along with another prominent founding member, Canon Hardwicke Rawnsley,[70] who was well known for his preservation efforts in England's northern Lake District. George Shaw Lefevre was also a member of the provisional council, which was presided over by the Duke of Westminster, both having long been involved in land preservation work. The trust would be created under the Joint Stock Companies Act as a nonprofit and "devised to act as general trustee for all property intended for the use and enjoyment of the nation at large."[71] It would complement existing preservation organizations with its capacity to hold property in perpetuity and provide an alternative vehicle for preservation in cases where local authorities were limited either by law or by other local considerations. Should the trust prove to be a success and accumulate significant property, more extensive powers would be sought at a later date, through a royal charter or special act of Parliament. And though it was clear that the group initially anticipated receiving land as gifts from wealthier benefactors, it was also expected that the purchase of land on a voluntary or even compulsory basis would follow once funds could be secured. Participants at the meeting in 1893 were quoted in the *Times*: "We see no reason why for public purposes a bit of beautiful scenery should not be the subject of a forced sale under equitable conditions just as much as a bit of ugly country for a railway." As if to underscore the point, on the same day, the *Daily News* reminded its readers of several recent sales of notable landmarks, such as the peak of Mount Snowdon and Lodore Falls near lake Derwentwater, both of which might have been saved from the market had the trust existed.[72]

Unlike the CPS, which began as an explicitly metropolitan concern, the National Trust, as its title implied, emphasized the importance of preservation for linking all of England to a shared national history and identity. The theme of national identity was certainly present in Hill's earlier writing on open spaces, but the connection became even more pronounced during the late-nineteenth and early-twentieth century, when, as Paul Readman has argued, the politics of land and the sensibilities of the urban middle class imbued particular landscapes with historical, political, and cultural meaning.[73] The Lake District would forever be known as the home of Wordsworth, the New Forest as a last remnant of England before the yoke of enclosure. For Rawnsley, the underdevelopment of institutions like the National Trust was seen as an international disgrace. "The idea of a Stonehenge or a Glastonbury Abbey in private hands would seem to be impossible in Brittany," he wrote; in a short time, he warned, "the object lessons which might, in years to come, have made men feel that it was good to have been English-born will have passed away."[74]

More pragmatically, a sense of national purpose also offered a way for the National Trust to differentiate itself from the work of local authorities. Despite changes to the law that had given local authorities the right to purchase commons and other lands for recreation, and despite a history of cooperation between both sites, the trust continued to view local government with some degree of ambivalence.[75] As Rawnsley put it, the founders of the trust felt "that local authorities with the best intentions will sometimes ruthlessly destroy for present gain what future generations would have held most dear. They realise that these local authorities, unless very wisely guided, are at other times tempted, in zeal for so-called *improvements*, to so improve the places committed to their care as to do irretrievable damage to the charm of object or site and scene."[76] This perception was informed by the experience of the CPS, which had not always found local authorities willing to cooperate in the protection of open spaces. Rawnsley, Hunter and Hill, for example, had all been active in the 1878–79 campaign to stop the city of Manchester from developing Thirlmere Lake as a water supply. Similarly, in 1892, the society fought the city of Birmingham's attempt to purchase the rights to fifty square miles of land in South Wales for a town water project. As Lefevre warned in 1910, "It is a mistake to suppose that such [town] bodies are wholly to be trusted in questions affecting public interests and rights over Commons and Open Spaces. . . . Experience shows that they often cannot resist the temptation to acquire for town improvements land which they think can be obtained at a low price."[77] One of the rationales for the trust, as articulated in its first published report, was that it would be uniquely able to take a broader, national perspective in protecting land from spoliation.

Another difference between the National Trust and earlier preservation campaigns was the greater emphasis on holding land in perpetuity. The trust's first report reassured members that no land or buildings given to or purchased by the trust "for the benefit of the nation" would ever "be sold, or otherwise dealt with in a manner inconsistent with the objects of the Trust," even in the case of bankruptcy or dissolution. "Thus," the report concluded, "the Association affords ample security for the permanent safe custody of all property committed to its care."[78] To be sure, the preservation of commons had always carried an implied sense of perpetuity, but the active mechanism in that case was the actual exercise of commoner rights, not the trustworthiness of a particular organization. The need to reassure potential property donors or investors that the objectives of the trust would be honored made sense in light of the institution's youthful status, but so too did it make sense in light of the risk that the accusation of shortsightedness thrown on local authorities might just as easily fall on the trust. What was to stop future members of the trust from taking advantage of commercial self-interest to undermine the nation's patrimony? How, in other words, could the limits of marketable property set by the trust be themselves trusted? In the short term—but only in the short term—the relatively small amount of property held by the trust rendered the question all but moot.

In fact, nearly a decade passed before the trust could report any substantial acquisitions. The first of these was the Brandelhow Park estate, consisting of 108 acres on the shores of Derwentwater, purchased for £6,500 in 1902 by a private agreement with the owner (see fig. 20). This purchase brought the total area of land held by the association to around 160 acres by the time of its tenth annual report in 1905.[79] The real breakthrough came in the following year with purchase of another estate in the Lake District and an extensive tract of common land in Surrey. The acquisition of Gowbarrow Fell (and the Aira Force waterfall), on the banks of Ullswater, was several years in the making and had begun in 1903, when Rawnsley was approached by the owner to see if the trust would be interested in purchasing 2,000 acres of land at a price of £30 per acre. The trust ultimately settled for 740 acres and a price of £12,000, and launched a public appeal in the summer of 1904.[80] Anticipating that objections might be raised over the purchase of a property that was not in any imminent danger of being placed on the open market, the trust cautioned that the very announcement of the campaign had brought neighboring properties to auction, with the risk that further properties might soon be purchased "for purely speculative purposes."[81]

FIGURE 20. Photograph of Derwentwater, in the Lake District, with the Brandlehow estate outlined at center right. Published in *The National Trust for Places of Historic Interest or Natural Beauty: Report for the Year 1900–1901*. Courtesy of the National Trust Archives.

Furthermore, the trust argued that securing the estate offered a unique opportunity to "nationalise the English Lake District" along similar lines to national parks recently established in Canada and the United States.[82] In the fall of 1905, the trust was approached again—this time by a local committee of the CPS, the Hindhead Preservation Committee—with an offer to purchase the manor rights to another 750 acres of common land in the Surrey hills. Hindhead Commons, in the manor of Witley, had been purchased at auction on behalf of the local committee, which now wished to transfer it to the National Trust.[83] The executive committee quickly agreed to the sale, and the next annual report noted that Hindhead Commons represented the most significant act of commons preservation since those of the City of London in Epping Forest and Burnham Beeches.[84] These two purchases, at Ullswater and Hindhead, represented by far the largest acquisitions of property undertaken up to that point.

Thus, by the beginning of 1906, the National Trust had increased its landed property tenfold, and with this success came renewed pressure to secure the stronger legal position promised at its inception. The annual report for that year hinted that "it will probably be necessary ere long to reconstitute the trust on a more authoritative basis, and to give it larger powers of management in relation to the lands it holds for the public."[85] Then, at the annual general meeting in June, the membership approved a motion to seek out an extension of powers. Hunter and the trust's solicitors were tasked with preparing a study of legal options.[86] Unfortunately, no copy of this report survives in the trust's present archives, nor was the report discussed in the minutes of the executive committee, council, or annual meetings. It is difficult, therefore, to know how the principle of inalienability discussed at the opening of this chapter evolved in the course of drafting the bill that become the National Trust Act of 1907. What is clear is how important the trust considered this clause, along with the other powers to create bylaws that were included in the legislation. In the first report published after the trust was reconstituted as a statutory corporation, the power to declare its possessions inalienable was taken to be the clearest "recognition of the Trust by Parliament as the national custodian in perpetuity of beautiful and interesting places" and would "vitally [strengthen] its position."[87]

That strength would come from the inherent trustworthiness implied in a designation that placed property of national importance beyond the limit of any further commercial exchange. Members of the trust and the public at large could rest certain that gifts and purchases of land would be protected from any further encroachments, developments, or desecrations. The principle of inalienability would not seriously be tested until after World War II, when the National Trust faced pressure from local authorities to revise designations of inalienable status for the purpose of local development. In 1968, a parliamentary joint select committee decided against the trust on a case involving a highway development in Plymouth, but the government later sided with the trust in reaffirming the principle of inalienability for a plot of land on the outskirts of Bath.[88] In 1907, however, the idea of inalienability epitomized the very particular encounters between advocates of landscape preservation, landowners, commoners, and the state that had shaped the commons and open spaces movement over the course of the previous four decades. If there was any irony in the passing of the act and the consolidation of the National Trust's position as guardian of the nation's sacred lands, it was in the acceptance that the best way to protect land from the logic of the market might well be to buy it. How fitting, then, that in 1925 the trust learned of another estate that would soon be on the market, and quickly set about raising funds to purchase it. The appeal for public support drew the signatures of the current prime minister, James Ramsay MacDonald, and a previous one, Asquith (now Earl of Oxford), and succeeded in raising more than £45,000 for 1,600 acres of land and manor rights to one of the most famous battlegrounds of the land preservation movement: Berkhamsted Common, the very same site where laborers once ripped down fences in the dark of night to defend against the sale of the people's land.[89] It remains, to the present day, owned and inalienable, a property of the National Trust.

The passing of the National Trust Act established new limits to the marketability of property in nineteenth- and early-twentieth-century Britain. To say that certain lands and open spaces in England and Wales had always been set apart from routine commercial exchange, or that the long history of enclosure entailed a process of gradually whittling away this endowment at a cost to some and a profit to others, is not the same as saying that there was such a thing as inalienable land—at least, not in the sense used by the land preservation movement at the turn of the twentieth century. The notion of inalienability expressed by witnesses to the 1865 select committee, who spoke of an older protection afforded to common land by the ambiguity of widely known but vaguely recorded customary rights, rested on assumptions, institutions, and practices that were significantly transformed over the following decades through legal and social contests over open spaces in and around London and throughout the rest of England. The land preservation movement reconfigured the meaning of inalienable land, and the limits of marketability, in a number of ways. First, it articulated a broader understanding of public right and access to commons, open spaces, and other sites of natural or historical importance—a public right premised on the benefits to the urban lower and middle classes of recreation, nature, health, and national identity. Second, it established new institutions—like the CPS, the National Trust, and various local committees—to advocate for, defend, acquire, and manage land and buildings on behalf of the public. Finally, land preservationists promoted the principle of holding these lands in perpetuity and removing them from the short-term calculations of urban development, market speculation, or other special interests.

The earmarking of special land as inalienable in this way made sense only in a world of normalized alienability, much like the earmarking of special monies that proliferated amid the growing nationalization of legal tender in the late nineteenth- and early twentieth-century United States.[90] The very same processes that drove the expansion and urbanization of the property market—suburban growth, demographic transformation, industrialization, and railway development—increased speculative and development pressure on the remaining common land and open space of England and Wales and provided new opportunities to contest the legal rights to and value of those spaces to the public. Rather than see the history of marketable and unmarketable property in opposition to each other, it is more useful to see them as entwined in the larger process of property marketization. The task of embedding land in new social relations of trust, custom, or national identity would be solved not by resisting the market, but by embracing it.

CONCLUSION

"Property for the Million"

> At present the land is held by the few, but a day is coming when it will belong to the many.
>
> —"Land and House Property for the Million," *Estates Chronicle*, April 15, 1898

In 1898, when the *Estates Chronicle* offered this prediction, one could easily have confused its message with the multitude of others sounding from the chorus of land reformers, an ensemble convinced that the solution to Britain's social, political, and economic troubles would come from reconnecting people and land. The key question was how. For the *Chronicle*, the answer would not come from "recourse to revolutionary expedients" like land taxation or nationalization.[1] All that was needed was patience and a steady faith in the power of the market. The "transfer of titles by purchase in equitable and just regard of the rights of those actually in possession" would gradually erode the steep banks of Britain's landed monopoly, leveling through natural means what others threatened to carry out with shovels and pickaxes.[2] Property "for the million" would come through "the operation of agencies already recognized as sound in principle"—agencies, not coincidentally, like the *Chronicle* itself and the information it could provide on the trends and fluctuations of the real property market.[3] The magazine considered house property and the recent move toward greater working- and middle-class homeownership to be a particularly "distinctive" sign of "a higher and advancing civilization."[4] The purchase of a house should not be taken lightly, however; it required careful attention and patience on the part of any would-be buyer. On the one hand, there was the general movement of house sales, which constituted a "stream, the rise and fall and trend of which" the *Chronicle* would "take proper cognizance" through reported sales at the London Auction Mart or through provincial reports of sales.[5] On the other hand, not all property should be treated alike. As the journal advised its readers in another column: "In the purchase of property, as in almost every other commodity, there are varying degrees of excellence, and property generally may be placed in three classes, viz., first, second, and third," depending on the local context.[6] Attention to individual variability was as important as the measurement of general tendencies. To effect the transfer of property from the few to the many, the *Estates Chronicle* thus instructed its readers to reimagine property as a commodity shaped, valued, sorted, and circulated through and by the kind of institutions and agencies discussed in this book.

However evocative it was to conceive of the property market as a fluid stream of transactions, what this metaphor missed was the very particular channels through which it was created and circulated. What I have called the marketization of property entailed a variety of historically contingent practices that collectively assembled and mobilized the legitimacy of real property in a commodity state. It was not a case of the *Estates Chronicle* being right or wrong in its depiction of the property market, so much as one of understanding where, when, and how its idea of commoditized property gained particular purchase. Though the *Chronicle* itself survived for just a single year before shifting its attention to the business of insurance, its belief in the property market as a measurable flow of commodity transactions was widely shared by others in the field of property journalism; by auctioneers, estate agents, and other mediators of property transaction; by those in the elite of the profession who designed and built tailored marketplaces for the sale of property; and by those who sought to reform the law of property to more closely approximate the penultimate commodities of British Victorian capitalism. In these times and places, through these networks, and for these people, the property market emerged as a visible and enduring field of economic exchange—a field with sufficient coherence to be offered as a tool for remaking a landed society into a society of landowners.

Like all markets, the development of the property market was decidedly uneven and contested. Asymmetries of information and the concentration of power, access, and resources repeatedly limited attempts at creating universal knowledge of property transactions. There would be no single marketplace for property, no comprehensive registry of sale histories, no universally agreed-on definition of value in the auction room or elsewhere. Though all markets face similar challenges, the market for real property was particularly limited through the inherent immobility of land, its fixed and locally variable nature. Immobility was only part of the issue, however. Of greater importance to the contingent development of the property market was the many-layered meaning of land in social, political, and cultural terms, the network of associations that fixed rights to land *in place* within a given community. The problem of marketability—the conditions under which a community would accept the commercial exchange of land—informed every discussion of how to reform, improve, or limit the buying and selling of property. Professional practice, notions of calculability, or the bureaucratic management of titles all required new answers to the persistent problem of how to conceive of land as a saleable commodity. This was particularly true for those who strove to protect certain special land from the market, such as the advocates for land preservation discussed in chapter 5. Both the statutory protection of commons and the declaration of National Trust lands as inalienable placed new limits on the exchange of certain properties designated of unique value to the public or the nation. These actions entailed a reconfiguration—rather than preservation in the strict sense of older understandings—of what market and nonmarket value would mean going forward, based on new understandings of public access, urban recreation, historical associations or natural beauty. The configuration of marketization thus emerged out of efforts to wrestle with the problem of marketability across a range of temporal and social spaces.

This history of the property market began in the eighteenth century, with the rise of new commercial practices like auction sales and the processes of urbanization and industrialization that diversified both the types of property for sale and the people willing to invest in them. It ends in the early twentieth century, in the years before and after World War I, when new patterns of land use, ownership, and exchange once more reconfigured the marketization of land and houses. Many of these patterns—such as the consolidation of legal ownership to leasehold and freehold tenure, or the growth of broadly communal forms of property ownership (as registered commons or National Trust properties) will already be familiar from discussions elsewhere in this book. At the risk of oversimplifying, however, many others can be clustered around the single greatest development of the twentieth century in terms of landownership, the expansion of homeownership and its associated impacts on land use, tenure, financing, public policy, and social attitudes. The numbers alone tell of a major social transformation in the organization of house property. In 1914, the tenurial landscape consisted overwhelmingly of rented accommodation, with homeowners making up, at best, 10 percent of the total. Then, during the interwar period, landlordism declined from 80 to 56 percent, offset by growth in owner occupation from 10 to 25 percent and in public housing from 1 to 10 percent. In 1981, the private rental market amounted to 8.5 percent of all housing, compared to over 60 percent in private ownership.[7] By 2003, following the retreat from public housing under the Thatcher government and the continuation of that policy under the Labour governments of Tony Blair, private homeownership peaked at 70.9 percent of all housing tenure—a figure higher even than in the United States.[8] The shift from one regime of property marketability to another was conditioned upon a new society of homeowners.

Before 1918, most working- and middle-class families in Britain lived in privately rented accommodation, consisting of higher density urban tenements (predominant in Scotland) or terrace houses, or in lower-density suburban detached or semidetached villas.[9] The house-hunting adventures discussed in chapter 2 grew out of this prevailing experience, albeit one that offered a great variety of quality, depending on one's ability to pay. Attitudes toward homeownership likewise reflected the prevalence of renting. Though the middle-class home gained increasing importance as a "sacred institution" of moral worth, that value was not necessarily premised on a particular form of tenure.[10] The Victorian market was diverse enough to accommodate a range of needs and social classes. Homeownership was generally restricted to more affluent districts of towns or to regions with particularly strong traditions of ownership, such as the mining communities of South Wales or the northeast of England. In Leicester, for example, rates of ownership could range from 4 to 15 percent across poorer and wealthier neighborhoods. Similarly, in the northeastern city of Durham, the rate of ownership in the mid-nineteenth century was around 17 percent, well above the overall rate for England and Wales. In Leeds, on the other hand, the rate was 4 percent.[11]

The basis for owner-occupied expansion was already evident in the late-Victorian and early Edwardian periods, with the continued growth of low-density suburbs and the development of new models for financing home purchases. Railways, of the kind that sent Edward Ryde tramping throughout the southwest of London, led the way in opening up hinterlands for housing development, followed by horse and electric tramways, underground lines, and buses.[12] By 1907, middle-class commuters could reach districts as far as twelve to thirty miles from the center of London; and in rapidly growing suburban hamlets like Ilford and Golders Green, ambitious developers and estate agents—the latter heeding professional advice to set up shop within convenient sight of commuter rail stations—marketed villas to trainloads of white-collar workers escaping the metropolis. "Edwardian Ilford," wrote one historian, "with its large estates of small houses built for sale, its parks and its sports clubs, its sponsored railway stations and its rows of busy shops, was in many ways the precursor of the host of new suburbs that were to flash into life around London in the twenties and thirties."[13] This urban exodus was sponsored in part through a variety of new forms of house finance. From the mid-nineteenth century, permanent building and freehold land societies offered a means for many middle-class families to acquire mortgage lending. As Luke Samy has demonstrated, building society financing was not always limited only to middle-class households. In the decades following its founding in 1884, for instance, the Co-operative Permanent Building Society specifically targeted its lending for nonspeculative, owner-occupied housing. More than half of its loans between 1884 and 1913 were for amounts under £300, mostly for single freehold properties with broadly working-class specifications.[14] Meanwhile, in Ilford, both local builders and the local authority offered subsidized loans and reduced cash payments to help middle-class families buy newly constructed homes.[15] When the above-mentioned *Estates Chronicle* launched its support for land nationalization via the private market, it also included a glowing review of the home-purchase program initiated by the British Homes Assurance Corporation, which tied purchase certificates to life and mortgage insurance policies.

The first World War and its aftermath added to and accelerated these earlier trends in transportation, migration, construction and financing. By far the single most important event during the war was the direct intervention of the state in regulating the property market through rent control. To be sure, the collapse of property values after 1905, the competition between real property and other forms of domestic and foreign investment, and the erosion of any political constituency willing to defend the private rental market all played a role in undermining the pillars of nineteenth-century landlordism.[16] Under the pressure of war conditions and rent strikes, however, the government in 1915 dealt the final blow in the form of the Increase of Rent and Mortgage Interest (War Restrictions) Act (5 & 6 Geo. 5, c. 97), which froze rent and mortgage rates to pre-war levels. Rent controls remained in varying form throughout the interwar period and had the effect of stifling any significant reinvestment in rental housing. Beyond rent control, the war also transformed public attitudes and expectations toward housing, with "Homes fit for Heroes" being the promise given to all returning soldiers and their families.[17] Even before the end of the war, in the spring of 1918, the Tudor Walters report on postwar local government housing set a standard for low-density, semidetached or short-terraced working-class homes that would become a major influence on both public and private postwar construction. Immediately after the war, the Housing, Town Planning, &c. Act of 1919 (9 & 10 Geo. 5, c. 35)—also known as the Addison Act—and a Housing (Additional

Powers) Act (9 & 10 Geo. 5, c. 99) mandated surveys for public housing needs by local authorities, fixed rents based on rent-controlled prices rather than building costs, and provided grants in aid for private builders of working-class homes.[18] This legislation was further enhanced by housing acts passed in the early 1920s. The result was an interwar boom in housing construction: four million homes in all, three million built for private ownership and one million for local authority public housing. By 1938 one-third of the housing stock in England and Wales had been constructed during the interwar period, and mostly on new suburban land, increasing the total urban area by 26 percent.[19]

The interwar expansion of homeownership was more than just a change in quantity; it also transformed the organization of estate development and home construction, marketing, finance, and ideology. Unlike the development of estates based on leasehold agreements that had been so common in the nineteenth century, many new housing estates were purchased as freehold property and later sold as freehold tenures. Thus, while the registration of titles made limited inroads in terms of the total area of land in England and Wales, the single largest category of transaction was for home properties; by the end of the century, approximately two-thirds of registered titles were held by private homeowners.[20] As in the nineteenth century, small builders remained prevalent in the home construction industry, but larger firms, likes New Ideal Homesteads or Henry Boot & Sons (the latter became the first publicly traded housing company in 1919), also emerged as significant builders of private and public housing.[21] The corporatization of construction was paralleled in the world of finance, and led by the growth of building societies. In 1920, 1,271 societies operated in Britain with combined assets of £87 million; by 1940 the assets of the remaining 952 societies amounted to £756 million, nearly a ninefold increase in mortgage lending.[22] Both builders and lenders also sought to market homes using easier lending terms and consumer messaging that framed home investment as a lifestyle and leisure activity. "Easy term" purchasing involving deposits as low as 5 percent, thirty-year mortgages terms, and tax deductions for interest payments made home investment available to a wider spectrum of families. Aspirations for homeownership were similarly cultivated through home exhibitions (the first Daily Mail Ideal Home Exhibition opened in 1908), relaxed sales techniques, and new genres of lifestyle magazines (*Homes and Gardens*, 1919, *Ideal Home*, 1920, *Good Housekeeping*, 1922, and *Woman & Home* 1926), many targeting women as the ideal consumer of a new domestic modernity.[23] Owning a home was now viewed as synonymous with full participation in middle-class respectability and liberal democracy. It was from this period that the phrase "property-owning democracy" first entered the political lexicon, only to be reused later in the century by the likes of Anthony Eden, Harold Macmillan, and, of course, Margaret Thatcher.[24]

A society so deeply organized around the principle of homeownership and all its attendant benefits, challenges, and contradictions was clearly very different from that which existed in the previous century. It should not be surprising, then, that continuity in respect to the marketization of property in Britain was accompanied by significant changes. Notwithstanding the *Times'* announcement that the property market had suddenly become a recognizable feature of daily life in the postwar period, the notion that it had achieved a new level of public recognition was not unwarranted, and annual reports on the state of the market were reported in the general and specialist press throughout the interwar period. At the same time, the sudden growth of homeownership underscored the further diversification of the market into retail and commercial investment sectors, among others. Though it is impossible to know what proportion of estate agency licenses were issued for the retail sector alone, the fact that the number of these licenses finally surpassed those for auctioneers in 1938 suggests a shift in professional practice as well, with auction sales declining relative to the sudden emergence of privately contracted retail home sales based on more uniform transactions. Behind each of these developments, new networks of association configured the times and spaces in which land and houses might be conceived of as alienable commodities. Accepted by some as a self-evident feature of everyday economic life, the property market was still, in the end, an achievement of particular, historically contingent practice.

Suburban development and town planning also brought renewed conflict over the limits of alienability, as the National Trust would discover during the second half of the twentieth century, when central and local governments repeatedly attempted to modify trust property through compulsory purchase orders. With the further development of town planning after 1945, the trust had adopted a practice of consulting with government authorities over development issues prior to making declarations of inalienability. In 1957, however, it briefly abandoned this practice when it declared inalienable the gift of a 291-acre farm outside Plymouth, despite having been informed by the government of plans to expand the width of a highway running over the property. The issue finally came before a joint select committee of Parliament in 1968 and was decided against the trust, much to the consternation of its executive leadership and members. Subsequent challenges, however, reaffirmed the principle of inalienability and its importance to the preservation of trust holdings. One of these cases was deliberated during the very same period as the select committee hearing in 1968, involving the Bath City Council's attempt to compulsorily acquire land held by the trust on the outskirts of the city, which the council had hoped to develop first as a housing estate and then as a fairground. In 1969 the minister of Housing and Local Government negated the council's order before the trust could invoke a parliamentary process.[25] The politics of preservation and planning clashed further in the 1960s and 1970s, with each instance involving public and private negotiations over when and where to draw the line between sacred and marketable land.

The dominant regime of homeownership that came to define twentieth-century Britain and that has often been taken to be a uniquely powerful tradition of Anglo-American culture has recently become more closely comparable with other parts of the world. From its peak in 2003, homeownership in Britain has fallen to a thirty-year low, the result of high home prices, rising economic inequality, and the global financial crisis of 2008.[26] At the same time, homeownership in Europe and elsewhere has continued to climb after World War Two. In 2012, for example, the average rate in the European Union was just under 71 percent, though this masked a pattern of enormous variation between high rates in the east and south of Europe and relatively more modest rates in countries like Germany (53.2 percent) and Austria (57.5 percent). Nevertheless, debate has now come to focus on the contagious ideological hegemony of homeownership and the belief that rates will inevitably converge around the structural features of global capitalism.[27]

It may be tempting to believe that, by the early twentieth century, the question of land's marketability had been definitively answered through the creation of a durable set of institutions and a firm societal commitment to the legitimacy and limits of property's marketability. Tempting, in other words, to accept that Britons—and perhaps even others living in fully marketized property regimes[28]—can finally free themselves from the question of whether land can or should indeed be sold, untethered from all its social, cultural, and political roots. This study has argued that a better approach would be to ask instead where, when, and how the commoditization of real estate takes place within and through these deeply rooted associations.[29] Moreover, one need only look to the most recent property crisis—which called into question the viability of Britain's property-owning democracy—to see that the creation of the property market remains an unsettled and evolving process.[30]

ACKNOWLEDGMENTS

This book would not have been possible without the support of a great many people and institutions. Financial support was made possible through the Social Sciences and Humanities Research Council of Canada; the University of California, Berkeley; the National Endowment for the Humanities (award FT61608–14); and the dean of Faculty and Department of History at Mount Holyoke College.

Historians would have nothing to write about if not for the hard work and generosity of librarians and archivists. My thanks go to the staff at the Bodleian Library, British Library, Cambridge University Library, Cambridgeshire Archives, Croydon Archives, East Sussex Record Office, London Metropolitan Archives, Museum of English Rural Life, National Archives, Parliamentary Archives, Royal Institution of Chartered Surveyors, Surrey History Centre, and Westminster Archives. The National Trust Records and Archives was being relocated when I attempted to visit, but Daz Beatson stepped in to send copies of materials by post and by email. Thanks also to Peter Mayer and staff at the HM Land Registry, who provided access to materials held there. At Mount Holyoke College, Bryan Goodwin and the staff at Library and Information Technology Services (LITS) make possible the idea of a research liberal arts college.

Over the years that it took to finish this book, I have had the privilege of presenting and discussing ideas with fellow presenters and attendees at the North American Conference on British Studies, Northeast Conference on British Studies, Canadian Historical Association, Business History Conference, Rethinking Modern British Studies Conference, Urban History Association, and five College History Seminar. Special thanks goes to participants of the Histories of Land, Economy, and Power Conference, held at Harvard University in 2012. I wish to thank Cambridge University Press for permission to reprint material previously published in "The London Auction Mart and the Marketability of Real Estate in England, 1808–1864," *Journal of British Studies* 55, no. 2 (April 2016), 295–319.

I am grateful for the unwavering support provided during the past six years by my colleagues in the Mount Holyoke Department of History: Dan Czitrom, Kavita Datla, Christine DeLucia, Harold Garrett-Goodyear, Lowell Gudmundson, Holly Hanson, Jeremy King, Fred McGuinness, Lynda Morgan, Mary Renda, Bob Schwartz, Holly Sharac, and Lan Wu. I am a better teacher, writer, and thinker thanks to the intelligent and indomitable students of Mount Holyoke College. Colleagues in other institutions have responded to drafts, discussed ideas, and offered suggestions. I thank all of them, even those whose names I forget to include here: Tim Alborn, Susanna Barrows, John Beckett, Elizabeth Blackmar, Tim Butler, Ben Cowell, Richard Dennis, Nadia Durbach, Margot Finn, Richard Harris, Alun Howkins, Jon Lawrence, David Lieberman, Peter Mandler, Richard Munton, Avner Offer, Chris Otter, Hugh Prince, Edmund Rogers, Brian Short, F. M. L. Thompson, Michael Turner, and Cathy Waters.

This book might feel substantial to the touch, but it is really made of sweat, tears, time, and friendship. James Vernon—advisor, critic, booster, mentor, and friend—has been there from the very beginning. Only he could have foreseen and nurtured the potential in this project. Paul Groth and Tom Laqueur offered me their encouragement, guidance, and wisdom. I am grateful for the encouragement and company of so many friends and fellow travelers: David Anixter, Susanne Cowan, Grahame Foreman, Aidan Forth, Simon Grote, Jo Guldi, Daniel Immerwahr, Andrew Keating, Riyad Koya, Radhika Natarajan, Joshua Rosenthal, Caroline Shaw, Chris Shaw, Alex Toledano, Daniel Ussishkin, Jonathan Weier, Nicholas Hoover Wilson, and Alexia Yates. I would not have conquered this figurative mountain were it not for Penny Ismay, who first suggested the metaphor and then insisted that we should climb together.

I could not have asked for a more enthusiastic and supportive team of professionals than those who work for the University of Chicago Press. Editors invariably come late to a book project, but Priya Nelson made up for lost time with her unwavering support, encouragement, and guidance. Dylan Joseph Montanari, Kristen Raddatz, Susan Karani, Tamara Ghattas, and many others helped shepherd the manuscript to publication. Johanna Rosenbohm worked tirelessly and patiently to transform a very rough manuscript into a polished one. David Robertson compiled the index. My thanks also to the three anonymous reviewers whose careful and critical reading pushed me to make a better book.

Finally, I wish to thank my family. My mother, sister, and stepfamily have never stopped cheering for me. My wife, Catherine Corson, lovingly endured too many days with a husband distracted with worry or lost in thought. Lastly, I dedicate this book to Geoffrey and Alex, for reminding me each and every day of the things that matter most in my life.

NOTES

Page numbers for *Estates Gazette* and *Property Market Review* citations refer to the bound holdings of the British Library, arranged in volumes by year.

INTRODUCTION

1. Jane Austen, *Persuasion*, ed. D. W. Harding (London: Penguin Classics, 1985), 45.

2. Austen, *Persuasion*, 53–54.

3. An Old Hand, "The Property Market," *Estates Gazette*, January 5, 1895, 19. See also F. M. L. Thompson, "The Land Market in the Nineteenth Century," *Oxford Economic Papers*, n.s., 9, no. 3 (October 1957): 285–308.

4. Laurent Feller and Chris Wickham, eds., *Le marché de la terre au Moyen Âge* (Rome: École Française de Rome, 2005); P. D. A. Harvey, ed., *The Peasant Land Market in Medieval England* (Oxford: Clarendon Press, 1984); B. J. P. Van Bavel, "The Organization and Rise of Land and Lease Markets in Northwestern Europe and Italy, c. 1000–1800," *Continuity and Change* 23, 1 (2008): 13–53; and Rory Naismith, "The Land Market and Anglo-Saxon Society," *Historical Research* 89, no. 243 (2016): 19–41.

5. An Old Hand, "The Property Market."

6. Matthew Cragoe and Paul Readman, *The Land Question in Britain, 1750–1950* (New York: Palgrave Macmillan, 2010); Roy Douglas, *Land, People & Politics: A History of the Land Question in the United Kingdom, 1878–1952* (New York: St. Martin's Press, 1976).

7. F. M. L. Thompson, "Cobden, Free Trade in Land, and the Road to the Abbey National," in *Rethinking Nineteenth-Century Liberalism: Richard Cobden Bicentenary Essays*, ed. Anthony Howe and Simon Morgan (Aldershot, UK: Ashgate, 2006), 68–79. For more on how land politics was voiced by different political constituencies, see Paul Readman, *Land and Nation in England: Patriotism, National Identity, and the Politics of Land, 1880–1914* (Woodbridge, UK: Royal Historical Society, 2008); and Ian Packer, *Lloyd George, Liberalism and the Land: The Land Issue and Party Politics in England, 1906–1914* (Rochester, NY: Royal Historical Society, 2001).

8. James Beal, *Free Trade in Land: An Inquiry into the Social and Commercial Influence of the Laws of Succession and the System of Entails*, [. . .] (London: Edward Truelove, 1855), viii.

9. *Times*, April 18, 1870.

10. F. F. Arbuthnot, "Free Trade in Land; or, A Few Remarks on the English Land Question in the Shape of an Address to the Wonerish District Liberal Association," John Johnson Collection, Bodleian Library, "Land and People," box 9.

11. Alfred Russel Wallace, *Land Nationalisation, Its Necessity and Its Aims: Being a Comparison of the System of Landlord and Tenant with That of Occupying Ownership in Their Influence on the Well-Being of the People*, 2nd ed. (London: Trübner, 1882), vii.

12. Henry George, *Progress and Poverty: An Inquiry into the Cause of Industrial Depressions and of Increase of Want with Increase of Wealth: The Remedy* (London: C. K. Paul, 1881), 365.

13. F. W. Newman, "Land as National Property," LNS pamphlet 7, 1, John Johnson Collection, Bodleian Library, "Land and People," box 3.

14. Newman, "Land as National Property," 7.

15. John Ruskin, *Time and Tide, by Weare and Tyne: Twenty-Five Letters to a Working Man of Sunderland on the Laws of Work* (London: Smith, Elder, 1872), 161.

16. Alfred Russel Wallace, "Land Nationalisation Manifesto," John Johnson Collection, Bodleian Library, "Land and People," box 3.

17. Clive Dewey, "Images of the Village Community: A Study in Anglo-Indian Ideology," *Modern Asian Studies* 6, no. 3 (1972): 291–328; and Dewey, "Celtic Agrarian Legislation and the Celtic Revival: Historicist Implications of Gladstone's Irish and Scottish Land Acts 1870–1886," *Past and Present*, no. 64 (August 1974): 30–70.

18. "About Land," John Johnson Collection, Bodleian Library, "Land and People," box 10. However, the Old Testament was hardly clear on the matter, as the United Committee for the Taxation of Land Values demonstrated with its own pamphlet, located in the same box and titled "The Bible and the Land Question." That author gestured to Leviticus 25:23: "The land shall not be sold for ever; for the land is mine; for ye are strangers and sojourners with me."

19. Edward Bristow, "The Liberty and Property Defence League and Individualism," *Historical Journal* 18, no. 4 (December 1, 1975): 761–89. See also Paul Readman, "Conservatives and the Politics of Land: Lord Winchilsea's National Agricultural Union, 1893–1901," *English Historical Review* 121, no. 490 (February 1, 2006): 25–69.

20. "Land," LPDL pamphlet (1885), and J. C. Spence, "Property in Land, a Defence of Individual Ownership," LPDL pamphlet (1892), John Johnson Collection, Bodleian Library, "Land and People," box 5.

21. Karl Polanyi, *The Great Transformation: The Political and Economic Origins of Our Time* (Boston: Beacon Press, 2001), 187; and John Lie, "Embedding Polanyi's Market Society," *Sociological Perspectives* 34, no. 2 (Summer 1991): 219–35. See also Chris Hann and Keith Hart, eds., *Market and Society: The Great Transformation Today* (Cambridge: Cambridge University Press, 2009).

22. Thompson, "The Land Market in the Nineteenth Century," 286.

23. On the importance of seeing representation and practice as co-constituted, see Timothy Mitchell, *Rule of Experts: Egypt, Techno-Politics, Modernity* (Berkeley: University of California Press, 2002), 5–6.

24. See Michel Callon, ed., *The Laws of the Markets*, Sociological Review Monographs (Oxford: Blackwell, 1997); Callon and Fabian Muniesa, "Peripheral Vision: Economic Markets as Calculative Collective Devices," *Organization Studies* 26, no. 8 (August 1, 2005): 1229–50; Koray Çalışkan and Callon, "Economization, Part 1: Shifting Attention from the Economy towards Processes of Economization," *Economy and Society* 38, no. 3 (August 2009): 369–98; and Çalışkan and Callon, "Economization, Part 2: A Research Programme for the Study of Markets," *Economy and Society* 39, no. 1 (April 2010): 1–32. For a closely related theory of socially constructed markets, see Pierre Bourdieu, *The Social Structures of the Economy* (Malden, MA: Polity, 2005).

25. The literature on landownership and development is vast. For some important surveys, see J. V. Beckett, "Landownership and Estate Management," in *The Agrarian History of England and Wales*, ed. G. E. Mingay, vol. 6, 1750–1850 (Cambridge: Cambridge University Press, 1989), 545–640; Beckett, *The Aristocracy in England: 1660–1914* (Oxford: Basil Blackwell, 1986); and David Cannadine, *Lords and Landlords: The Aristocracy and the Towns, 1774–1967* (Leicester, UK: Leicester University Press, 1980). Some effort to explore the intermediaries of the market has recently been carried out by James Anderson; see Anderson, "The Operation of the Early Nineteenth-Century Property Market," *Construction History* 24 (January 1, 2009): 63–81.

26. Kenneth Lipartito, "Reassembling the Economic: New Departures in Historical Materialism," *American Historical Review* 121, no. 1 (February 1, 2016), 113; and William H. Sewell, "A Strange Career: The Historical Study of Economic Life," *History and Theory* 49, no. 4 (December 2010), 146. For some examples of recent work in this quickly expanding subfield, see Sven Beckert, *Empire of Cotton: A Global History*, reprint ed. (New York: Vintage, 2015); Jonathan Levy, *Freaks of Fortune: The Emerging World of Capitalism and Risk in America* (Cambridge, MA: Harvard University Press, 2012); Julia C. Ott, *When Wall Street Met Main Street: The Quest for an Investors' Democracy* (Cambridge, MA: Harvard University Press, 2011); and Stephen Mihm, *A Nation of Counterfeiters: Capitalists, Con Men, and the Making of the United States* (Cambridge, MA: Harvard University Press, 2007).

27. See Jean-Christophe Agnew, "Anonymous History," in *Capitalism Takes Command: The Social Transformation of Nineteenth-Century America*, ed. Michael Zakim and Gary J. Kornblith (Chicago: University of Chicago Press, 2012), 277–84; and Kenneth Lipartito, "Connecting the Cultural and the Material in Business History," *Enterprise & Society* 14, no. 4 (December 2, 2013): 686–704. On materiality in British history, see Frank Trentmann, "Materiality in the Future of History: Things, Practices, and Politics," *Journal of British Studies* 48, no. 2 (April 2009): 282–307.

28. See, for example, Paul Johnson, *Making the Market: Victorian Origins of Corporate Capitalism* (Cambridge: Cambridge University Press, 2010), 12–21.

29. For some important recent examples, see Johnson, *Making the Market*; Frank Trentmann, *Free Trade Nation: Commerce, Consumption, and Civil Society* (Oxford: Oxford University Press, 2008); James Taylor, *Creating Capitalism: Joint-Stock Enterprise in*

British Politics and Culture, 1800–1870 (London: Royal Historical Society, 2006); Natasha Glaisyer, *The Culture of Commerce in England, 1660–1720* (London: Royal Historical Society, 2006); Margot C. Finn, *The Character of Credit* (Cambridge: Cambridge University Press, 2003); Timothy L. Alborn, *Conceiving Companies: Joint-Stock Politics in Victorian England*, 1st ed. (New York: Routledge, 1998); and G. R. Searle, *Morality and the Market in Victorian Britain* (Oxford: Clarendon Press, 1998).

30. The patterns of development varied enormously, but for useful examples, see Cannadine, *Lords and Landlords*; H. J. Dyos, *Victorian Suburb: A Study of the Growth of Camberwell* (Leicester, UK: Leicester University Press, 1961); and Richard Dennis, *English Industrial Cities of the Nineteenth Century: A Social Geography* (Cambridge: Cambridge University Press, 1984).

31. Joshua Williams, *Principles of the Law of Real Property: Intended as a First Book for the Use of Students in Conveyancing*, ed. Thomas Cyprian Williams (London, 1892), 1–32.

32. See V. T. H. Delany, "English and Irish Land Law-Some Contrasts," *American Journal of Comparative Law* 5, no. 3 (1956): 471–77; and Richard Rodger, *The Transformation of Edinburgh: Land, Property and Trust in the Nineteenth Century* (Cambridge: Cambridge University Press, 2001). For a useful explanation of Scottish property law, see *Report of the Royal Commission on the Housing of the Industrial Population of Scotland, Rural and Urban*, c. 8731 (1917), 226–29.

33. Historians once termed this transformation of eighteenth-century consumer culture a "consumer revolution." Neil McKendrick, John Brewer and J. H. Plumb, *The Birth of a Consumer Society: The Commercialization of Eighteenth-Century England* (Bloomington: Indiana University Press, 1982), 1. See also John Brewer and Roy Porter, eds., *Consumption and the World of Goods* (New York: Routledge, 1993); Brewer, *The Pleasures of the Imagination: English Culture in the Eighteenth Century* (New York: Farrar Straus Giroux, 1997); and Maxine Berg and Helen Clifford, *Consumers and Luxury: Consumer Culture in Europe 1650–1850* (Manchester University Press, 1999). More recently, Frank Trentmann has taken a broader temporal and geographical perspective. See *Empire of Things: How We Became a World of Consumers from the Fifteenth Century to the Twenty-First* (New York: Penguin, 2017).

34. James Vernon, *Distant Strangers: How Britain Became Modern* (Berkeley: University of California Press, 2014).

35. Avner Offer, "Farm Tenure and Land Values in England, C. 1750–1950," *Economic History Review*, 2nd ser., 44, no. 1 (February 1991): 12.

36. On the former view, see Robert C. Allen, "The Price of Freehold Land and the Interest Rate in the Seventeenth and Eighteenth Centuries," *Economic History Review*, 2nd ser., 41, no. 1 (February 1988): 33–50; and Christopher Clay, "The Price of Freehold Land in the Later Seventeenth and Eighteenth Centuries," *Economic History Review*, 2nd ser., 27, no. 2 (May 1974): 173–89. The view that landed estates represented a distinct market—one separated from other land sales by considerations of family and status—belongs most notably to John Habakkuk, "English Landownership, 1680–1740," *Economic History Review* 10, no. 1 (February 1940): 2–17; and Habakkuk, *Marriage, Debt, and the Estates System*. See also J. V. Beckett, "The Pattern of Landownership in England and Wales, 1660–1880," *Economic History Review*, 2nd ser., 37, no. 1 (February 1984): 1–22.

37. See Gregory Clark, "Land Hunger: Land as a Commodity and as a Status Good, England, 1500–1910," *Explorations in Economic History* 35, no. 1 (January 1998): 59–82; and Offer, "Farm Tenure and Land Values."

38. Cited in Beckett, "Landownership and Estate Management."

39. See John C. Weaver, *The Great Land Rush and the Making of the Modern World, 1650–1900* (Montreal: McGill-Queen's University Press, 2006); Patrick McAuslan, "Land Law and the Making of the British Empire," in *Modern Studies in Property Law*, vol. 4, ed. Elizabeth Cooke (Portland, OR: Hart Publishing, 2007), 239–62; Peter Karsten, *Between Law and Custom: "High" and "Low" Legal Cultures in the Lands of the British Diaspora—The United States, Canada, Australia, and New Zealand, 1600–1900* (Cambridge: Cambridge University Press, 2008); and Ranajit Guha, *A Rule of Property for Bengal: An Essay on the Idea of Permanent Settlement* (Durham, NC: Duke University Press, 1996).

40. On the general importance of empire to British cultural formation, see Andrew Thompson, *The Empire Strikes Back? The Impact of Imperialism on Britain from the Mid-Nineteenth Century* (London: Pearson, 2005).

41. Andrew Sartori, *Liberalism in Empire: An Alternative History*, Berkeley Series in British Studies, vol. 8 (Berkeley: University of California Press, 2014).

42. See Alexia Yates, *Selling Paris: Property and Commercial Culture in the Fin-de-Siècle Capital* (Cambridge, MA: Harvard University Press, 2015), 12–14.

43. Yates, 85–95.

CHAPTER ONE

1. Don Slater and Fran Tonkiss, *Market Society: Markets and Modern Social Theory* (Cambridge: Polity, 2001), 7–10; Karl Polanyi, *The Great Transformation: The Political and Economic Origins of Our Time* (Boston: Beacon Press, 2001); and Jean-Christophe Agnew, *Worlds Apart: The Market and the Theater in Anglo-American Thought, 1550–1750* (Cambridge: Cambridge University Press, 1988).

2. Emma Rothschild, *Economic Sentiments: Adam Smith, Condorcet, and the Enlightenment* (Cambridge, MA: Harvard University Press, 2002).

3. See, for example, E. P. Thompson, *Customs in Common: Studies in Traditional Popular Culture* (New York: New Press, 1991).

4. Neil McKendrick, John Brewer, and J. H. Plumb, *The Birth of a Consumer Society: The Commercialization of Eighteenth-Century England* (Bloomington: Indiana University Press, 1982), 20–29. See also Brian Learmount, *A History of the Auction* (Iver, UK: Barnard & Learmount, 1985).

5. James Vernon, *Distant Strangers: How Britain Became Modern* (Berkeley: University of California Press, 2014), 101. See also Joel Mokyr, *The Enlightened Economy: An Economic History of Britain 1700–1850* (New Haven, CT: Yale University Press, 2012), 368–91.

6. David Kynaston, *The City of London: A World of Its Own 1815–1890*, vol. 1 (London: Chatto & Windus, 1994), 10; and Ranald C. Michie, *The London Stock Exchange: A History* (Oxford: Oxford University Press, 2001). On the general transformation of institutional space, see Michael Reed, "The Transformation of Urban Space, 1700–1840," in

The Cambridge Urban History of Britain, vol. 2, ed. Peter Clark (Cambridge: Cambridge University Press, 2000), 615–40.

7. Brian William Cowan, *The Social Life of Coffee: The Emergence of the British Coffeehouse* (New Haven, CT: Yale University Press, 2005), 134.

8. Learmount, *A History of the Auction*, 30–31. East India Company goods were required by statute to be sold by auction.

9. Peter Ash, "The First Auctioneer: Origins of Sales by Auction of Real Property," *Estates Gazette: Centenary Supplement*, May 3, 1958, 35–37. See also Ralph Cassady, *Auctions and Auctioneering* (Berkeley: University of California Press, 1967); and Robin Myers, "Sale by Auction: The Rise of Auctioneering Exemplified in the Firm of Christopher Cock, the Langfords, and Henry, John and George Robins (c. 1720–1847)," in *Sale and Distribution of Books from 1700*, ed. Robin Myers and Michael Harris (Oxford: Oxford Polytechnic Press 1982), 126–63.

10. F. M. L. Thompson has suggested that development of sales by order of the Chancery Court was another important condition for the development of auction sales. Thompson, *Chartered Surveyors: The Growth of a Profession* (London: Routledge & K. Paul, 1968), 47. Bankruptcy and estate sales were routinely noted in advertisements for auctions at the turn of the century.

11. Satomi Ohashi, "The Auction Duty Act of 1777: The Beginning of Institutionalisation of Auctions in Britain," in *Auctions, Agents and Dealers: The Mechanisms of the Art Market 1660–1830*, ed. Jeremy Warren and Adriana Turpin (Oxford: Beazley Archive & Archaeopress, 2007), 21–31.

12. "Auctions in London, No. II," *Penny Magazine of the Society for the Diffusion of Useful Knowledge* 13, no. 768 (1844): 105.

13. "Auctions in London, No. II," 107.

14. Charles W. Smith, *Auctions: The Social Construction of Value* (Berkeley: University of California Press, 1990), x–xi.

15. John Habakkuk, *Marriage, Debt, and the Estates System: English Landownership, 1650–1950* (Oxford: Clarendon Press, 1994), 397–400; and F. M. L. Thompson, "The Land Market in the Nineteenth Century," *Oxford Economic Papers*, n.s., 9, no. 3 (October 1957): 285–308. Thompson's effort to gauge the proportion of auction sales to total sales of real property produced a range of 10 to 50 percent.

16. Albert J. Schmidt, "Marketing Property in Eighteenth-Century England: Lawyer History in the Huntington Library's Stowe Collection," *Huntington Library Quarterly* 62, no. 1 (1999): 123–26.

17. Beckett, "Aristocratic Financial Troubles and the Operation of the Land Market: The Sale of Astwell and Falcutt in 1774–78," *Northamptonshire Past & Present* 8, no. 5 (1993): 378.

18. [?] Salmon to the Duke of Wellington, September 30, 1837, Wellington Estate Collection, Museum of English Rural Life, Wellington/1652. Emphasis in the original.

19. Particulars of sale for the Rushall Estate (to be sold June 19, 1838), Wellington Estate Collection, Museum of English Rural Life, Wellington/1652; A. P. Baggs, D. A. Crowley, Ralph B. Pugh, Janet H. Stevenson, and Margaret Tomlinson, "Parishes: Rushall," in *A History of the County of Wiltshire*, vol. 10, ed. Elizabeth Crittall (London: Victoria

County History, 1975), 136–46, *British History Online*, http://www.british-history.ac.uk/vch/wilts/vol10/pp136-146.

20. Habakkuk, *Marriage, Debt, and the Estates System*, 378; and W. Unwin, "A Nineteenth-Century Estate Sale: Wetherby 1824," *Agricultural History Review* 23, no. 2 (1975): 116–38.

21. Habakkuk, *Marriage, Debt, and the Estates System*, 413–76. On the debate over new men of wealth and the purchase of land, see W. D. Rubinstein, "New Men of Wealth and the Purchase of Land in Nineteenth-Century Britain," *Past & Present* 92 (August 1981): 125–47; F. M. L. Thompson, "Life after Death: How Successful Nineteenth-Century Businessmen Disposed of Their Fortunes," *Economic History Review*, 2nd ser., 43, no. 1 (February 1990): 40–61; William D. Rubinstein, "Cutting Up Rich: A Reply to FML Thompson," *Economic History Review*, 2nd ser., 45, no. 2 (May 1992): 350–61; and Thompson, "Stitching It Together Again," *Economic History Review*, 2nd ser., 45, no. 2 (May 1992): 362–75.

22. B. A. Holderness, "The English Land Market in the Eighteenth Century: The Case of Lincolnshire," *Economic History Review*, 2nd ser., 27, no. 4 (November 1974): 557–76.

23. Duncan George Forbes MacDonald, *Estate Management* (London, 1868), 226.

24. Daniel Defoe, *A Tour through the Whole Island of Great Britain*, ed. Philip Nicholas Furbank, W. R. Owens, and Anthony J. Coulson (New Haven, CT: Yale University Press, 1991), 7; and Reed, "The Transformation of Urban Space" 617.

25. Jerry White, *A Great and Monstrous Thing: London in the Eighteenth Century* (Cambridge, MA: 2013), 68–76. See also H. J. Dyos, "The Speculative Builders and Developers of Victorian London," in "Symposium on the Victorian City," supplement, *Victorian Studies* 11 (1968): 641–90. Dyos rightly warns against drawing too strong a distinction between speculative and planned building. He specifically discusses the work of James Burton on the Bedford Estate; Thomas Cubitt in Belgravia and Pimlico; and Edward Yates in South London.

26. Dyos, *Victorian Suburb*, 117–18.

27. The following is based on a database compiled by the author of unique auction advertisements published in the *Times* (one of London's four main daily newspapers at the time) for ten days in June and July of 1805 and 1810 (June 1, June 3–8, and July 1–3, 1805; June 1, June 2, June 4–8, and July 2–4, 1810). The database consists of 399 advertisements for real property only and has been used here to explore and illustrate the marketing of property, not necessarily its actual sale (hereafter cited as Auction Advertisement Database). Though auction advertisements were routinely published on the last page of many newspapers, the *Times* tended to publish the largest number and to offer the widest coverage.

28. *Times*, June 1, June 6, July 1, and July 2, 1805.

29. John Chisholm, ed., *Green's Encyclopaedia of the Law of Scotland*, vol. 1 (Edinburgh, 1896), 349–52. See also M. P. Brown, *A Treatise on the Law of Sale* (Edinburgh, 1821).

30. John Gibson, *Comparative View of the Respective Modes of Auction-Sale of Land Estates as Practised in Scotland and England* (Edinburgh, 1826), 17.

31. Alfred Cox, *The Landlord's and Tenant's Guide: A Compendium of Information upon the Procuring, Occupying, and Disposing of Estates and Houses, and Many Collateral Subjects; with a Gazetteer of Great Britain* (London, 1853), 34.

32. See *An Address to the Auctioneers of the Metropolis, Containing Proposals for Forming an Establishment to Promote Their General Accommodation and Interest, Embracing a System Advantageous to Their Principals and Eminently Beneficial to the Profession* (London, 1807).

33. Rudolf Ackermann, "View of the Grand Saloon at the Auction Mart," *Repository of Arts, Literature, Commerce, Manufactures, Fashions and Politics* 6, no. 32 (August 1811): 93–96.

34. *An Address to the Auctioneers of the Metropolis*, 7.

35. *An Address to the Auctioneers of the Metropolis*, 7.

36. Learmount, *A History of the Auction*, 52. In a sample of 183 advertisements published in 1805, 166 were for auctions to be held at Garraway's. Auction Advertisements Database.

37. *An Address to the Auctioneers of the Metropolis*, 12.

38. *An Address to the Auctioneers of the Metropolis*, 26.

39. *An Address to the Auctioneers of the Metropolis*, 26.

40. Alexia Yates, *Selling Paris: Property and Commercial Culture in the Fin-de-Siècle Capital* (Cambridge, MA: Harvard University Press, 2015), 140–43. Unlike in London, the auction room in Paris was a more highly regulated institution, with attendance limited to legal officials acting on behalf of clients.

41. Auction Mart Register of Proprietors, 1808–1823, National Archives, J/90/1476; "Auction Mart," *Times*, September 21, 1808, 3; "Auction Mart," *Morning Chronicle*, September 21, 1808, 3.

42. "Sales by Auction," *Times*, January 5, 1810, 4; and "Sales by Auction," *Times*, January 12, 18, and 25, 1810.

43. Myers, "Sale by Auction," 139; and *Oxford Dictionary of National Biography*, s.v. "Robins, George Henry (1777–1847)," by Robin Myers (Oxford: Oxford University Press, 2004), http://www.oxforddnb.com/view/article/23824. Most of what can be said of the earliest real estate auctioneers in London comes from those who would claim them as founders of present-day auction and real estate corporations. For references to Richard Winstanley, John Prickett, and Harry Phillips, respectively, see the history pages of www.us.jll.com, www.prickettandellis.com, and www.phillips.com (all accessed October 5, 2014). The remaining company directors were G. E. Shuttleworth, Charles H. Hoggart, George Adams, Daniel R. Munn, John A. Hermon, and William Snell.

44. I. O. Chance, "The Auction and Its Role in Commerce," *Journal of the Royal Society of Arts* 119, no. 5177 (April 1, 1971), 294–300. In addition to the abovementioned auctioneers, James Christie, John Thompson, and Peter Coxe were also founders of the Select Society and investors in the London Auction Mart.

45. Auction Mart Register of Proprietors, 1808–1823, National Archives, J/90/1476. The following analysis is based on cross-referencing those holding original shares in the London Auction Mart with the auction mart's prospectus and the author's Auction Advertisement Database for 1805 and 1810.

46. *A Detailed Prospectus of the Auction Mart: Instituted 1808* (London: Auction Mart, 1809), 6.

47. For descriptions of the subscription rooms at Lloyd's, which may well have been the inspiration for the London Auction Mart's design, see Rudolf Ackermann, *The Microcosm of London or London in Miniature*, vol. 2 (London, 1904), 174–75.

48. *Detailed Prospectus*, 10. These perceived advantages were similarly emphasized in later city guidebooks. Charles Frederick Partington, *National History and Views of London and Its Environs; Embracing Their Antiquities, Modern Improvements, &c. &c. from Original Drawings by Eminent Artists* (London, 1834), 157; and Thomas Pennant and John Wallis, *London: Being a Complete Guide to the British Capital* (London, 1814), 453.

49. David Morier Evans, *The City; or, The Physiology of London Business* (London, 1845), 62–63. On the history of the London Stock Exchange, see Michie, *The London Stock Exchange*, 38–40.

50. Despite the provision of space for both personal and real property sales, the dominance of the latter was reflected in later pressure to convert the upper-floor rooms for estate sales. The board seriously considered investing in such renovations on at least one occasion in July 1848. National Archives, J/90/1475, Auction Mart Board of Directors Minute Book, 1848–65.

51. Kynaston, *The City of London*, 9–10; and Garrett Ziegler, "The City of London, Real and Unreal," *Victorian Studies* 49, no. 3 (Spring 2007): 431–55.

52. *Detailed Prospectus*, 9.

53. *Detailed Prospectus*, 9–23.

54. *Detailed Prospectus*, 22.

55. *Detailed Prospectus*, 22. Despite its founders' hope that the London Auction Mart would become an imperial real estate marketplace, the majority of sales that took place at the mart were of British land and estates. The occasional exceptions often attracted public attention. On April 2, 1831, for example, the *Times* reported a successful sale at the auction mart of a 3,400 acre estate in Jamaica, "together with 190 negroes, and 100 head of horned cattle." The same report also noted the presence of two antislavery activists who denounced the sale as "irreligious and injust."

56. "Auctions in London, No. II," 106.

57. I use the term *disinterested* in two senses throughout this chapter. The first, reflected in this example, refers to a visual mode of calculation that was meant to encompass all property within a single field of exchangeable value. This form of disinterestedness was prescribed in the arrangement of space and the reification of protocols for operating within it. A second sense, explored later in this chapter, refers to moments in which participants in an auction sale sought to frame their interactions in ways that disentangled and limited social obligations beyond the transaction itself, often thought of as being at "quits." For more on the value of disentangling as a framework for understanding processes of economic abstraction, see Don Slater, "From Calculation to Alienation: Disentangling Economic Abstractions," *Economy and Society* 31, no. 2 (January 1, 2002): 234–49.

58. "Auctions in London, No. II," 105.

59. Evans, *The City*, 164.

60. James Grant, *Portraits of Public Characters*, vol. 2 (London, 1841), 263–65.

61. Grant, 266.

62. The question of whether spaces like the London Auction Mart are ever anything more than simple ideological representations of reality (versus actual mechanisms for disentangling social relations) has been much debated by critics of Michel Callon. Following Callon's suggestion that social entanglement and disentanglement are produced through each other, I would argue that the London Auction Mart allows us to localize in time and space a particularly visible instance in which this dynamic of marketization emerged for real estate in England. See *The Laws of the Markets*, 17–19; Daniel Miller, "Turning Callon the Right Way Up," *Economy and Society* 31, no. 2 (May 2002): 218–33; Michel Callon, "Why Virtualism Paves the Way to Political Impotence: A Reply to Daniel Miller's Critique of *The Laws of the Markets*," *Economic Sociology: European Electronic Newsletter* 6, no. 2 (February 2005): 3–20; and Miller, "Reply to Michel Callon," *Economic Sociology: European Electronic Newsletter* 6, no. 3 (July 2005): 3–13.

63. Ackermann, "View of the Grand Saloon at the Auction Mart," 95.

64. Julia Pardoe, "Purchasing a Property," *Ainsworth's Magazine* 2 (July 1842): 459–65.

65. Pardoe, 461.

66. Pardoe, 463.

67. Thomas Frewen to William Nanson, April 9, 1841, FRE/3101, Frewen Family Archive, East Sussex Record Office.

68. Thomas Frewen to William Nanson, July 13, 1858, FRE/3707, Frewen Family Archive, East Sussex Record Office.

69. "Memoranda and Notes by Thomas Frewen [. . .]," FRE/327, Frewen Family Archive, East Sussex Record Office.

70. Benjamin Adam to Thomas Frewen, February 2, 1869, FRE/9543, Frewen Family Archive, East Sussex Record Office.

71. Benjamin Adam to Thomas Frewen, February 19, 1869, FRE/9550, Frewen Family Archive, East Sussex Record Office.

72. Benjamin Adam to Thomas Frewen, February 22, 1869, FRE/9552, Frewen Family Archive, East Sussex Record Office.

73. Benjamin Adam to Thomas Frewen, March 18, 1869, FRE/9556, Frewen Family Archive, East Sussex Record Office.

74. Edward Ryde, diary entry, September 16, 1847, Surrey History Centre, SHC reference 1262/4.

75. Julia Thomas, *Shakespeare's Shrine: The Bard's Birthplace and the Invention of Stratford-upon-Avon* (Philadelphia, PA: University of Pennsylvania Press, 2012), 40–43.

76. Quoted in Thomas, 45.

77. John Summerson, *The Unromantic Castle and Other Essays* (New York: Thames & Hudson, 1990), chap. 11; Iain S. Black, "Spaces of Capital: Bank Office Building in the City of London, 1830–1870," *Journal of Historical Geography* 26, no. 3 (July 2000): 351–75.

78. NA J/90/1475. On the efforts to increase revenues, see board minutes, April 3, 1858, and December 3, 1859 (in which the board considered refitting the saloon as office space). Demand for the lot previously had come from an unsolicited offer of £60,000 from

the Liverpool and London Fire and Life Insurance company, received by the board in December 1858. The board presented the offer to shareholders, who nonetheless equivocated at a general meeting held in January 1859. This failed offer presaged the successful sale that came in 1864.

79. "New Auction Mart," *Estates Gazette*, December 15, 1864, 620.

80. "New Auction Mart, Tokenhouse Yard," *Builder*, December 7, 1867, 889–91.

81. Thompson, "The Land Market in the Nineteenth Century," 297–98.

82. Unidentified clipping (1867), London Guildhall Library A, 34/13 P.1817.

83. H. B. Wheatley, *London Past and Present: Its History, Associations, and Traditions* (London: Murray, 1891), 79.

84. "Busy Centres of City Life: Tokenhouse Yard, the Headquarters of the Real Estate Market," *London* (June 27, 1895), 501–2.

85. Onlooker, "Mems from the Mart," *Estates Gazette*, February 10, 1894, 129.

86. Onlooker, "Mems from the Mart," *Estates Gazette*, March 17, 1894, 263.

87. Expertus, "Week at the Mart," *Property Market Review*, November 30, 1895, 998–99.

88. "Week at the Mart," November 30, 1895. Conflicts over family or inheritance-related issues seem to have broken out at the London Auction Mart with relative frequency, though this is difficult to judge from media reports alone. For other examples, see Onlooker, "Mems from the Mart," *Estates Gazette*, June 23, 1894; and Expertus, "Week at the Mart," *Property Market Review*, July 17, 1897, 602–3.

89. Onlooker, "Mems from the Mart," *Estates Gazette*, June 23, 1894.

90. Expertus, "Week at the Mart," *Property Market Review*, September 14, 1895, 773.

91. Expertus, "Week at the Mart: Lady Bidders and Buyers," *Property Market Review*, March 2, 1895, 154.

92. Expertus, "Lady Bidders and Buyers," 155.

93. "Sales by Auction," *Times*, April 7, 1888, 18.

94. "Sale of an Irish Estate," *Reynolds's Newspaper*, April 22, 1888, 6.

95. "Sale of an Irish Estate."

96. See *Report of the Royal Commissioners Appointed to Inquire into the Law and Existing Practice as to the Sale, Exchange, and Resignation of Ecclesiastical Benefices. Minutes of Evidence and Appendix*, Parliamentary Papers, c. 2507 (1880).

97. "The Traffic in Souls," *Northern Echo*, June 29, 1882, 3.

98. "The Sale of Church Livings," *Bristol Mercury and Daily Post*, July 8, 1882, 6. See also "The Sale of Church Livings," *Manchester Times*, July 1, 1882, 8; "The Curates' Alliance and the Sale of Church Livings," *Birmingham Daily Post*, July 3, 1882, 8; and "The Sale of Church Livings," *Bristol Mercury and Daily Post*, July 31, 1882, 3.

99. "The Sale of Church Livings," *Bristol Mercury*, 6.

100. Thompson, "The Land Market in the Nineteenth Century," 299.

101. Quoted in "New Sale Rooms at Shrewsbury," *Estates Gazette*, April 8, 1893, 316.

102. "George Lovett & Son," advertisement, *Estates Gazette*, December 28, 1895, 906.

103. "Nicholson, Greaves, Barber and Hastings," advertisement, *Estates Gazette*, December 28, 1895, 906.

104. A Chartered Surveyor, *Auctioneering as a Profession; or, Hints to Success as an Auctioneer and Estate Agent* (London, 1909), 42.

105. "New Auction Offices at Hammersmith," *Estates Gazette*, June 10, 1899, 1012.

106. "Portrait Gallery: Mr. Howard Frank," *Estates Gazette*, October 29, 1910, 718. The overseas expansion has continued to the present day, with the company operating 165 offices in more than thirty-six countries.

107. The other firms, all in the West End, were Hampton and Sons in St. James Square, Goddard and Smith in Piccadilly, and Harrods's estate operations on Brompton Road. The paper also noted the continuing use of town halls and Winchester House, which had been arranged as a temporary substitution for the London Auction Mart following the closure of Tokenhouse Yard. "The Estate Market, Another New Mart," *Times*, April 22, 1921, 8.

108. "The Auction Mart: Proposed Sale," *Estates Gazette*, November 2, 1918, 420.

109. "The Auction Mart, Tokenhouse Yard: Sale Confirmed," *Estates Gazette*, November 9, 1918, 444.

110. "The Auction Mart, Tokenhouse Yard: Sale Confirmed," 444.

111. "Future of the Auction Mart: Views of Prominent Professional Men," *Estates Gazette*, November 16, 1918, 467.

CHAPTER TWO

1. F. M. L. Thompson, *Chartered Surveyors: The Growth of a Profession* (London: Routledge & K. Paul, 1968), 109–27.

2. Edward Ryde, diary entry, September 16, 1847, Surrey History Centre, SHC reference 1262/4. See also his diary entries on June 21, 1849, and May 10, 1855.

3. Edward Ryde, *A General Text Book for the Constant Use and Reference of Architects, Engineers, Surveyors, Solicitors, Auctioneers, Land Agents, and Stewards* [. . .] (London: J. Weale, 1854).

4. Edward Ryde, "Railway Companies and Landowners: To the Editor of the Times," *Times*, January 2, 1864, 6–7.

5. Edward Ryde, "Surveyor of Woking: Diaries," Surrey History Centre, SHC reference 1262/6, 1262/12, 1262/21, 1262/29.

6. Thompson, *Chartered Surveyors*; D. H. Chapman, *The Chartered Auctioneers' and Estate Agents' Institute: A Short History* (London: Chartered Auctioneers' and Estate Agents' Institute, 1970); and A. M. Carr-Saunders, *The Professions* (Oxford: Clarendon Press, 1933).

7. Thompson, *Chartered Surveyors*, 159–60. On the relative subordination of these property middlemen to the legal profession, see Avner Offer, *Property and Politics, 1870–1914: Landownership, Law, Ideology, and Urban Development in England* (Cambridge: Cambridge University Press, 1981), 98–100.

8. Carr-Saunders, *The Professions*, 194.

9. Arjun Appadurai, "Commodities and the Politics of Value," in *The Social Life of Things: Commodities in Cultural Perspective*, ed. Appadurai (Cambridge: Cambridge University Press, 1986), 13.

10. On the importance of alienation over and above theories of economic calculation, see Don Slater, "From Calculation to Alienation: Disentangling Economic Abstractions," *Economy and Society* 31, no. 2 (January 1, 2002): 234–49. Slater offers a useful interven-

tion on the extensive debate between Daniel Miller and Michel Callon on the analytical limits of social and market entanglement; see Miller, "Turning Callon the Right Way Up," *Economy and Society* 31, no. 2 (May 2002): 218; Miller, "Reply to Michel Callon," *Economic Sociology: European Electronic Newsletter* 6, no. 3 (July 2005): 3–13; and Slater, "From Calculation to Alienation."

11. David Cannadine, *Lords and Landlords: The Aristocracy and the Towns, 1774–1967* (Leicester, UK: Leicester University Press, 1980); J. T. Ward and R. G. Wilson, eds., *Land and Industry: The Landed Estate and the Industrial Revolution* (Newton Abbot: David & Charles, 1971); F. M. L. Thompson, *Hampstead: Building a Borough, 1650–1964* (London: Routledge & Kegan Paul, 1974); and David Spring, *The English Landed Estate in the Nineteenth Century: Its Administration* (Baltimore: Johns Hopkins University Press, 1963).

12. James Anderson, "The Operation of the Early Nineteenth-Century Property Market," *Construction History* 24 (January 1, 2009): 63–81.

13. H. J. Dyos, "The Speculative Builders and Developers of Victorian London," in "Symposium on the Victorian City," supplement, *Victorian Studies* 11 (1968): 641–90; and Dyos, *Victorian Suburb: A Study of the Growth of Camberwell* (Leicester, UK: Leicester University Press, 1961).

14. Harry Kirk, *Portrait of a Profession: A History of the Solicitor's Profession, 1100 to the Present Day* (London: Oyez Publishing, 1976), 125–54.

15. M. Miles, "Eminent Practitioners: The New Visage of County Attorneys c. 1750–1800," in *Law, Economy and Society, 1750–1914: Essays in the History of English Law*, ed. G. R. Rubin and David Sugarman (Abingdon: Professional Books, 1984), 470–503. This portion of income from conveyancing fees seems to have remained similar through to the twentieth century. See Offer, *Property and Politics*, 19.

16. Offer, *Property and Politics*, 11. See also Kirk, *Portrait of a Profession*, 127–31.

17. William Marshall, *On the Landed Property of England: An Elementary and Practical Treatise: Containing the Purchase, the Improvement, and the Management of Landed Estates* (London, 1804), 23.

18. R. Campbell, *The London Tradesman: Being a Compendious View of All the Trades, Professions, Arts, Both Liberal and Mechanic, Now Practised in the Cities of London and Westminster. Calculated for the Information of Parents, and Instruction of Youth in Their Choice of Business* (London: T. Gardner, 1747), 78–79. For more on solicitors and the world of business, see M. Miles, "The Money Market in the Early Industrial Revolution: The Evidence from West Riding Attorneys C. 1750–1800," *Business History* 23, no. 2 (1981): 127–46; and Peter Mathias, "The Lawyer as Businessman in Eighteenth-Century England," in Donald Cuthbert Coleman, Peter Mathias, and Charles Wilson, eds., *Enterprise and History: Essays in Honour of Charles Wilson* (Cambridge: Cambridge University Press, 1984), 151–67.

19. Jane Austen, *Persuasion*, ed. D. W. Harding (London: Penguin Classics, 1985), 42–54.

20. Thompson, *Chartered Surveyors*, 158–68; Philip Aylett, "A Profession in the Marketplace: The Distribution of Attorneys in England and Wales 1730–1800," *Law and History Review* 5, no. 1 (1987): 1–30; Albert J. Schmidt, "Marketing Property in Eighteenth-Century England: Lawyer History in the Huntington Library's Stowe Collection," *Huntington*

Library Quarterly 62, no. 1/2 (1999): 115–43; and Spring, *The English Landed Estate in the Nineteenth Century: Its Administration.*

21. Andrew McRae, "To Know One's Own: Estate Surveying and the Representation of the Land in Early Modern England," *Huntington Library Quarterly* 56, no. 4 (1993): 332–57.

22. William Leybourn, *A Platform for Purchasers, a Guide for Builders, a Mate for Measurers* (London: Thomas Raw, 1685), ii.

23. Thompson, *Chartered Surveyors*, 26.

24. On surveying in colonial contexts, see John C. Weaver, *The Great Land Rush and the Making of the Modern World, 1650–1900* (Montreal: McGill-Queen's University Press, 2006), 216–63. For the role of surveyors in the public acquisition of land, see Thompson, *Chartered Surveyors*, 51, 63, and 127.

25. *The London Directory . . . Containing an Alphabetical Arrangement of the . . . Merchants, Manufacturers and Principal Traders of the Cities of London and Westminster, the Borough of Southwark and Their Environs* (London, 1789).

26. Post Office London, *Post Office Annual Directory* (London, 1802); *The Post Office London Directory* (Kelly's Directories, 1841). This rough periodization corresponds with similar figures compiled in later professional narratives. In a paper read at the Auctioneers' Institute in 1896, James F. Field calculated that there were 100 practicing auctioneers in London in 1810, 350 in 1845, and 920 in 1896.

27. Satomi Ohashi, "The Auction Duty Act of 1777: The Beginning of Institutionalisation of Auctions in Britain," in *Auctions, Agents and Dealers: The Mechanisms of the Art Market 1660–1830*, ed. Jeremy Warren and Adriana Turpin (Oxford: Archaeopress, 2007), 25–26.

28. *Twelfth Report of the Commissioners of Inquiry into the Excise Establishment, and into the Management and Collection of the Excise Revenue* (London, 1835). Auction duty applied to auctioneers throughout Great Britain and Ireland, though there seems to have been widespread evasion of the duty in both Scotland and Ireland. In 1811, for example, per capita returns from England were approximately five times greater than in Scotland, and Scottish witnesses to the Excise Commission reported widespread exemptions and abuses; see ibid., appendixes 4 and 28.

29. HC Deb 02 May 1861 vol 162 cc1376–7; Deb 31 May 1861 cc437–9; Deb 06 June 1861 vol 163 cc671–6.

30. W. Frederick Nokes, *The Auctioneers' Manual*, 5th ed. (London, 1898), 56.

31. These data include auctioneers who would not have been primarily involved in the sale of real estate, but rather with sales of personal property, such as art, books, or farm animals. Published directories for England and Wales, which claimed to distinguish between auctioneers of merely "local interest" and those involved with sales of land and houses, were fairly consistent in suggesting that between 60 percent and 70 percent of auctioneer licenses involved some form of real estate business. See Henry Allnut, *The Auctioneers', Land Agents, Valuers, and Estate Agents' Directory* (London: Estates Gazette,1862).

32. Offer, *Property and Politics*, 53.

33. License data did not identify the gender balance in either field, but census returns indicate that female participation in the property professions was limited. Of the nearly fourteen thousand auctioneers, appraisers, valuers, and house agents enumerated in the

1901 census, only fifty-four were women. For estimates of solicitors, see Kirk, *Portrait of a Profession*, 108; for surveyors, see Thompson, *Chartered Surveyors*, 349–50.

34. "Census of Auctioneers," *Estates Gazette*, October 21, 1893, 371.

35. *Tenth Decennial Census of the Population of Scotland Taken 5th of April 1891*, vol. 2, part 2, Parliamentary Papers C. 7134 (1893), 5. The sum represents agents in the boroughs of Glasgow and Edinburgh as well as their surrounding counties of Lanark and Edinburgh, a total of 663 agents.

36. M. J. Daunton, *House and Home in the Victorian City: Working-Class Housing 1850–1914*, Studies in Urban History 7 (London: Edward Arnold, 1983), 109, 173–74.

37. *Forty-Seventh Report of the Commissioners of His Majesty's Inland Revenue*, Parliamentary Papers (1904), 60–61.

38. Daunton, *House and Home in the Victorian City*, 168. See also Duncan Sim, "The Scottish House Factoring Profession," *Urban History* 23, no. 3 (December 1996): 351–71; and Richard Rodger, *The Transformation of Edinburgh: Land, Property and Trust in the Nineteenth Century* (Cambridge: Cambridge University Press, 2001).

39. Robert Squibbs, *Auctioneers: Their Duties and Liabilities*, 2nd ed. (London: Crosby Lockwood and Son, 1891), 260.

40. Henry Mayhew, *London Labour and the London Poor: A Cyclopaedia of the Condition and Earnings of Those That Will Work, Those That Cannot Work, and Those That Will Not Work* (G. Woodfall, 1851), 298.

41. "George Robins at Home," *Punch, or the London Charivari* 8–9 (1845), 57; and *Oxford Dictionary of National Biography*, s.v. "Robins, George Henry (1777–1847)," by Robin Myers (Oxford: Oxford University Press, 2004), http://www.oxforddnb.com/view/article/23824.

42. Robin Myers, "Sale by Auction: The Rise of Auctioneering Exemplified in the Firm of Christopher Cock, the Langfords, and Henry, John and George Robins (c. 1720–1847)," in *Sale and Distribution of Books from 1700*, ed. Myers and Michael Harris (Oxford: Oxford Polytechnic Press, 1982), 126–63.

43. "George Robins: Prince of Auctioneers," *Estates Gazette*, October 26, 1895, 570.

44. Myers, "Sale by Auction," 139–41.

45. Myers, "Sale by Auction," 142–43. On the Ormonde sales, see John Habakkuk, *Marriage, Debt, and the Estates System: English Landownership, 1650–1950* (Oxford: Clarendon Press, 1994), 376–78.

46. "Sales by Auction," *Morning Post*, June 18, 1832, 4.

47. "Sales by Auction," 4.

48. "Sales by Auction," 4.

49. "Sales by Auction," *Morning Post*, June 12, 1837, 8.

50. Ad copy quoted from more than two hundred particulars of sale—several authored by Robins—collected by a Lewes firm of surveyors. East Sussex Record Office, Archive of Messrs. Fuller and Askew (FAA), ACC 5500/1/19; "FAIRY LAND" copy from *Morning Post*, June 12, 1837, 8.

51. George Robins, "Sales," *Tait's Edinburgh Magazine* 3:18 (1833), 722–26. See also "Sketches of Society," *Literary Gazette*, June 23, 1832, 395.

52. "Important to Unmarried Capitalists," *Punch, or the London Charivari* 5, no. 119 (1843): 173. Criticisms of Robins reflected, in part, much more general concerns with the

impact of auctions on both trade and morality in modern commercial society. The most well-known attack on auctions in Britain came earlier in the century from a disgruntled bookseller; see *The Ruinous Tendency of Auctioneering, and the Necessity of Restraining It for the Benefit of Trade: Demonstrated in a Letter to the Right Hon. Lord Bathurst, President to the Board of Trade* (London: E. Wilson, 1812). For the wider transatlantic debate on auctions, see Brian Learmount, *A History of the Auction* (Iver, UK: Barnard & Learmount, 1985), 81–99.

53. Thomas Carlyle, *The Collected Works of Thomas Carlyle* (Chapman and Hall, 1864), 141–42.

54. Sam Sambok, *A Letter to the Editor of the Times Newspaper, Containing Observations on Mr. George Robins's El Dorado, at the Cape of Good Hope: With Hints to Those Who Are Disposed to Hire Moon Shine at One Shilling per Acre, in That Colony* (London: William Gilling, 1843), 36–37.

55. "The Poetry of the Hammer," *London Review of Politics, Society, Literature, Art, & Science*, October 3, 1863, 355.

56. "The Age of Veneer: The Science of Puffing," *Fraser's Magazine for Town and Country*, January 1852, 88–89.

57. "The Age of Veneer," 89.

58. Joseph Bateman, *The Auctioneer's Guide, Containing a Practical Treatise on the Law of Auctions, with a Complete Series of Conditions of Sale, Rules for Valuing Property, the Law of Distress, and Numerous Forms, Tables, and Precedents*, 3rd ed. (London: W. Maxwell, 1846). Bateman's guide to auction law and practice was first issued in 1838 and ran through eleven subsequent editions, the last in 1954. While not the earliest professional guidebook for auction law and practice, it was certainly one of the more prominent and enduring references.

59. Bateman, 41. Private treaty contracts were accorded more flexibility, though it was not uncommon for particulars and conditions of sale to be included in private contracts made subsequent to an auction.

60. Bateman, 42.

61. Squibbs, *Auctioneers*, 16.

62. See, for example, Joseph Henry Dart, *A Compendium of the Law and Practice of Vendors and Purchasers of Real Estate* (Banks, Gould, 1851); and William Frederick Webster, *The Law Relating to Particulars and Conditions of Sale on a Sale of Land* (Stevens, 1889).

63. Webster, *Particulars and Conditions of Sale*, 1–2.

64. Webster, 10–11.

65. Bateman, *The Auctioneer's Guide*, 42.

66. Webster, *Particulars and Conditions of Sale*, 23–25.

67. Francis Cross, *Landed Property: Its Sale, Purchase, Improvement, and General Management*. (London: Simpkin, Marshall, 1857), 100.

68. Webster, *Particulars and Conditions of Sale*, 23.

69. Squibbs, *Auctioneers*, 23, 263.

70. Douglas Jerrold, "The Auctioneer," in *Heads of the People: Or, Portraits of the English*, ed. Kenny Meadows (London: Robert Tyas, 1840), 103–4.

71. Cynthia Wall, "The English Auction: Narratives of Dismantlings," *Eighteenth-Century Studies* 31, no. 1 (Fall 1997): 21. See also Charles W. Smith, *Auctions: The Social Construction of Value* (Berkeley: University of California Press, 1990).

72. Michel Callon, ed., *The Laws of the Markets*, Sociological Review Monograph (Oxford: Blackwell, 1997), 6.

73. See the exchange between H. & R. Powell and Edmund Robins: "George Robins," letter to the editor, *Estates Gazette*, February 15, 1860, 57; "George Robins," letter to the editor, *Estates Gazette*, March 1, 1860, 73; and "George Robins," letter to the editor, *Estates Gazette*, March 15, 1860, 89. Edmund Robins mounted another defense against a similar attack in 1881; "The Modern Mr. Robins," editorial, *Land: A Journal for All Interested in Landed and House Property*, July 16, 1881, 533; Edmund Robins, "Modern Mr. Robins," *Land: A Journal for All Interested in Landed and House Property*, July 23, 1881, 544–45.

74. W. H. Taylor, *Handbook of Law Relating to the Sale and Purchase of Real Property. Specially Adapted for the Use of Auctioneers, Surveyors, and Estate Agents, Etc* (London, 1910), 86–87.

75. Walter Simms, "The Humours of Auctioneering II," *Estates Gazette*, December 28, 1895, 861; and "George Robins: Prince of Auctioneers," *Estates Gazette*, October 26, 1895, 569.

76. Herbert George Wells, "House-Hunting as an Outdoor Amusement," in *Certain Personal Matters: A Collection of Material, Mainly Autobiographical* (Lawrence & Bullen, 1898), 78–85.

77. As another example of such stiff competition, the London Metropolitan Archives holds a packets of forty-five letters sent by advertisers and estate, house, and land agents to one firm of solicitors to solicit commissions for the sale of the Hanworth Park estate in 1873–74. ACC/1023/256.

78. John Burnett, *A Social History of Housing*, 2nd ed. (New York: Methuen, 1986), 97. See also Leonore Davidoff and Catherine Hall, *Family Fortunes: Men and Women of the English Middle Class, 1780–1850*, rev. ed., (New York: Routledge, 2002), 357–96.

79. Mrs. Isabella Beeton, *The Book of Household Management* (London: S. O. Beeton, 1861; Adelaide: eBooks@adelaide, 2006), http://ebooks.adelaide.edu.au/b/beeton/isabella/household/.

80. George Augustus Sala, "Houses to Let," *Household Words*, March 20, 1852, 6.

81. Sala, 6. On patterns of middle-class housing, see Richard Trainor, "The Middle Class," in *The Cambridge Urban History of Britain*, ed. M. J. Daunton, vol. 3 (Cambridge: Cambridge University Press, 2000), 673–714.

82. Burnett, *A Social History of Housing*, 140–41; and Jose Harris, *Private Lives, Public Spirit: A Social History of Britain, 1870–1914* (Oxford: Oxford University Press, 1993).

83. *The Cambridge Urban History of Britain*, s.v. "Migration," by David Feldman (Cambridge: Cambridge University Press, 2000), 3:185.

84. *The Cambridge Urban History of Britain*, s.v. "Modern London," by Richard Dennis (Cambridge: Cambridge University Press, 2000), 3:117; and David Englander, *Landlord and Tenant in Urban Britain, 1838–1918* (Oxford: Oxford University Press, 1983), 8–9. See also Dennis, *English Industrial Cities of the Nineteenth Century: A Social Geography* (Cambridge: Cambridge University Press, 1984); and Colin G. Pooley, "Residential

Differentiation in Victorian Cities: A Reassessment," *Transactions of the Institute of British Geographers* 9, no. 2 (1984): 131–44.

85. Alfred Cox, *The Landlord's and Tenant's Guide: A Compendium of Information upon the Procuring, Occupying, and Disposing of Estates and Houses, and Many Collateral Subjects; with a Gazetteer of Great Britain* (London, 1853), 5–7.

86. "House-Hunting," *Literary Magnet*, January 1827, 201.

87. Edward Ryde, diary entry, July 7, 1860, Surrey History Centre, SHC reference 1262/17.

88. P. D., "House Hunting," *London Society: An Illustrated Magazine of Light and Amusing Literature for the Hours of Relaxation*, July 1867, 21–23.

89. Alexander Rainy, *A Brief Exposition of Some Existing Abuses Regarding the Transfer of Real Property by Public Auction and Private Contract* (London: T. Brettell, 1838), 13. See also Rainy, *On the Transfer of Property by Public Auction and Private Contract, the Reciprocity or Allowance System, Etc Being the Substance of a Statement Made at a Meeting Held on the 8th of July, 1845* (London, 1845).

90. "The Employment of Estate Agents," *Estates Gazette*, February 1, 1859, 43; and editorial, *Estates Gazette*, December 1, 1858, 9.

91. R. Ernest, *How to Become a Successful Estate Agent*, 3rd ed. (London: Ernest & Co., 1905), 23.

92. Ernest, 208–9.

93. William Ellison, *A Handy Guide to Property: Or, House-Hunting Made Easy* [. . .] (London: W. H. and L. Collingridge, 1874).

94. The first mention came from J. H. Townsend Green, president of the Auctioneers' Institute, during his inaugural address. "Central Property Register," *Estates Gazette*, October 31, 1903, 721; and "Meeting of the Auctioneers' Institute," *Estates Gazette*, January 16, 1904, 102.

95. A. D. S., "The Public and Estate Agents," letter to the editor, *Estates Gazette*, September 12, 1903, 443.

96. A. J. W., letter to the editor, *Estates Gazette*, September 19, 1903, 485; E. M. L., letter to the editor, *Estates Gazette*, September 19, 1903, 485; and J. W. Turner, letter to the editor, *Estates Gazette*, September 26, 1903, 513.

97. "Meeting of the Auctioneers' Institute."

98. "Meeting of the Auctioneers' Institute."

99. Experientia Docet, "The Estate Agency Question," letter to the editor, *Estates Gazette*, January 23, 1904, 146.

100. Quote from the chair: "The Estate Exchange Annual Meeting," *Estates Gazette*, March 5, 1904, 398; correspondents to *Estates Gazette*: C. J. Howell Thomas, "The Estate Agency Question," letter to the editor, *Estates Gazette*, March 19, 1904, 472; and Simplictat, "Plea for 'Single Registration,'" letter to the editor, *Estates Gazette*, March 26, 1904, 528.

101. Simplicitat, "Plea for 'Single Registration.'"

102. "Meeting of the Auctioneers' Institute."

103. Ernest, *How to Become a Successful Estate Agent*, 28.

104. Ernest, 30.

105. Advertisement for Lyle property card register, in Ernest, back pages.

106. W. Frederick Nokes, *The Auctioneers' Manual: Describing the Preparation for and Conduct of Sales by Auction of Real Property, Furniture, Stock-in-Trade, Etc., Dilapidations, House Agency, Distraints, Ejectments, War Emergency Legislation, and Various Forms of Agreement for Letting and Selling Property, Scales and Charges; also Specimens of Particulars of and Conditions of Sale and Title Pages of Catalogues*, 8th ed. (London: Estates Gazette, 1919), 105–6.

107. Peter Becker and William Clark, eds., *Little Tools of Knowledge: Historical Essays on Academic and Bureaucratic Practices* (Ann Arbor, MI: University of Michigan Press, 2001), 1. See also Michel Callon, "What Does It Mean to Say That Economics Is Performative?," in *Do Economists Make Markets? On the Performativity of Economics*, ed. Donald MacKenzie, Fabian Muniesa, and Lucia Siu (Princeton, NJ: Princeton University Press, 2007). Callon makes a similar point when referring to "economics in the wild" and the role that a variety of tools, instruments, and methods can play in bringing into existence ideas about the economy. Callon, "What Does It Mean," 336–41.

108. Wells, "House-Hunting as an Outdoor Amusement," 79.

109. A. R., " 'This House to Let,' " *London Reader of Literature, Science, Art and General Information*, June 15, 1867, 165. In a similar story, written by the same author, a bachelor chances upon a lost romance who calls to view his own house, recently advertised to let. A. R., "To Let; Inquire Within," *London Reader of Literature, Science, Art and General Information*, June 16, 1866, 218.

110. L., "House-Hunting," *Saint Paul's Magazine*, September 1870, 592–95.

111. Thomas De Longueville, "House-Hunting," *Saturday Review*, January 4, 1879, 10–11. The article was reprinted in the *Estates Gazette* and *Land*, and later included in a collected volume of works. De Longueville, *The Platitudes of a Pessimist* (Kegan Paul, Trench, Trübner, 1897).

112. De Longueville, "House-Hunting," 10.

113. George Robert Sims, ed., *Living London: Its Work and Its Play, Its Humour and and Its Pathos, Its Sights and Its Scenes*, vol. 2 (Cassell, 1902), 216–21.

114. Sims, 219.

115. Nokes, *The Auctioneers' Manual*, 7th ed., 57.

116. Ernest, *How to Become a Successful Estate Agent*, 115–16.

CHAPTER THREE

1. On the function of calculation in markets, see Michel Callon and Fabian Muniesa, "Peripheral Vision: Economic Markets as Calculative Collective Devices," *Organization Studies* 26, no. 8 (August 1, 2005): 1229–50.

2. See *A Detailed Prospectus of the Auction Mart: Instituted 1808* (London: Auction Mart, 1809), 25.

3. The best account of the history of financial news remains Wayne Parsons, *The Power of the Financial Press: Journalism and Economic Opinion in Britain and America* (Aldershot, UK: Edward Elgar, 1989). See also Mary Poovey, *The Financial System in Nineteenth-Century Britain* (Oxford: Oxford University Press, 2002), 25–32.

4. The one exception was the regular "Journal of Property" column in the *Law Times*, discussed below. I have avoided discussing one further source of property sales: that

concerning the sale of individual and publicly notable properties. The auction of Shakespeare's Stratford home, carried out by Edmund Robins in 1847, provides a good example. The *Morning Chronicle* described the scene as a "national event" of "universal interest" that had attracted large crowds interested in knowing the fate of the property. "Sale of Shakespeare's House," *Morning Chronicle*, September 17, 1847, 2. Reports of similar sales could often be quite detailed, but were clearly aimed at recording a singular event rather the operations of a more general property market.

5. Joanne Shattock and Michael Wolff, *The Victorian Periodical Press: Samplings and Soundings* (Leicester, UK: Leicester University Press, 1982); Jerry Don Vann and Rosemary T. VanArsdel, *Victorian Periodicals and Victorian Society* (Toronto: University of Toronto Press, 1994); and Chris Hosgood, "The Shopkeeper's 'Friend': The Retail Trade Press in Late-Victorian and Edwardian Britain," *Victorian Periodicals Review* 25, no. 4 (Winter 1992): 164–72.

6. David J. Moss, "'Circular to Bankers': The Role of a Prototypical Trade Journal in the Evolution of Middle-Class Professional Consciousness," *Victorian Periodicals Review* 25, no. 3 (Fall 1992): 129–36.

7. *Oxford Dictionary of National Biography*, s.v. "Crockford, John (1824/5–1865)," by Brenda Hough, revised by H. C. G. Matthew, accessed February 3, 2010, (Oxford: Oxford University Press, 2004), http://www.oxforddnb.com/view/article/37324. Reliable estimates of the paper's circulation are all but impossible to estimate. Cox himself was quite aggressive in promoting his business, going so far as to publish under a pseudonym a *Handbook for Advertisers*, in which it was stated that the *Journal* counted a circulation of 2,250 per issue. In a scathing review in 1854, however, the *Athenaeum* revealed that Excise Office figures for the *Law Times* had been used to inflate the estimates for several other Cox publications, all of which shared the same stamp. The *Journal* had initially claimed a circulation of five thousand. *Journal of Auctions*, August 20, 1853; and *Athenaeum*, October 28, 1854.

8. Following the first impulse, the paper gradually expanded its targeted readership to include house and estate agency, freehold land societies, and limited liability company news. It ultimately dissolved in 1866 with the intention of transforming yet again, into separate papers for property news and company news. Neither of these projects appears to have been realized.

9. This chapter is centrally concerned not with the advertisements for property sales but with the calculation and analysis of sale results. It should be clear, however, that advertisements were the financial basis on which all of the periodicals discussed here depended. Many of them admitted as much and hoped to garner enough advertisements to build a sustainable financial footing and to justify their claim to be a necessary medium for auctioneers and agents. Market analysis, therefore, was more of a luxury feature geared toward a more specific target audience of investors and professionals.

10. "Introduction," editorial, *Journal of Auctions*, August 6, 1853, 1.

11. "Property Reporter," *Journal of Auctions*, August 6, 1853, 2.

12. "Introduction," *Journal of Auctions*.

13. "To Our Readers," *Journal of Auctions*, August 20, 1853, 25–26.

14. "Property Reporter," *Journal of Auctions*, August 13, 1853, 15.

15. "To Auctioneers," *Journal of Auctions*, August 20, 1853, 26. The request was

made again a few months later. "To Readers," *Journal of Auctions*, October 1, 1853, 97; and "Auction Reports," *Journal of Auctions*, October 15, 1853, 125.

16. Editorial, *Journal of Auctions*, November 5, 1853, 174.

17. "To the Auctioneers of the United Kingdom," *Journal of Auctions*, September 3, 1853, 49.

18. "Auctions," *Journal of Auctions*, June 1, 1854, 529. A similar request was made of country auctioneers two weeks later, and the issue again arose from further correspondence with auctioneers later that summer. "To Auctioneers," *Journal of Auctions* June 15, 1854, 554; and "Bought In," *Journal of Auctions*, August 1, 1854, 628.

19. Mary Poovey, "Writing about Finance in Victorian England: Disclosure and Secrecy in the Culture of Investment," *Victorian Studies* 45, no. 1 (Autumn 2002): 17–41; and Poovey, *The Financial System in Nineteenth-Century Britain*, 25.

20. "Correspondence," *Journal of Auctions*, September 10, 1853, 61.

21. "Review of Sale and Value of Property," *Journal of Auctions*, August 1, 1854, 628; and "Review of Sales—Value of Land," *Journal of Auctions*, August 15, 1854, 651–52.

22. "The Land Market," *Law Times*, October 27, 1855, 68. The scope of the annual values report was heavily skewed toward the southeast, with over half of the 131 reported values located in home counties. Not surprisingly, the *Law Times* regularly reprinted the reports from its sister journal, but I can find no evidence of a broader circulation of reports in any daily papers (as would happen later in the century—see below).

23. The earliest holdings in the British Library newspaper collection dates from 1869, though the paper continued publishing as the *Glasgow Advertiser and Property Circular* until 1932.

24. F. M. L. Thompson, "The Land Market in the Nineteenth Century," *Oxford Economic Papers*, n.s., 9, no. 3 (October 1957): 295–96.

25. David Spring, introduction to John Bateman, *The Great Landowners of Great Britain and Ireland*, 4th ed. (Leicester: Leicester University Press, 1971).

26. Avner Offer, *Property and Politics, 1870–1914: Landownership, Law, Ideology, and Urban Development in England* (Cambridge: Cambridge University Press, 1981), part 2.

27. From the midcentury onward, for example, insurance companies and building societies helped create smaller and more easily purchased units of real property. P. Scott, *The Property Masters: A History of the British Commercial Property Sector*, 1st ed. (London: Chapman & Hall, 1996), 19.

28. On the transformations in patterns and perceptions of late-Victorian and Edwardian property, see Jose Harris, *Private Lives, Public Spirit: A Social History of Britain, 1870–1914* (Oxford: Oxford University Press, 1993), 96–122; and Paul Readman, *Land and Nation in England: Patriotism, National Identity, and the Politics of Land, 1880–1914* (Woodbridge, UK: Royal Historical Society, 2008).

29. Mary Poovey, "Beneath the Horizon of Cultural Visibility," *Journal of Cultural Economy* 1, no. 3 (November 2008): 337–47; and Poovey, "Writing about Finance in Victorian England."

30. The proliferation of journals is one sign that property market news was attracting a wider audience. Circulation figures are notoriously difficult to judge, but it is clear that many of these new journals were aimed at wider audiences. Price was one indication.

The issue price of *Land*, at six pence, clearly marked it for elite consumption; but later papers, such as the *Property Market Review* and *Estates Journal*, were priced at the more popular rate of a penny. The price of a single issue of the *Estates Gazette* was three pence (1885). Moreover, several of the new papers clearly marketed their content in more popular tones. The *Estates Chronicle*, for instance, included an article in its inaugural issue on "Land and House Property for the Million," in which it promised to help "nationalise the land on the basis of individual ownership." April 15, 1898, 2.

31. "Estates Exchange," *Land: A Journal for All Interested in Landed and House Property*, February 12, 1881, 2.

32. The *Estates Gazette* may have been inspired by the publishers of *Land: A Journal for All Interested in Landed and House Property*, which ran from 1881 to 1883, and which had offered a summary of weekly public sales similar in format to the *Journal of Auctions*. In January 1883 it also printed a retrospective assessment of the land market, based on estate exchange figures, in which it tried to argue that more recent declines in volumes were a reflection of growing confidence in values, which would soon translate into more property put on the market once agents felt prices had bottomed out. "The Position of the Land Market," *Land: A Journal for All Interested in Landed and House Property*, January 13, 1883, 374.

33. "Property Market: The London Auction Mart," *Estates Gazette*, March 6, 1886, 113.

34. "Property Market," *Estates Gazette*, June 19, 1886, 297.

35. "The New Year's Land Market," *Estates Gazette*, January 2, 1886, 4-5.

36. "The Land Sales of 1890," *Estates Gazette*, January 17, 1891, 49.

37. "A Year's Land Values," *Estates Gazette*, January 17, 1891, 56.

38. To a certain extent, the change in editorship reflected both the growing professionalization of property market expertise and the narrowing of interests associated with market practice. Allnutt's more eclectic interests were reflected in a book published on the Franco-Prussian War and in his active involvement in commons and footpath preservation. He served as secretary to the Footpaths Preservation Society and remained involved in open-access movements throughout his life. Wilson's interests seem to have been much more professionally focused on the auctioneering and property agency professions, as suggested by his expansion of the *Estates Gazette*'s publishing activities to other areas of specialist interest.

39. "A New Year Book," *Estates Gazette*, January 28, 1893, 81.

40. *Property Index. 1884 A Reliable Guide to All Interested in Ascertaining the Present Market Value of Lands, Buildings, and Heritable Securities in Glasgow and West of Scotland* (Glasgow: John C. King, 1885). The *Estates Gazette* regularly paid for advertisements in the *Glasgow Property Circular*, which suggests that it was aware of developments in Scottish property market reporting, and, while there is no direct evidence of the English version of a property index being modeled on its Scottish counterpart, it is possible that such was the case.

41. *Property Index*, 3–4.

42. The paper's property reporter used this principle to explain the dearth of auction advertisements seen in the week of October 1, 1853.

43. The correspondents' reports remained a prominent feature of the paper in the 1920s.

44. "The Year 1892," *Estates Gazette*, January 7, 1893, 6.

45. "The Year 1892," *Estates Gazette*, January 7, 1893, 7.

46. "The Year 1892," *Estates Gazette*, January 21, 1893, 50.

47. "The Year 1892," *Estates Gazette*, January 28, 1893, 82.

48. "The Year 1890," *Estates Gazette*, January 3, 1891, 5.

49. "Land Sales of 1890," *Cheshire Observer*, January 24, 1891, 4.

50. "Land in Leicestershire in 1890," *Leicester Chronicle and the Leicestershire Mercury*, January 10, 1891, 3; "The Derbyshire Land Market," *Derby Mercury*, January 10, 1894, 2; "The Land Market in 1891," *Jackson's Oxford Journal*, February 6, 1892, 3; "Improved Outlook for Agricultural Properties in North and South Oxon.," *Jackson's Oxford Journal*, January 7, 1899, 2; and "Property in Bristol," *Bristol Mercury*, January 10, 1899, 3.

51. "Improved Prospects in the Land Market," *Manchester Weekly Times*, January 8, 1892, 6.

52. "Improved Prospects in the Land Market."

53. "The Property Market," *Financial Times* June 25, 1894, 3. The *Financial Times* would later defend its early investment in property market journalism when the *Times* tried to claim that its daily market reports were new in 1919.

54. "The Estate Market," *Estates Gazette*, February 5, 1898; "The Estate Market," *Daily Mail*, February 5, 1898, 2; and "The Estate Market," *Times*, February 5, 1898, 9.

55. "Multiple Market News," *Financial Times*, April 13, 1896, 4.

56. "Glasgow Property Market: Statistical Summary of Transactions during 1905," *Glasgow Advertiser and Property Circular*, February 6, 1906, 3.

57. "Glasgow Property Market: Resume of the Year 1908," *Glasgow Advertiser and Property Circular*, January 5, 1909, 2.

58. "Sales of Land and House Property in 1911," *Economist*, January 6, 1912, 5. The journal began weekly reports on the property market in September 1916.

59. "The Property Market in 1912," *Economist*, January 11, 1913, 66.

60. On the problem of uncertainty and calculation, see Theodore M. Porter, *Trust in Numbers: The Pursuit of Objectivity in Science and Public Life* (Princeton, NJ: Princeton University Press, 1995).

61. *Estates Gazette*, July 1, 1893.

62. Indeed, given the prominent display of estate sales in both the professional and daily press, general readers could be forgiven for thinking that the market was largely to do with estates. The argument that estate sales needed to be compared with other, less glamorous forms of property was an interesting example of representing the market as a more uniform space in which the social distinctions between properties were less important than their contribution to the health of the market as a whole.

63. "The Real Estate Market," *Estates Gazette*, July 15, 1893, 37. See also "Occasional Notes," *Estates Gazette*, August 5, 1893, 109.

64. Expertus, "Week at the Mart," *Property Market Review*, November 27, 1897, 998.

65. Expertus, "Week at the Mart—the Press and the Market," *Property Market Review*, February 12, 1898, 122; see also "The Estate Market," *Estates Gazette*, February 5, 1898, 218.

66. Expertus, "Week at the Mart—the Press and the Market," *Property Market Review*, February 12, 1898, 122.

67. Segrave, Browett, and Taylor, letter to the editor, *Property Market Review*, February 19, 1898, 150.

68. Segrave, Browett, and Taylor, letter to the editor.

69. Expertus, "Week at the Mart—the Press and the Market," *Property Market Review*, February 12, 1898, 122. The *Estates Gazette* defended its analysis by falling back on the veracity of the weekly figures it had quoted. "Ground Rents at the Mart," *Estates Gazette*, February 12, 1898, 266.

70. Brian Short, *Land and Society in Edwardian Britain* (Cambridge: Cambridge University Press, 1997); and Ian Packer, *Lloyd George, Liberalism and the Land: The Land Issue and Party Politics in England, 1906–1914* (Rochester, NY: Royal Historical Society, 2001).

71. "The Budget at Close Quarters," *Estates Gazette*, May 8, 1909, 815.

72. "The Estate Market," *Times*, May 8, 1909, 11.

73. "Property and the Budget," *Estates Gazette*, July 31, 1909, 185.

74. HC Deb 17 August 1909 vol 9 cc1115–6.

75. "The Land of Illusions," *Estates Gazette*, August 21, 1909, 320.

76. Quoted in "The Auctioneers' Institute: The Finance Bill Memorial," *Estates Gazette*, August 28, 1909, 353.

77. Quoted in "The Auctioneers' Institute," August 28, 1909.

78. See "The Auctioneers' Institute: The Finance Bill Memorial," *Estates Gazette*, September 4, 1909, 394.

79. "The Auctioneers' Institute," August 28, 1909.

80. "The Auctioneers' Institute," August 28, 1909; and "Correspondence: Auctioneers' Institute Memorial," *Estates Gazette*, September 11, 1909, 434.

81. "The Profession and the Budget," *Estates Gazette*, September 18, 1909, 475–76.

82. "The Land of Illusions," *Estates Gazette*, August 21, 1909, 320.

83. "Occasional Notes," *Estates Gazette*, August 14, 281.

84. "Correspondence: The Auctioneers' Institute Memorial," *Estates Gazette*, September 25, 1909, 514.

85. "The Estate Market," *Times*, September 18, 1909, 13.

86. "Occasional Notes," *Estates Gazette*, March 29, 1919, 349.

87. "England Changing Hands," *Times*, May 10, 1919, 9.

88. "England Changing Hands," *Times*, June 24, 1919, 16.

89. "England Changing Hands: A Silent Revolution," *Times*, June 2, 1919, 17. The rest of the series ran June 7 and June 9–11.

90. For the ongoing debate over the accuracy and importance of this estimate of turnover, see F. M. L. Thompson, *English Landed Society in the Nineteenth Century* (London: Routledge & K. Paul, 1963), 332–33; John Beckett and Michael Edward Turner, "End of the Old Order? F. M. L. Thompson, the Land Question, and the Burden of Ownership in England, c.1880–c.1925," *Agricultural History Review* 55, no. 2 (2007): 269–88; Beckett and Turner, "Land Reform and the English Land Market, 1880–1925," in *The Land Question in Britain, 1750–1950*, ed. Matthew Cragoe and Paul Readman (New York: Palgrave Macmillan, 2010), 219–36; Michael Thompson, "The Land Market, 1880–1925: A Reappraisal Reappraised," *Agricultural History Review* 55, no. 2 (2007): 289–300.

91. "The Estate Market: Land Sales in 1919," *Times*, December 31, 1919, 4.

92. "Nothing New Under the Sun," *Financial Times*, January 2, 1920, 4.

CHAPTER FOUR

1. Solomon Atkinson, *An Essay on Marketable or Doubtful Titles to Real Estate* (London: J. S. Littell, 1838), 1–2.

2. *Report from the Select Committee of the House of Lords on the Burdens Affecting Real Property; Together with the Minutes of Evidence Taken Before the Said Committee, and Index*, Parliamentary Papers, c. 441 (1846), 457.

3. On the growth of special conditions with respect to real property contracts, see J. Stuart Anderson, "Property," in *The Oxford History of the Laws of England*, ed. William Cornish, J. Stuart Anderson, Ray Cocks, Michael Lobban, Patrick Poldan, and Keith Smith, vol. 12, *1820–1914 Private Law* (Oxford: Oxford University Press, 2010), 94–109.

4. Anderson, 105–6.

5. Avner Offer, *Property and Politics, 1870–1914: Landownership, Law, Ideology, and Urban Development in England* (Cambridge: Cambridge University Press, 1981); Offer, "The Origins of the Law of Property Acts 1910–25," *Modern Law Review* 40, no. 5 (September 1977): 505–22; and J. Stuart Anderson, *Lawyers and the Making of English Land Law, 1832–1940* (Oxford: Oxford University Press, 1992).

6. J. Stuart Anderson, "Changing the Nature of Real Property Law," in *The Oxford History of the Laws of England*, ed. William Cornish, J. Stuart Anderson, Ray Cocks, Michael Lobban, Patrick Poldan, and Keith Smith, vol. 12, *1820–1914 Private Law* (Oxford: Oxford University Press, 2010), 179–231.

7. Richard Rodger, "Property Transfers and the Register of Sasines: Urban Development in Scotland since 1617," *Urban History Yearbook* 15 (May 1988): 49–57; C. F. Kolbert and N. A. M. Mackay, *History of Scots and English Land Law*, Studies in Land Economy (Berkhamsted, UK: Geographical Publications Limited, 1977); and V. T. H. Delany, "English and Irish Land Law-Some Contrasts," *American Journal of Comparative Law* 5, no. 3 (1956): 471–77.

8. *Second Report Made to His Majesty by the Commissioners Appointed to Inquire into the Law of England Respecting Real Property*, Parliamentary Papers, c. 575 (1830), 3. Jeremy Bentham was among those who preferred a systematic revision of property similar to that found in the French civil code. See Bentham, "Observations on the Actual State of the English Law of Real Property, with the Outline of a Code," *Westminster Review* 6 (1826): 446–506; and Mary Sokol, "Jeremy Bentham and the Real Property Commission of 1828," *Utilitas* 4, no. 2 (1992): 225–45.

9. *Second Report to Inquire into the Law*, 6.

10. James Stewart, "A Few Words to the Members of Agricultural Societies and Others Interested in Land," letter to the editor, *Times*, October 22, 1846, 5.

11. *Second Report to Inquire into the Law*, 17.

12. See the evidence and correspondence of Thomas George Fonnereau and Thomas Jefferson Hogg, *Second Report to Inquire into the Law*, 11, 97, 52–53. The idea of title registration was not new: Andrew Yarranton and John Asgill, both writing in the

late-seventeenth century had suggested the idea, though in their cases the more common analogy was to other traditional registries, such as for births or marriage. Yarranton did prophesy registered titles operating "as equal as Cash in a mans hands," but the metaphor was meant less to prescribe reform than to evoke the potential for more secure credit. See Andrew Yarranton, *England's Improvement by Sea and Land: To Out-Do the Dutch without Fighting* [. . .] (London, 1677), 12; and John Asgill, *An Essay on a Registry, for Titles of Lands* (London, 1698).

13. Anderson, *Lawyers and English Land Law*, 65.

14. *Second Report to Inquire into the Law Respecting Real Property*, 52.

15. *Second Report to Inquire into the Law*, 52.

16. *Second Report to Inquire into the Law*, 97.

17. Robert Wilson, *Outlines of a Plan for Adapting the Machinery of the Public Funds to the Transfer of Real Property* (London 1844); and Wilson, *Registration of Title to Land; What It Is, Why It Is Needed, and How It May Be Effected* (London, 1863). For contemporaneous calls for title registration and discussion of Wilson's influence, see Anderson, *Lawyers and English Land Law*, 64–68.

18. Prior to 1896, contemporaries generally referred to this act as the Transfer of Land Act of 1862. In 1896, it was renamed the Land Registry Act of 1862.

19. Anderson, *Lawyers and the English Land Law*, 68.

20. Wilson, *Outlines of a Plan*, 13.

21. Wilson, *Registration of Title to Land*, 1–10.

22. Wilson, *Outlines of a Plan*, 15.

23. Wilson, 18.

24. Wilson, 20.

25. Wilson, *Registration of Title to Land*, 69.

26. Wilson, 70.

27. Wilson, *Outlines of a Plan*, 26–27.

28. Wilson, 27–30.

29. Wilson, 30.

30. Wilson, 39 and 52.

31. Anderson, "Changing the Nature of Real Property Law," 192–93.

32. The phrase is typically associated with a speech by Richard Cobden, given shortly before his death in 1865; but it circulated much earlier, and Cobden's belated commitment to it was largely tactical. F. M. L. Thompson, "Cobden, Free Trade in Land, and the Road to the Abbey National," in *Rethinking Nineteenth-Century Liberalism: Richard Cobden Bicentenary Essays*, ed. Anthony Howe and Simon Morgan (Aldershot, UK: Ashgate, 2006).

33. James Stewart, letter to the editor, *Times*, October 22, 1846.

34. Letters to the editor, *Times*, October 29 and November 7, 1846. S. P., who wrote to the editor in support of Stewart on November 11, 1846, referred to Wilson's pamphlet as "a most able, luminous, and in every way business-like statement."

35. John Stuart Mill, *Principles of Political Economy* (Amherst, NY: Prometheus Books, 2004), 809.

36. Thompson, "Cobden, Free Trade in Land," 71.

37. James Beal, *Free Trade in Land: An Inquiry into the Social and Commercial Influence of the Laws of Succession and the System of Entails*, [. . .] (London, 1855), 129.

38. In later commentaries, the most common comparison was with the sale of ships—a metaphor most associated with Robert Torrens registration reforms, but one that also circulated in earlier English debates. Joseph Kay, *Free Trade in Land* (London, 1879); John Macdonell, *The Land Question, with Particular Reference to England and Scotland* (London: MacMillan, 1873); and Offer, *Property and Politics*, 32.

39. J. M. Ludlow, "Stock Registers, Share Registers, and Land Registers," in *Papers Read Before the Juridical Society* (London, 1863), 141–42.

40. Ludlow, 163.

41. Edward P. Wolstenholme, "Simplification of Title to Land Preferable to the Introduction of Novel Modes of Assurance, with an Outline of a Plan," *Papers Read Before the Juridical Society* 2 (1863): 533–52.

42. Wolstenholme, 537.

43. Wolstenholme, 538.

44. Anderson, "Changing the Nature of Real Property Law," 195; and Offer, *Property and Politics*, 31–32.

45. *Report of the Commissioners Appointed to Consider the Subject of the Registration of Title with Reference to the Sale and Transfer of Land*, Parliamentary Papers, c. 2215 (1857) 2.

46. *Report to Consider Registration of Title*, 23–24.

47. Anderson suggests that Wilson was unwilling to see a partial implementation of his plan, and he could not accept the commission's conclusion against compulsion and an expensive public map index. Anderson, *Lawyers and the English Land Law*, 91 and 95; and *Report to Consider Registration of Title*, 19–20.

48. *Report to Consider Registration of Title*, 35.

49. *Report to Consider Registration of Title*, 35–36.

50. HC Deb 11 February 1859 vol 152 cc280–1.

51. HC Deb 17 February 1862 vol 165 cc358.

52. Advertisement, *Estates Gazette*, April 23, 1864, 157.

53. Anderson, *Lawyers and English Land Law*, 109–10.

54. *Royal Commission to Inquire into Operation of Land Transfer Act, and Condition of Registry of Deeds for County of Middlesex*, Parliamentary Papers, c. 20 (1870), xiv.

55. *Royal Commission to Inquire into Land Transfer Act*, xxvi.

56. *Royal Commission to Inquire into Land Transfer Act*, xxvi–xxvii.

57. See "The Lord Chancellor's Bill as to Land Transfers," *Economist*, May 17, 1873, 586–87; and G. Shaw-Lefevre Eversley, *English and Irish Land Questions: Collected Essays* (London, 1881), 105.

58. Anderson, "Changing the Nature of Real Property Law," 199.

59. "Registration and the Land Market," *Estates Gazette*, March 10, 1888, 124.

60. For British perspectives on the land question, see Roy Douglas, *Land, People & Politics*; and Matthew Cragoe and Paul Readman, *The Land Question in Britain, 1750–1950*. On the history of title registration in England only, see Anderson, *Lawyers and English Land Law*; and Offer, *Property and Politics*.

61. Edmund Rogers, "The Impact of the Australian Torrens System on the Land Transfer Debate in the United Kingdom, 1858–1914," *ANZLH E-Journal* Refereed Paper No. 4

(2006); and Rogers, "The Impact of the New World on Economic and Social Debates in Britain, c. 1860–1914" (PhD diss., University of Cambridge, 2009).

62. *Oxford Dictionary of National Biography*, s.v. "Torrens, Sir Robert Richard Chute (1812–1884)," by P. A. Howell (Oxford: Oxford University Press), http://www.oxforddnb.com/view/article/27566.

63. Robert Richard Torrens, *Transfer of Land by "Registration of Title": As Now in Operation in Australia* (Dublin, 1863), 18.

64. Gary B. Magee and Andrew S. Thompson, *Empire and Globalisation: Networks of People, Goods and Capital in the British World, c.1850–1914* (Cambridge: Cambridge University Press, 2010).

65. See, for example, Peter Karsten, *Between Law and Custom: "High" and "Low" Legal Cultures in the Lands of the British Diaspora—The United States, Canada, Australia, and New Zealand, 1600–1900* (Cambridge: Cambridge University Press, 2008); Patrick McAuslan, "Land Law and the Making of the British Empire," in *Modern Studies in Property Law*, vol. 4, ed. Elizabeth Cooke (Hart Publishing, 2007), 239–62; and John C. Weaver, *The Great Land Rush and the Making of the Modern World, 1650–1900* (Kingston: McGill-Queen's University Press, 2006).

66. Peter Gray, "The Peculiarities of Irish Land Tenure, 1800–1914: From Agent of Impoverishment to Agent of Pacification," in *The Political Economy of British Historical Experience, 1688–1914*, ed. Donald Winch and Patrick K. O'Brien (Oxford: Oxford University Press, 2002), 139–64.

67. Jonathan Pim, *The Condition and Prospects of Ireland: And the Evils Arising from the Present Distribution of Landed Property: With Suggestions for a Remedy* (Dublin, 1848), 263–66. English reformers were quick to notice Pim's recommendations and incorporate them into their own proposals. James Stewart, *On the Means of Facilitating the Transfer of Land, 3 Lectures* (1848), 92–95.

68. Peter Gray, *Famine, Land and Politics: British Government and Irish Society 1843–1850* (Dublin: Irish Academic Press, 1999), 196–226.

69. Quoted in W. L. Burn, "Free Trade in Land: An Aspect of the Irish Question," *Transactions of the Royal Historical Society*, 4th ser., 31 (January 1, 1949): 61–74.

70. Burn, 68.

71. Gray, *Famine, Land and Politics*, 223–24.

72. J. A. Dowling, "Of Ships and Sealing Wax: The Introduction of Land Registration in Ireland," *Northern Ireland Legal Quarterly* 44, no. 4 (1993): 363.

73. Dowling, 363–64.

74. *Report of to Consider Registration of Title*, 16–18.

75. *Report to Consider Registration of Title*, 47.

76. *Report to Consider Registration of Title*, 47–48.

77. HC Deb 11 February 1859 vol 152 cc282.

78. HC Deb 11 February 1859 vol 152 cc285.

79. HC Deb 11 February 1859 vol 152 cc289.

80. See Cairns's comments before the select committee in 1879, when he said that he would have preferred in 1875 to have established an Estates Court. *Report from the Select Committee on Land Titles and Transfer, Together with the Proceedings of the Committee, Minutes of Evidence, and Appendix*, Parliamentary Papers, c. 244 (1879), 147.

81. J. A. Dowling, "The Landed Estates Court, Ireland," *Journal of Legal History* 26, no. 2 (August 2005): 149.

82. Dowling, "Of Ships and Sealing Wax," 364–67.

83. Dowling, 371–73.

84. Torrens, *Transfer of Land by "Registration of Title."* His engagement with English debates started even earlier. The *Estates Gazette* reprinted his correspondence to the *South Australian Register*, where he had compared Cairns's bill with the act recently passed in the colony. "Three Letters Contrasting the Landed Estates Bill and the Land Registry Bill of Sir Hugh Cairns, with the South Australia Real Property Act," *Estates Gazette*, April 2, 1860, 105–6; see also *Estates Gazette*, April 16 and May 1, 1860.

85. HC Deb 25 May 1865 vol 179 cc842 and cc845. Hugh Cairns, the attorney general, later suggested that the public had become interested in the subject of title registration through having learned of its success elsewhere (cc852).

86. "Registration of Title," *Estates Gazette*, April 11, 1891.

87. Rogers, "The Impact of the Torrens System"; and Rogers, "The Impact of the New World."

88. Rogers, "The Impact of the Torrens System," 5.

89. *Report on Land Titles and Transfer*, 165.

90. Robert Torrens, *An Essay on the Transfer of Land by Registration under the Duplicate Method Operative in British Colonies* (London, 1882), 28–31.

91. Torrens, *Transfer of Land*, iii–iv.

92. *Report on Land Titles and Transfer*, 20.

93. Rogers, "The Impact of the New World," 31.

94. Timothy Mitchell, *Rule of Experts: Egypt, Techno-Politics, Modernity* (Berkeley: University of California Press, 2002), chap. 2.

95. Peter Becker and William Clark, eds., *Little Tools of Knowledge: Historical Essays on Academic and Bureaucratic Practices* (Ann Arbor, MI: University of Michigan Press, 2001).

96. See, for example Patrick Carroll-Burke, "Material Designs: Engineering Cultures and Engineering States—Ireland 1650–1900," *Theory and Society* 31, no. 1 (February 2002), 75–114; C. Otter, *The Victorian Eye: A Political History of Light and Vision in Britain, 1800–1910* (Chicago: University of Chicago Press, 2008); James Vernon, *Hunger: A Modern History* (Cambridge, MA: Belknap Press of Harvard University Press, 2007); and Alain Pottage and Martha Mundy, *Law, Anthropology, and the Constitution of the Social: Making Persons and Things* (Cambridge: Cambridge University Press, 2004).

97. See Westbury's discussion of the practice, HD Deb 17 Feb 1862 vol 165, c. 353.

98. Alain Pottage, "The Measure of Land," *Modern Law Review* 57, no. 3 (May 1994), 361–84. On the origins of written documents in conveyancing, see A. W. B. Simpson, *A History of the Land Law*, rev. ed. (Oxford: Clarendon Press, 1986).

99. Bentham, "English Law of Real Property," 486. See also Anderson, *Lawyers and English Land Law*, 5. On law stationary workers, see Offer, *Property and Politics*, 20–22.

100. HC Deb 17 February 1862 vol 165 cc356–359.

101. Charles Fortescue Brickdale, *The Practice of the Land Registry under the Transfer of Land Act, 1862, Etc* (London, 1891), 40.

102. HL Deb 21 April 1864 vol 174 cc1412–17.

103. "A Land Certificate," *Estates Gazette*, May 9, 1864.

104. *Registration and Conveyancing Commission: First Report of the Commissioners*, appendix 7.

105. Ludlow, "Stock Registers, Share Registers, and Land Registers," 152.

106. *Registration and Conveyancing Commission: First Report*, 486.

107. *Registration and Conveyancing Commission: First Report*, 468.

108. *Registration and Conveyancing Commission: First Report*, 487.

109. Ludlow, "Stock Registers, Share Registers, and Land Registers," 149. Emphasis in the original.

110. *Royal Commission on the Land Transfer Acts: Appendix to First Report of the Commissioners: Minutes of Evidence*, Parliamentary Papers, c. 4510 (1909), 23.

111. *Royal Commission on the Land Transfer Acts: Appendix*; Charles Fortescue Brickdale, William Robert Sheldon, and Great Britain, *The Land Transfer Acts, 1875 and 1897* (London, 1899), 392–93. The fee for producing these certificates was subsequently dropped.

112. *Report on Land Titles and Transfer*, 146.

113. *Royal Commission on the Land Transfer Acts. Minutes of Evidence Taken Before the Royal Commission on the Land Transfer Acts*, vol. 2, Parliamentary Papers, c.5494 (1911), 272. Another witness, C. A. Elgood, noted that "they [owners] look upon their title deeds with the greatest reverence. The parchments, in practice, the deeds, the plans, and one thing and another, mean a great deal more to owners than that they are mere sheepskin." On the question of issuing clean certificates and on the physical condition of certificates, see Brickdale's testimony, ibid., 483–84; and the testimony of J. S. Beale, ibid., 369.

114. Peter Mayer, *Ten Chief Land Registrars, 1862–1996* (H.M. Land Registry, n.d.), 16.

115. HC Deb 30 April 1900 vol 82 cc388.

116. The phrase is borrowed from Andrew Pickering's study of the reciprocal relationship between material and human agency in the constitution of scientific practice. Pickering, *The Mangle of Practice: Time, Agency, and Science* (Chicago: University of Chicago Press, 1995), 1–23.

117. The following section draws on the excellent work of Alain Pottage, who has demonstrated how the practice of registration in various contexts transformed the meaning of property. See Pottage, "The Measure of Land"; Pottage, "The Originality of Registration," *Oxford Journal of Legal Studies* 15, no. 3 (Autumn 1995): 371–401; and Pottage, "Evidencing Ownership," in *Land Law: Themes and Perspectives*, ed. Susan Bright and John Dewar (Oxford: Oxford University Press, 1998), 129–50.

118. Pottage, "The Measure of Land," 365.

119. Pottage, 370–80.

120. Pottage, 362.

121. *Registration and Conveyancing Commission: First Report*, 15–16.

122. *Registration and Conveyancing Commission: First Report*, 484. See also Wilson, *Outlines of a Plan*, 25.

123. Pottage, "The Measure of Land," 364.

124. The report did recommend that maps be used, however, as it admitted that they were "now in almost universal use." *Royal Commission to Inquire into Land Transfer Act*, xxix.

125. Pottage, "The Measure of Land," 381.

126. J. Stuart Anderson, "The 1925 Property Legislation: Setting Contexts," in *Land Law: Themes and Perspectives*, ed. Susan Bright and John Dewar (Oxford: Oxford University Press, 1998), 107–28.

127. Elizabeth Cooke, *Land Law* (Oxford: Oxford University Press, 2006), 8–9.

128. Offer, "The Origins of Property Acts."

129. Pottage, "The Originality of Registration."

CHAPTER FIVE

1. Gordon Biddle, *The Railway Surveyors: The Story of Railway Property Management 1800–1990* (London: Ian Allan, 1990).

2. *The Cambridge Urban History of Britain*, s.v. "The Political Economy of Urban Utilities," by Robert Millward (Cambridge: Cambridge University Press, 2001), 3:315–50; and Harriet Ritvo, *The Dawn of Green: Manchester, Thirlmere, and Modern Environmentalism* (Chicago: University of Chicago Press, 2009).

3. Michael Taggart, *Private Property and Abuse of Rights in Victorian England: The Story of Edward Pickles and the Bradford Water Supply*, Oxford Studies in Modern Legal History (Oxford: Oxford University Press, 2002).

4. P. Readman, "Preserving the English Landscape, C. 1870–1914," *Cultural and Social History* 5, no. 2 (2008): 197–218; Jeremy Burchardt, *Paradise Lost: Rural Idyll and Social Change in England Since 1800* (New York: I. B. Tauris, 2002), 89–111; and Avner Offer, *Property and Politics, 1870–1914: Landownership, Law, Ideology, and Urban Development in England* (Cambridge: Cambridge University Press, 1981), 328–49.

5. National Trust Act, 7 Edw. 7, c. 136.

6. See, for example, David Cannadine, "The First Hundred Years," in *The National Trust: The Next Hundred Years*, ed. Howard Newby (London: National Trust, 1995), 11–31.

7. Karl Polanyi, *The Great Transformation: The Political and Economic Origins of Our Time* (Boston: Beacon Press, 2001), 189–91.

8. Alun Howkins, "The Use and Abuse of the English Commons, 1845–1914," *History Workshop Journal* 78, no. 1 (2014): 107–32. For more on the period of parliamentary enclosure, see Michael Turner, *English Parliamentary Enclosure: Its Historical Geography and Economic History* (Folkestone: Dawson, 1980); and J. M. Neeson, *Commoners: Common Right, Enclosure and Social Change in England, 1700–1820* (Cambridge: Cambridge University Press, 1993).

9. Howkins, "Use and Abuse of Commons," 110. See also J. R. Wordie, "The Chronology of English Enclosure, 1500–1914," *Economic History Review*, 2nd ser., 36 (1983).

10. Inclosure Act, 1845, 8 & 9 Vict., c. 118, sections 14, 15, 27, and 30.

11. "Enclosure of Wandsworth Common," *Times*, 2 September, 1863.

12. J. C. Buckmaster, "To the Editor of *The Times*: Enclosures on Wandsworth Common," *Times*, September 3, 1863.

13. Buckmaster, "Enclosures on Wandsworth Common."

14. See the testimony of James Anderson Rose, *Second Report from the Select Committee on Open Spaces (Metropolis)*, Parliamentary Papers, c. 390 (1865), 2–9.

15. *First Report from the Select Committee on Open Spaces (Metropolis)*, Parliamentary Papers, c. 178 (1865), 18–29.

16. HC Deb 21 February 1865 vol. 177 c502. A similar motion to examine commons and open spaces had passed at the end of the previous session of Parliament, but without sufficient time to be carried out. In seconding the motion to form the committee in 1865, Alderman Rose, MP for Southampton and former mayor of London, cited Wandsworth as an example of the threat posed to Wimbledon and other commons.

17. HC Deb 21 February 1865 vol. 177, c504–5.

18. For general overviews on the law of commons, see [?] Cole, "Our Commons and Open Spaces," *Fraser's Magazine for Town and Country* 73 (1866): 652–66; and Sir Robert Hunter, *The Preservation of Open Spaces, and of Footpaths and Other Rights of Way: A Practical Treatise on the Law of the Subject*, 2nd ed. (London, 1902).

19. Howkins, "Use and Abuse of Commons," 118–23.

20. *First Report on Open Spaces*, 30.

21. *Second Report on Open Spaces*, 81.

22. *Second Report on Open Spaces*, 80. See also page 53 for similar views of the lord of the manor for Peckham Rye.

23. Testimony of Henry Peale Bird, steward of the manor of Tooting, *Second Report on Open Spaces*, 83.

24. *First Report on Open Spaces*, 75.

25. *First Report on Open Spaces*, 56.

26. *Second Report on Open Spaces*, 56.

27. *Second Report on Open Spaces*, 55–56.

28. Cole, "Our Commons and Open Spaces," 656; and George Shaw-Lefevre, *English Commons and Forests: The Story of the Battle during the Last Thirty Years for Public Rights over the Commons and Forests of England and Wales* (London: Cassell, 1894), 11–13. A copy of the Statute of Merton was included in *Second Report on Open Spaces (Metropolis)*, appendix 4.

29. *Second Report on Open Spaces*, 88–95.

30. *Second Report on Open Spaces*, 94.

31. *Second Report on Open Spaces*, 91.

32. *Second Report on Open Spaces*, vii.

33. *Second Report on Open Spaces*, v.

34. HC Deb 20 March 1866 vol 182 c628.

35. HC Deb 20 March 1866 vol 182 c636–7.

36. M. J. D. Roberts, "Gladstonian Liberalism and Environment Protection, 1865–76," *English Historical Review* 128, no. 531 (2013): 292–322. For the only published general history of the CPS, see Shaw-Lefevre, *English Commons*.

37. Leslie Stephen, "Memorandum by Secretary as to the Mode of Carrying out the Objects of the Society, to Be Submitted to the Meeting of the Committee" (Commons Preservations Society, November 10, 1865), Surrey History Centre, Robert Hunter Papers, SHC reference 1621, box 2/9. Though the society declined to campaign against the Statute of Merton in 1865, it never abandoned hopes of seeing the legislation repealed, and this was eventually achieved in 1893 through the Law of Commons Amendment Act (56 & 57 Vict., c. 57). See Shaw-Lefevre, *English Commons*, 343–56.

38. Shaw-Lefevre, *English Commons*, 64–67.

39. Ben Cowell, "The Commons Preservation Society and the Campaign for Berkhamsted Common, 1866–70," *Rural History* 13, no. 2 (2002): 145–61. On the importance of fence breaking in earlier periods, see E. P. Thompson, *Customs in Common: Studies in Traditional Popular Culture* (New York: New Press, 1991), 116–21; and Neeson, *Commoners*, 259–93.

40. *Commons Preservation Society: Report of Proceedings, 1868–9* (London, 1869), Surrey History Centre, Robert Hunter Papers, SHC reference 1621, box 2/9. The CPS combined legal action with advocating for further legislative reform and the application of the Metropolitan Commons Act.

41. *Commons Preservation Society: Report*, 12.

42. F. M. L. Thompson, *Hampstead: Building a Borough, 1650–1964* (London: Routledge & Kegan Paul, 1974), 193–98.

43. Commons Preservation Society, *A Glance at the Commons & Open Spaces near London* (London, 1867), 26.

44. Commons Preservation Society, memorandum, 1870, 8, Surrey History Centre, Robert Hunter Papers, SHC reference 1621, box 2/9.

45. Shaw-Lefevre, *English Commons*, 150–51.

46. Shaw-Lefevre, *English Commons*, 158. For more on Robert Hunter's contribution to the CPS, see G. Murphy, *Founders of the National Trust* (London: Christopher Helm, 1987), 23–41.

47. *Commons Preservation Society: Report of Proceedings, 1876–80* (London, 1880), 20–21, Surrey History Centre, Robert Hunter Papers, SHC reference 1621, box 2/9; and Shaw-Lefevre, *English Commons*, 272.

48. *First Report on Open Spaces*, 10–12.

49. *Second Report on Open Spaces*, 164–65.

50. Shaw-Lefevre, *English Commons*, 188–211.

51. Shaw-Lefevre, 195.

52. Burchardt, *Paradise Lost*, 93. For more on the National Footpaths Preservation Society, which merged with the CPS in 1899, see Jan Marsh, *Back to the Land: The Pastoral Impulse in England, from 1880 to 1914* (London: Quartet Books, 1982), 39–59. The founder of the Footpaths Preservation Society was none other than Henry Allnutt, founder of the *Estates Gazette*. On the Kyrle Society, see Robert Whelan, "'The Poor, as Well as the Rich, Need Something More Than Meat and Drink': The Vision and Work of the Kyrle Society," in *"Nobler Imaginings and Mightier Struggles": Octavia Hill, Social Activism and the Remaking of British Society*, ed. Elizabeth Baigent and Ben Cowell (London: Institute of Historical Research, 2016), 91–117.

53. Elizabeth Baigent and Ben Cowell, eds., *"Nobler Imaginings and Mightier Struggles": Octavia Hill, Social Activism and the Remaking of British Society* (London: Institute of Historical Research, 2016). Hill's contribution to the land preservation movement is discussed in a number of essays, including those by Astrid Swenson, Melanie Hall, and Ben Cowell, collected in this broader examination of her contribution to Victorian activism.

54. Octavia Hill, *Our Common Land* (London: Macmillan, 1877), 13–14.

55. Murphy, *Founders of the National Trust*, 51.

56. Ben Cowell, "For the Benefit of the Nation: Politics and the Early National Trust," in *"Nobler Imaginings and Mightier Struggles": Octavia Hill, Social Activism and the Remaking of British Society*, ed. Elizabeth Baigent and Ben Cowell (London: Institute of Historical Research, 2016), 304–5.

57. Letter from Robert Hunter to unknown recipients, July 21, 1884, Surrey History Center, Hunter Family: Letters and Papers, 1260/4.

58. Letter from Octavia Hill to Robert Hunter, August 22, 1884, Surrey History Center, Hunter Family: Letters and Papers, 1260/4.

59. Robert Hunter, *A Suggestion for the Better Preservation of Open Spaces* (London: Commons Preservations Society, 1884); and Cowell, "For the Benefit of the Nation," 306–7.

60. Hunter, *Better Preservation of Open Spaces*, 6–8.

61. Hunter, 9.

62. Hunter, 9.

63. Hunter, 16.

64. Quoted in Murphy, *Founders of the National Trust*, 104.

65. David Owen, "The City Parochial Charities: The 'Dead Hand' in Late Victorian London," *Journal of British Studies* 1, no. 2 (1962): 115–35.

66. "Draft Statement Presented to the Charity Commissioners by the Commons Preservation Society and the Kyrle Society," December 14, 1887, Surrey History Centre, Robert Hunter Papers, SHC reference 1621, box 10/3. This statement was followed up with a further printed letter sent sometime during the summer of 1888.

67. "Statement as to the Powers of the Society for Improving the Condition of the Labouring Classes [SICLC]," Surrey History Centre, Robert Hunter Papers, SHC reference 1621, box 10/3. Included with this memorandum was a copy of the SICLC's royal charter and a letter to Robert Hunter from Ralph Thicknesse, January 31, 1888, which detailed the communication that had taken place with Octavia Hill on the matter.

68. Owen, "The City Parochial Charities," 128–30.

69. There was also an important, though often neglected, transatlantic connection between the National Trust and a similar organization, the Trustees of Public Reservations, incorporated in the state of Massachusetts in 1891. Charles S. Sargent, one of the named trustees in Massachusetts, was nominated to sit on the council of the National Trust soon after the trust was incorporated in 1895. The National Trust for Places of Historic Interest or Natural Beauty: Report of the Council, March 1896–July 1896 (London, 1896), 12. My thanks to Daz Beatson at the National Trust for providing me with copies of the trust's annual reports and minutes. For more on the transatlantic connections shaping the trust, see Melanie Hall, "Octavia Hill and the National Trust," in *"Nobler Imaginings and Mightier Struggles": Octavia Hill, Social Activism and the Remaking of British Society* (London: Institute of Historical Research, 2016), ed. Elizabeth Baigent and Ben Cowell, 214–18.

70. Murphy, *Founders of the National Trust*, 70–100.

71. "The National Trust for Places of Historic Interest or Natural Beauty," *Times*, November 17, 1893.

72. "A National Trust for Places of Beauty and Interest," *London Daily News*, November 17, 1893.

73. Readman, "Preserving the English Landscape," 203–5; and Readman, *Land and Nation in England: Patriotism, National Identity, and the Politics of Land, 1880–1914* (Royal Historical Society, 2008).

74. H. D. Rawnsley, "The National Trust," *Cornhill Magazine* Ser. 3, v. 2 (1897): 245–49.

75. Cowell, "For the Benefit of the Nation: Politics and the Early National Trust," 307–8. Cowell argues that the trust's overall view toward local authorities was more complementary than antagonistic and that the trust could provide mechanisms for moving between the limitations of different state entities.

76. Rawnsley, "The National Trust," 247.

77. George Shaw-Lefevre (Lord Eversley), *Commons, Forests and Footpaths: The Story of the Battle during the Last Forty-Five Years for Public Rights over the Commons, Forests and Footpaths of England and Wales*, rev. ed. (Cassell, 1910), 275–76. Lefevre's revised edition includes an entire chapter dedicated to examples of local authorities encroaching on commons. For the earlier campaign against Manchester, see Ritvo, *The Dawn of Green*; and James Winter, *Secure from Rash Assault: Sustaining the Victorian Environment* (Berkeley: University of California Press, 1999), 166–88.

78. *National Trust Report of Provisional Council, 1895*, 4.

79. *The National Trust for Places of Historic Interest or Natural Beauty: Report of the Council, 1904–1905*, appendix A, 15–17.

80. See the National Trust executive committee minutes, April 20, 1903, May 11, 1903, and June 20, 1904.

81. *The National Trust & Gowbarrow* (Beaver Press, 1904), 6.

82. *The National Trust & Gowbarrow*, 1.

83. "The Preservation of Hindhead," *Times*, October 30, 1905.

84. *The National Trust for Places of Historic Interest or Natural Beauty: Report of the Council, 1905–1906*, 5–6.

85. *National Trust: Report, 1905–1906*, 13.

86. Minutes for the Ordinary General Meeting of Members, June 28, 1906; minutes of the National Trust Council, July 16, 1906.

87. *National Trust for Places of Historic Interest or Natural Beauty: Report of the Council, to the 21 August, 1907, when the Trust Was Reconstituted*, 3–4.

88. Gaze, *Figures in a Landscape*, 231–33.

89. Cowell, "The Commons Preservation Society and the Campaign for Berkhamsted Common, 1866–70," 156; and *National Trust for Places of Historic Interest or Natural Beauty: Report of the Council, 1925–1926*, 5–6.

90. Viviana A. Zelizer, *The Social Meaning of Money* (Princeton, NJ: Princeton University Press, 1997), 201–4.

CONCLUSION

1. "Land and House Property for the Million," *Estates Chronicle*, April 15, 1898, 2.

2. "Land and House Property for the Million."

3. "Land and House Property for the Million."

4. "About Ourselves," *Estates Chronicle*, April 15, 1898.

5. "About Ourselves."

6. "House Property Purchase," *Estates Chronicle*, June 15, 1898.

7. Colin G. Pooley and Michael J. Harmer, *Property Ownership in Britain C. 1850–1950: The Role of the Bradford Equitable Building Society and the Bingley Building Society in the Development of Homeownership* (Cambridge: Granta Editions, 1999), 22; Mark Swenarton and Sandra Taylor, "The Scale and Nature of the Growth of Owner-Occupation in Britain between the Wars," *Economic History Review*, n.s., 38, no. 3 (August 1985): 373–92; and Richard Harris and Chris Hamnett, "The Myth of the Promised Land: The Social Diffusion of Home Ownership in Britain and North America," *Annals of the Association of American Geographers* 77, no. 2 (June 1987): 173–90.

8. Christine Whitehead and Peter Williams, "Causes and Consequences? Exploring the Shape and Direction of the Housing System in the UK Post the Financial Crisis," *Housing Studies* 26, no. 7/8 (November 2011): 1157–69; and Robert Home, "Land Ownership in the United Kingdom: Trends, Preferences and Future Challenges," in "Land Use Futures," supplement, *Land Use Policy* 26 (December 2009): S103–8. Homeownership in the United States peaked during the second quarter of 2004 at a rate of 69.2 percent. US Census Bureau, "Quarterly Residential Vacancies and Homeownership, Fourth Quarter 2016," CB 17-05, January 31, 2017, https://www.census.gov/housing/hvs/files/qtr416/Q416press.pdf.

9. M. J. Daunton, *House and Home in the Victorian City: Working-Class Housing 1850–1914*, Studies in Urban History 7 (London: Edward Arnold, 1983); and John Burnett, *A Social History of Housing, 1815–1985* (Methuen, 1986).

10. Burnett, *A Social History of Housing*, 98.

11. Richard Dennis, *English Industrial Cities of the Nineteenth Century: A Social Geography* (Cambridge: Cambridge University Press, 1984), 143.

12. Alan A. Jackson, *Semi-Detached London*, 2nd ed. (London: Wild Swan Publications, 1991), 26–30.

13. Jackson, 70.

14. Luke Samy, "Extending Home Ownership before the First World War: The Case of the Co-operative Permanent Building Society, 1884–1913," *Economic History Review* 65, no. 1 (February 2012): 168–93; and Samy, "The Building Society Promise: The Accessibility, Risk and Efficiency of Building Societies in England c.1880–1939" (PhD diss., University of Oxford, 2010).

15. Jackson, *Semi-Detached London*, 63.

16. M. J. Daunton, *A Property-Owning Democracy? Housing in Britain* (London: Faber and Faber, 1987); and Avner Offer, *Property and Politics, 1870–1914: Landownership, Law, Ideology, and Urban Development in England* (Cambridge: Cambridge University Press, 1981).

17. Peter Scott, *The Making of the Modern British Home: The Suburban Semi and Family Life between the Wars* (Oxford: Oxford University Press, 2013), 35–36; and Mark Swenarton, *Homes Fit for Heroes: The Politics and Architecture of Early State Housing in Britain* (London: Heinemann Educational Books, 1981).

18. Scott, *The Modern British Home*, 37–38.

19. Scott, 99.

20. Home, "Land Ownership in the United Kingdom," S104.

21. Scott, *The Modern British Home*, 76–82.

22. Pooley and Harmer, *Property Ownership in Britain*, 41.

23. Scott, *The Modern British Home*, 120–21; Deborah S. Ryan, "'All the World and Her Husband': the Daily Mail Ideal Home Exhibition 1908–39," in *All the World and Her Husband: Women in Twentieth-Century Consumer Culture*, ed. Maggie Andrews and Mary M. Talbot (London: Cassell, 2000), 10–22; and Judy Giles, *The Parlour and the Suburb: Domestic Identities, Class, Femininity and Modernity*, 1st ed. (Oxford: Bloomsbury Academic, 2004).

24. Reba N. Soffer, *History, Historians, and Conservatism in Britain and America: The Great War to Thatcher and Reagan* (Oxford: Oxford University Press, 2009), 297.

25. John Gaze, *Figures in a Landscape: A History of the National Trust* (London: Barrie & Jenkins in association with the National Trust, 1988), 231–33.

26. Rupert Jones, "Home Ownership in England at a 30-Year low, Official Figures Show," *Guardian*, March 2, 2017, www.theguardian.com/money/2017/mar/02/home-ownership-in-england-at-a-30-year-low-official-figures-show.

27. For rates, see *Living Conditions in Europe* (Luxembourg: Publications Office of the European Union, 2014), 50. For more on the theme of convergence in homeownership rates, see Jim Kemeny and Stuart Lowe, "Schools of Comparative Housing Research: From Convergence to Divergence," *Housing Studies* 13, no. 2 (March 1998): 161–76; and R. Ronald, *The Ideology of Home Ownership: Homeowner Societies and the Role of Housing* (New York: Palgrave Macmillan, 2008).

28. An argument popularized recently in Hernando de Soto, *The Mystery of Capital: Why Capitalism Triumphs in the West and Fails Everywhere Else*, repr. ed. (New York: Basic Books, 2003). For criticism of this view, see Timothy Mitchell, "The Properties of Markets," in *Do Economists Make Markets? On the Performativity of Economics*, ed. Donald MacKenzie, Fabian Muniesa, and Lucia Siu (Princeton, NJ: Princeton University Press, 2007), 244–75.

29. For an excellent discussion of the "microstructures" of property marketization in contemporary Britain, see Susan Smith, Moira Munro, and Hazel Christie, "Performing (Housing) Markets," *Urban Studies* 43, no. 1 (January 2006): 81–98; Munro and Smith, "Calculated Affection? Charting the Complex Economy of Home Purchase," *Housing Studies* 23, no. 2 (March 2008): 349–67; and Smith and Munro, *The Microstructures of Housing Markets* (London: Routledge, 2013).

30. Deborah Orr, "The Notion of Britain as a Property-Owning Democracy Is in Tatters," *Guardian*, August 31, 2011, http://www.guardian.co.uk/commentisfree/2011/aug/31/tory-housing-idea-in-tatters.

INDEX

References to figures are denoted by an "f" in italics following the page number.